Learning to Fly

Marisha McDowell

Library of Congress Control Number: 2021900729

ISBN: 978-0-578-84016-1

DEDICATION

To my dear.

TABLE OF CONTENTS

"It was the pure Language of the World. It required no explanation, just as the universe needs none as it travels through endless time. What the boy felt at that moment was that he was in the presence of the only woman in his life, and that, with no need for words, she recognized the same thing. He was more certain of it than of anything in the world. He had been told by his parents and grandparents that he must fall in love and really know a person before becoming committed. But maybe people who felt that way had never learned the universal language. Because, when you know that language, it's easy to understand that someone in the world awaits you, whether it's in the middle of the desert or in some great city. And when two such people encounter each other, and their eyes meet, the past and the future become unimportant. There is only that moment, and the incredible certainty that everything under the sun has been written by one hand only. It is the hand that evokes love, and creates a twin soul for every person in the world. Without such love, one's dreams would have no meaning."

— Paulo Coelho, *The Alchemist*

AUTHORS NOTE

This story surrounds and focuses on a very specific part of my life. I want to be clear – Much of the topic is about my husband, yet it is about my thoughts, my feelings, and my emotions. My memories may be imperfect; however, they are accurate to the best of my knowledge and how I personally recall those events happening. Many individuals are unnamed out of respect for their own interpretation of occurrences.

My husband is an integral part of my life, as he is my partner. We committed to sharing a life together; for better or worse, in sickness and in health. With that, we are two very singular people who have chosen each other.

Realistically, when I started writing I was not sure I had anything to say.

Yet, it is something that needed to physically find its way out of me.

I knew that I cannot continue to happily live my life being haunted by my own thoughts.

No part of me could have predicted this part of our story. The part where my worst dreams became a reality. The part where the silent fears that turned round and round in my head and kept me up at night became a reality of a rollercoaster I could not seem to get off of.

This tale does not define me, nor my husband. It is a part of us and our journey together. Parts of this book are excerpts of my journal writing that takes the reader back into time, in a first-person narrative of what I was candidly experiencing in the moment. It is raw and unembellished.

Asking a person to enjoy reading seems odd to me, as it is the enjoyment of some of the most heartbreaking moments of my life.

Instead, I ask for *grace*.

Grace to enable the power of healing; reading my words and realizing through this process, I can finally let go.

BEFORE

part I

What does it mean to die? Does your physical body have to perish? Or is death merely the act of continuously having air pumped through your lungs and blood flowing through your veins? Is death losing the ability to communicate and foster relationships? Death and dying can mean different things. There are medical and dictionary definitions that inform the meaning of each, but I believe that it is different for each person. Can the mortal body die, and the soul live? In some circumstances, sure. However, in my experience I believe the opposite is more likely – a person's soul can die, and their body lives on. The soul is the essence of a human being. I believe that souls are interconnected and have the power to save one another. For me, the entwining of souls is at the heart of living.

On March 9, 2013 I met my future husband. We both happened to be at a dive bar downtown Olympia, Washington where we both called home. On that Spring night we were surrounded by trees, a light breeze, and those first tingling of what turned into the greatest love of my life.

I remember the afternoon perfectly.

It was one of the first pretty Spring days that year, and I decided to go for a nice long run. I recall thinking how pretty it was outside; still cool, the rain and Winter had been slowly lifting. I could finally see the sky and Spring was near. I came home feeling content and at ease. That night I made a big pot of chili for my friends before we decided to go out downtown.

The bar itself was very linear – from the far end, you can see the length of the full bar to the entrance. I had been there already with friends, enjoying the evening. I had fun when we went out together, it felt as if that is what you are supposed to do in your early twenties, and we did often. It had taken me most of my life thus far to feel as if I was included, and I felt relaxed within my friend group.

I often amused myself with people watching and keeping track of our group, and those around us. Even though I felt comfortable with the people I was with, I did not feel at ease within the general public. Small talk is not something that I enjoy. Instead, I watch people's mannerisms and how they choose to present themselves to the world.

The bar scene in itself is a social experiment, the people act as if they are flies drawn to their sweet intoxicating drinks. I would watch the inherent buzzing and flitting about asking myself questions about human nature. Was it all just an act? Did the flight of the bumblebee mean anything? Or was it all innate, the circle of life repeating itself? I rarely interacted with people I did not know, my hesitance to trust was, and is fairly high.

That night when Josh walked in, I immediately saw him walk toward the table near ours, where another group of people already were. He was greeted by hugs and cheers; it appeared he was clearly well liked. It seemed silly, like all the romantic stories you hear growing up, but in that moment as he was walking toward the table, time really did slow down for me. I just knew that this person was meant to be in my life.

After a while his friend came up to me asking about playing shuffleboard. I was disappointed. I had been hopeful that Josh would be the one to come up and talk to me first. Much to my luck, he invited Josh over to chat. That initiated the cataclysm that changed the trajectory of my whole life.

Josh and I started our connection exchanging various small talk which continued into the night. I surprisingly was intrigued by him; Josh captivated my attention. Throughout that evening my friends left me at the bar, wanting to move on to other places, but I stayed. I was entranced with this boy who had the biggest and bluest eyeballs that I just couldn't look away from. That night, he told me he was a professional mountain guide.

I have grown up in Washington State, the heart of the Pacific Northwest my whole life. Seeing Mt. Rainier looming out of the sky on a clear day was normal for me. Weather reports on any television station would report whether "the mountain was out", signifying the clearness, or the majestic quality that the day had in store.

The next evening Josh and I went on our first official date. We met at a restaurant that I had never been to. I stressed out choosing what to wear. What do you wear on a date with someone who has such an established job and has it all together? I had voluntarily dedicated my year to service, working with AmeriCorps and living far below the poverty line. I was assisted with federal programs helping me to pay rent and grocery shop. I was nowhere near having a reputable career like a mountain guide.

I ended up wearing my trusted favorite jeans, a shirt out of my "work clothes pile" and a mustard yellow peacoat I had "borrowed" from a friend. I felt as if I was dressing up for a job interview. In normal life, my daily attire was any sort of shirt found at Target and hoodie in order to keep warm. In my nice unwrinkled shirt, I thought to myself that this is what professional people wear on real dates.

During dinner it was strange thinking that I had only met this person the day before. Where was this going? First dates are always so awkward, and to this day most forms of small talk make me cringe. I asked myself how in the world can I relate to this person. He literally climbs mountains as a job. Before yesterday I didn't even totally know what that meant. At dinner I ordered macaroni and cheese, where Josh had ordered a burger. It was not until a long time after that I found out Josh thought it was curious that I had ordered macaroni and cheese on a date. To this day, I find nothing strange about it, as macaroni and cheese is one of the best parts of life.

After we finished eating, Josh invited me to continue to talk at his sister's house where he was staying just a few miles down the road. I agreed, but would have to follow him because I was not familiar with this part of town. Driving just a few miles down the road felt remote, and I wondered where in the world we were going.

I hoped he was not leading me to some obscure location. In college I heard a comedian that made a joke about this very scenario, which she ended asking the audience to always ask themselves if they think they're going to be chopped up in the woods in a little box. If so, immediately halt whatever situation you were in. This thought occurred to me on this unlit road, but I never had the dark-box-in-the-woods feeling. Then suddenly, we were in a very conventional neighborhood and I pushed that thought aside.

Inside, we continued our conversation getting to know one another. Noticing that I was cold, Josh turned on the electric fireplace in the corner of the living room. We sat on the floor, right in front. That was the start of Josh's never-ending observation of me being cold in any given situation.

While we talked, he told me he would be leaving for Vietnam for the next two months to go outdoor rock climbing with a friend. I of course, in my early twenties, previously being subjected to pretty crappy dates, and no one who truly was interested in me, realistically thought that our date that night would be the last. It was wonderful while it lasted. I felt as if I actually had a real connection with this person, even though I was incredibly nervous. I did not think that I was polished enough to be with this person who had so much poise, adventure and daring. I mean, really – Vietnam. How foreign and so out of my wheelhouse. Josh had the perfect excuse to leave for his trip and never look back.

However, he didn't.

Much to my surprise we exchanged emails and he wrote. I confidently assured him that I had a Skype account and quickly signed up and gave myself a crash course on how to use the service. Due to unforeseen circumstances while travelling, he and his friend discovered they were not able to go to Vietnam. Josh had started to send me emails at that point, and he expressed his frustrations. Unbeknownst to me, this was the first example shown to me that "going with the flow" is something that is very foreign to Josh's nature.

If it were me, I would have probably dissolved into a puddle of anxiety. Josh however, had another friend that happened to be vacationing on a remote beach in Southern Thailand. So, they headed there. Josh took two months from real life to travel halfway across the world only to find out that he must change plans. They ended up in a totally different country then planned and were seemingly okay with the decision. I cannot imagine what I would have been thinking but being okay seems out of the ordinary. Reading his emails was something out of a fantasy book for me. I had a stable job and worked every traditional workday since I was eighteen. The idea of just escaping everyday life for weeks, let alone months at a time seemed unreal to me.

In Thailand, Josh called me every few days. Of course, I knew that Thailand was a country, but besides that it was hard for me to conceptualize that it was a place. It was so foreign, and at that point I had never traveled anywhere outside of the United States, let alone a very small and remote village at the bottom of Thailand.

Josh told me that they had found these huts in the jungle to rent, describing them as small tree houses, more like shacks a bit above ground, with mosquito netting across the top. After about a week or so of Josh living in the jungle, he said he upgraded to more bungalow style living. This included a complimentary breakfast – to this day, a major Josh selling point, and a real room with walls and a mattress. He upgraded to spending five U.S. dollars per day at this place, and stated it was worth every penny.

Josh would usually call me after he had breakfast, but because of the time difference, it would be during my evening, the day prior. Unknowingly, this was the start of us spending quality time together zones apart. Later, it was comforting to me knowing that if he was calling me "in the future" our love would at least last into the coming times of that next day.

I imagined what TonSai Beach would be like. Josh described the huge rock formations, the restaurants on the beach and living this exotic island life. We spent the first two months of our relationship strictly relegated to phone calls, emails, and an eleven-hour time difference. It was unlike any relationship that I had ever experienced. When Josh would call me, I would hear monkeys and birds in the background of our phone calls. The jungle felt so close over the phone, yet so far. We continued this pattern of chatting every few days, and I would look forward to hearing his sweet voice over the phone.

Josh came home two months later. He asked me out for the first Friday evening he was home to meet him and a small group of his friends for happy hour. This would be followed by seeing the Luminary Procession at Arts Walk. Olympia does a yearly Arts Walk festival every April. The Friday of the designated weekend, there is a procession at night where people create costumes having to do with nature and creatures.

Because the parade is at night, the creations also must have some form of light.

I had never been to the Luminary Procession but agreed to meet Josh there. I distinctly remember I had declined happy hour with his friends because I did not want to fall too fast for him. I wanted to go on a long run, for myself. I wanted to maintain individualism, or rather, tricking my brain that I had not already fallen head over heels. There is a blurry photo of us from that night, marking our first photo together. In it, we look so ridiculously young and full of bliss. As with most young couples, we had no idea the twists and turns our story would take.

Later that weekend we went on our "second real first date" where he took me on a ferry ride to Seattle. That day I was distracted, having just had a disagreement with one of my best friends. I am not perfect, and I had unconsciously hurt someone I cared about. Josh was kind, offering himself up as a scapegoat if I had to take care of anything. I was impressed with his ability to put whatever I was going through first but decided that forcing the issue would not be beneficial. I needed time to play its part.

We sat in his car awaiting the ferry, and he asked me if I would be his girlfriend, which of course I said yes.

We talked about how we felt as if we were tied to each other since the day we met two months ago. In that moment both of us admitted we felt awkward, having to define our relationship. Both of us felt certain that yes, we were together and now it really was official.

On the ferry ride Josh showed me a photo slideshow from Thailand. I remember being confused, thinking that I honestly didn't know what to think of the situation. Again, here was this super cute guy – we had been talking for two months, he literally went to Thailand, and here he is in a peacoat with a laptop and case showing me these exotic photos. I am not sure why I was so hung up with his laptop case, but anyone in my book that has a case for their computer must have it all together.

For the record, my laptop was (and is) old, sticky, and on any given day decides what keys want to work. In no realm of my world that I had experienced could I imagine a guy like Josh liking me. Except, much to my surprise, he did.

We travelled to Seattle and ate the most delicious sushi I had ever had. It was endearing to me that while we ate sushi that Josh struggled with chopsticks. Hadn't he just spent two months in a country eating with chopsticks? It was such a minor thing, but it made me feel as if we were on a little bit more of an equal playing field. I did not feel as intimidated by this unskilled chopstick using guy.

Two weeks after that, Josh started guiding on Mt. Rainier. That is when I gained a sliver of knowledge of what being a mountain guide was. And, most importantly, what it means to be a partner to someone who is a mountain guide. At the time, a handful of Josh's friends worked with him, as well.

Josh invited me to visit his first weekend that he was working in the office to come up to stay in Ashford and "hang out with him and the guides." In the Wintertime the town itself is sleepy and feels forgotten about, with only a convenience store to purchase limited items and a barber shop. In the Summer however, there are a couple seasonal restaurants open and the town has a constant stream of travelers. The town is bustling with people visiting Mt. Rainier National Park, climbers and working mountain guides.

My first experience in this tiny mountain town was the guide community. There was a camaraderie and a brotherhood. Most everyone that I met was kind. They asked me questions about myself and they were genuine.

Much of it could be due to their friendship with Josh, however I appreciated their care, nonetheless.

This care has translated itself into lifelong friendships for both of us. Diving into any sub-culture can be a learning experience, and the guiding industry is incredibly few in numbers, but expansive across the globe. I met other guides who lived out of their cars, or only rented storage units to keep their few, prized belongings as most of the year they spent living on the side of a mountain, often in a different country.

In addition to guiding throughout the week, that Summer Josh held an additional position of Weekend Operations Manager. Being Weekend Operations Manager had some perks. It meant that Josh had his own private storage closet, lined with boxes and boxes of old files, as well as a cot to sleep on. The next few Summers, when I went to visit him on the weekends that is where we would stay. Over the years, the boxes would multiply, constricting the space even more. It was cramped, uncomfortable, and often there were spiders lurking in the shadows, always in the back of my mind. Yet, it became a part of normal life for many Summers following. We would have evening bonfires with other guides, cook dinner on the grill and of course, indulge in some Rainier beer. It felt like Summer camp.

I still didn't fully understand what being a mountain guide meant, but being around others, in their realm in Ashford was a bit telling. Every hour of the day you heard the radio go off, transmitting fuzzy calls to those who were on Mt. Rainier and Josh deciphering the coded messages of crackle.

On Josh's first weekend working Operations, as well as my first weekend visiting, there was a rescue that Josh had to help coordinate. He of course was stressed trying to balance all the systems in play and keeping people safe, while not actually directly part of the situation on the mountain. It was a very immediate window into the life of a guide and how even in the best circumstances the mountains are always in control.

I realized that being in this profession you are performing an act of service every time that you work. It is not a career that has household distinguishment such as the paramedic or fire service, but they serve at an equally high risk every single day. Mountain guides not only put their life on the line for other guides, but for their clients. If, and when a client is ill-equipped, out of their element and incompetent the guide picks up the slack and puts themselves in jeopardizing situations.

Over the years I have learned that even when mountain guides are seldom around each other in everyday life, hardly any time passes in the instances of when they do see one another. The idea of how average coworkers interact in your general office setting is flipped in the guiding world. It does not necessarily matter if you like the person, because the stakes are higher. You and your coworkers are bound to life equally. The accountability of having your lives intertwined in such a high-risk environment translates to a real-life relationship. It was apparent that the camaraderie ran deep.

Every Summer the company Josh would work for would host a huge party with one of their sponsors. They would rent out lodging and space in the middle of the woods for everyone in attendance. I had never experienced parties on that level. Mountain guides could definitely party. Every year that Josh and I attended we stayed in a different, themed cabin. It was a distinct experience each time and one of the things that we looked forward to each year.

As an outsider, being sincerely welcomed into this culture, felt surreal. It was as if there was this club of people who were exceptionally strong, driven, and fearless. All characteristics I wouldn't describe myself as. Yet, they took me in, and it was as if I was an extension of Josh. The relationship of brotherhood, translated through him to me, as his partner.

When Josh was on his longest trip to date, one of the senior guides had reached out to me saying they were needing to send out additional gear mid-expedition and asked if there was anything I would like to send as well. I had put together a small care package for Josh and we arranged a time for him to stop by, as he said he would be in town. When he arrived, I found out he had driven two hours to me, with no other errands. I implored him to stay, have a drink or go to dinner to no avail. Two hours to me, and two hours back for a mere ten minutes on the side of the curb outside of our apartment just so I could send a little love to Josh. As he left, I asked him the chances of the trip succession. I was still new to the idea of mountain guiding, and each major expedition seemed dire to me.

He promised Josh would return home.

I held onto that little bit of hope every single day he was gone.

Climbing in Argentina was one of Josh's yearly Winter trips. It was about three and a half weeks total. This expedition itself never really bothered me. It was just enough time for him to be gone that I would start to miss him and then he would return home. Communication was always fairly decent, so I would hear from Josh every few days when he was away, and it was a relatively safe mountain.

However, much to my actual irritation it so happened that for this trip Josh was most always scheduled for the climb that would be over Christmas, missing the holiday at home. Sometimes we would have Christmas Eve together, with Josh set to be at the airport usually in the wee hours of the morning on Christmas Day. We never celebrated New Years together until many years into our relationship.

One time prior to the trip, I had asked one of the other co-guides if I could send a stocking with small gifts inside so Josh would have something to open on Christmas morning. He agreed, and we set a date for him to stop by next time he was in town. On that day in December, it was classic Pacific Northwest weather – rainy, cold and very wet. He showed up on our doorstep drenched.

What I discovered was that his car was in the repair shop and he had walked all the way across town to pick up a stocking for Josh. Seven miles in the pouring rain. I of course thought he was crazy and asked why. I would have been happy to drop off the stocking or meet somewhere close to him. He responded, "We walk up and down mountains through the rain and snow all the time. What's the difference if it's in town?" I expressed profuse gratitude for going over and beyond.

I had to talk him into accepting a ride back home.

These are only a few instances of what the culture of mountain guides are like. The dedication that they have for one another is unmatched. Over the course of my life I have had long lasting great friends and friendly coworkers. I would describe my own nature to go over and beyond for people to deliver gifts or provide a good holiday.

Putting myself in the shoes of potentially risking my life for them I ashamedly hesitate. I would probably weigh the options in my head and all the what-if scenarios. For mountain guides, it's reversed. Having the responsibility of another's life is not a question, nor an option – it is the job. Going over and beyond in "real life" is the option, yet in my experience it is not a question and is followed through on every single time.

At the end of that first Summer, Josh left to guide for his longest trip to date. He was going to China and Nepal to guide Cho Oyu and Ama Dablam, back to back for three months. I think looking back, I had an inkling of what this path would be like. I didn't yet know the emotional toll it would take on me, and on us as a couple. I did however know that those next three months were probably going to be pretty terrible.

I had just moved into a teeny, tiny apartment and was pretty much alone, minus my beloved cat Mushu, plus all of Josh's things. Another mountain guide trait – partners get stuck with all the gear and clothing storage. Really, I did not mind… his things made me feel less alone. I would fall asleep curled up with one of his sweatshirts every night because they smelled like him.

One thing that comforted me was like Thailand, all communication with Josh would be "in the future", or rather, in my future. Due to where we call home, over the course of all his trips there was only one expedition that my time was ahead of his. It soothed me to know that our love and phone calls were taking place, in a sense futuristically. It forced me to imagine a world where Josh continued to be safe and okay, even if it was just a half a day's difference.

I only remember parts of how I occupied my time when he was gone. Josh had, and still has a major sweet tooth and I had purchased a big thing of cookie dough which I remember making three to four cookies at a time, each night thinking of him.

As we were driving to the airport, Josh handed me a zip drive. He had put together a video diary for me with files to open every single day when he was away. The video diary was hilarious, and sweet, and so incredibly Josh. It featured cameos from friends, and him doing activities "together" with me, such as eating a double cheeseburger and him trying to teach me how to play football with the play that I had deemed, "Benjamin Button-hook."

I went back to spending more time with friends, but also a lot of time alone. I had lived on my own for many years, but up until this point, I always had roommates. This felt different in a lot of ways. I had recently started a new job where I would work on-call hours and never had a set shift. I felt as if there was not a huge amount of structure in my life and my life felt very quiet. This was my first experience with Josh on a mountain very far away from home, and our communication was dependent on weather, service, and availability. It was not frequent, nor was it planned.

Desmond Tutu said, "Much depends on your attitude. If you are filled with negative judgment and anger, then you will feel separate from other people. You will feel lonely. But if you have an open heart and are filled with trust and friendship, even if you are physically alone, even living a hermit's life, you will never feel lonely."

It was years after Josh guiding that I read this quote. It reminded me much of the times that I did spend alone and what isolation can feel like. I held resentment toward the many mountains that were so loved by him. How in the world can something cold, angular, and remote provide such amounts of love and devotion? It was truly a window into the soul of Josh, a window I can only still partially see through. Depending on the mountain or part of the world, the amount of trust I had that Josh would come home would fluctuate. That aided the amounts of loneliness or alone-ness I would feel.

When Josh came home from his China and Nepal trip, I hardly recognized him at the airport. He had lost a good amount of weight from the trip. I took a good double take and waited for him to talk for me to be able to truly recognize him by his voice. I knew what him being gone had felt like for me – the emotional stress, coupled with a good dose of anxiety and depression. I hadn't realized how much of a toll the act of guiding, as a verb would take on him.

He had come home literal skin and bone, allergic to antibiotics he had taken, and covered in hive-like spots. We went to a concert that weekend. Looking back at the photos, both of us are fairly unrecognizable. I had not yet realized, but limiting the food I had allowed myself every night had taken its toll on my body, too.

When Josh was not guiding, he had the option to substitute teach. He filled some time with that, but the work was taxing, and he was coming off working day and night for three months straight. In the Winter season, he would work week-long seminars on Mt. Rainier and continue to guide trips in Mexico and Argentina.

Suddenly, we were celebrating our first anniversary. We went to Seattle and stayed at a hotel on the water. We had sushi at the original restaurant we went to and discovered Josh's chopstick skills had not improved over time. This time the year before Josh was coming back from Thailand, preparing for Mt. Rainier season. This year however, he left for the month of May to guide Mt. Bona in Alaska before starting his Summer work.

We had been together for a little over a year, and Josh had already guided in four countries, not including the two months in Thailand. When we were able to spend time together in person, it was few and far between, but special. This became our lifestyle. It was very unconventional. Most of my friends did not understand what dating a mountain guide was like. The only somewhat similar comparison was a military life. However, in the military there was usually always someone there. The community of people waiting for their partners were strong, you had a built-in support system of people going through the same thing.

In mountain guiding, in theory you sometimes had a support system, but in reality, it was rare. There wasn't really a built-in network of people and partners going through a similar thing together at the same time. And if there was, there was not much communication. Most guides at that time did not have partners they were tied down to. Living life constantly moving countries and climbing mountains made it hard to maintain a stable relationship, let alone build a family.

Over the years and many days, I was alone in my thoughts. I had lots of practice being alone, growing up as a quiet only child. It was only as an adult that I felt as if I fit in with people the same age as me. Many days I was okay feeling alone. When Josh was guiding there would be some days that I wouldn't even have a conversation with anyone, and it would go weeks between having a hug with a friend as any physical contact.

Sometimes I would make it a game to see how long I could go without uttering any verbal words to another person. Though, I would talk to my cat Mushu, which made me feel less alone. Now, looking back it seems as if that came to be only because of extreme loneliness. Other days in between I missed having a human connection. A coworker intuitively recognized that and would force me into hugs. I usually keep myself at arm's length away from people, emotionally and physically. My coworker did not care and hugged me anyway. I was secretly grateful.

When Josh was home it was like he was the life of our home party. He brought laughter, conversation and brought out my own emotions. When he would leave, it was as if all the light, fun and chaos would be sucked into a chasm. I would always come home from dropping him off to the airport and think that the house would feel so empty.

Since Josh was often travelling over Christmas, we would celebrate the holiday on different days. One year I came home after dropping Josh off at the airport and my cat had knocked over our Christmas tree. She had stowed all her stuffed toys under the branches. It seemed like a pretty accurate metaphor for how I felt as well.

It usually took about a week or so for that emptiness to dissipate a bit at home and within myself. Solitude became something very ordinary to me. I would not say that solitude and I became friends, but we also were not mortal enemies. The times that I would lean into the solitude made it easier. The times that I would challenge it proved to be more difficult. Challenging it brought on a monster I knew well.

I have always struggled with anxiety, but it was not until I was an adult that I had a name for what I was feeling. That feeling in the pit of my stomach, the racing thoughts, the dread of what could potentially come was my normal. This of course, was exacerbated when Josh was in other countries, guiding on various mountains. This form of anxiety morphed itself into a different form than the times I had previously come to know it as.

It was never the loneliness that was hard. It was that aching feeling, always in the background of whatever I was doing. Because of the high danger level that his job entailed, I was constantly worrying and wondering if Josh was alive. Every time he would call or message me,

I would breathe a sigh of relief. It alleviated my stress for a few hours, and then those thoughts would slowly creep back into my psyche.

Some days he would plan to call and wouldn't be able to due to weather, or other circumstances outside of his control. Those days were the worst. The company that Josh worked for provided an online blog that followers could read and follow along as the trips commenced.

Our families followed it religiously.

I refused to read it.

The blog only talked about "sunshine and daisies", as it were. It did not talk about the nitty gritty, how my dear was doing, or if anything terribly unsafe happened. The blog was a rose-colored lens of mountain guiding, and it wasn't necessarily reality.

When I spoke with our family members, they would constantly quote the online blog, asking me clarifying questions, with this terribly upbeat undertone. It would infuriate me. No one really understood why I chose not to read it. Nor did they understand what it was like having a partner in a remote, high risk job. Other coworkers had partners that traveled, but if you needed to get a hold of them in an emergency, you could. Josh and I did not have that luxury.

Mountain guiding is not a perfect art and cannot be counted on. At the end of everyday Mother Nature is in charge, and sometimes things would not go to plan. Of course, Josh and other mountain guides would adjust based on their knowledge and skills. More often than not, the adjustments would turn out okay and no one would be the wiser, especially reading the blog. However, a minor line of "adjustment" might have had true consequences glossed over.

Some people with spouses or friends in high risk jobs don't actually want to know the details. They want the drama, or rather, the blog-worthy moments. Not knowing the true reality never really served me well. I am sure there were plenty of things Josh chose not to tell me, but what he did share would be honest and not always "socially appropriate", in which I found much more value.

I wish I could say that I filled all of my extra time with really productive things, such as learning another language, writing this book, or really focusing on learning a new skill. I however just tried to quiet the inner voice in my head as much as possible. It took active practice to be able to find balance. That meant, distracting myself and wrapping myself up into other people's stories. I used work, random television shows

(Netflix was a great investment), books and running to distract myself. It never worked one hundred percent, but significantly helped. Depending on what mountain Josh was on, the bits of contact that we had were across time zones and lying in bed reading awaiting the Skype ringtone became my idea of perfection.

Running helped more than anything. Even to this day I would not describe myself as "a runner", even though I run regularly. Running has positive benefits to your body, maintaining a healthy heart, endurance and the overall strength it takes to run long distances. However, for me running was all mental. It became a way of life for me, something that I would and continue to force myself to do, even on my darkest of days.

I returned back to myself, back to the day that I had met Josh where I had chosen to go on a run. In the moment, running would take the panic out of me. My body forced me to remember to breathe; in and out, in and out. If I held my breath when I ran, or let myself get overwhelmed with worst-case Josh scenarios, I could not achieve the necessary stride. It's Washington, and depending on the time of the year, there is a good chance it was wet outside. But I ran.

The idea of running to maintain sanity is still difficult to wrap my head around, and I am not sure why it helps. It is not fun. It is hard and sweaty work and most of the time I would run to the point of exhaustion. Yet, the effects of running are so significant I could not deny it. I continued, breath after breath, one step at a time.

BEFORE

part II

Being a partner of an international mountain guide, it was not long until pretty much everyone that we would encounter would ask me if I also climbed mountains. At this point in my life I enjoyed day hikes, spending time in nature, kayaking in the Puget Sound and being outside. But... mountain climbing? Not so much.

I have stared at Mt. Rainier my entire life, every day that it unveiled itself from the clouds and rainfall regarding it as beautifully majestic. The idea of climbing it to the tippy top never came across my wildest dreams. Yet, that became everyone's first go-to question when having conversations with me.

I started telling people that Josh would not let me. That went over really well, because then I put the responsibility on him having to explain away to the question seekers. I guess it was a bit of a sneaky way for me to see how tired he would get having to answer that question.

As a result, three years later on Friday, July 18, 2015 I summitted Mt. Rainier for the first time, via the Disappointment Cleaver route.

Most people spend months, often the greater part of a year planning and physically training to climb Mt. Rainier. It is never a guarantee because Mt. Rainier creates its own weather system, independent of what is around it. If you choose to go with a guide service, your dates are usually set eight to ten months prior to when you actually climb it. Even the best forecasters cannot predict that far out.

Once you start to climb, you also are burdened with how your body adapts to altitude. Mt. Rainier sits at 14, 411 feet above sea level. Some bodies adapt well to the climbing, thinning air. Some do not. My high point before this was about 6,000 feet, which I only hit the year prior climbing Mt. Ellinor in Olympic National Park with Josh.

That Summer, Josh came home from a climb on a Tuesday with the rest of the week off, him working in the office that weekend. After years of people inquiring if I was ever going to climb, he finally asked me if I wanted to climb Mt. Rainier. I had heard that if you can run a straight seven miles you can climb Mt. Rainier. To this day, I have no idea how accurate that statement is, but in the moment, it made me feel better, as seven miles was easy for me. With only one day's notice, we went up to Ashford the following night, ready to get an early Thursday morning start to the climb.

I did not tell my mom where we were going, only that we were going "camping" and "probably" would not have service. I let my boss and a couple coworkers know, all who panicked a bit at the idea. My boss had requested text check-ins, and my coworkers were responsible for my cat if for some reason I died.

I can't say that I blame them for being nervous. It is a big thing to try and accomplish, especially without warning. I however did not have time to panic or let myself get worried since we were leaving in twenty-four hours. In a way, that was almost better. I was filled with nervous excitement, disbelief that this was really going to finally happen.

Mt. Rainier Visitor Center is located at Paradise, where many people across the world come to visit, hike, as well as start their summit climbs. I had been to Paradise as a kid, plus a handful of times with Josh and various others. I had done some of the day hikes that took you around the base of the mountain, viewing the wildflowers, all on relatively flat ground. I had never ventured far off the maintained trails, or far into the snow or to a point where you required anything other than hiking boots.

W alking up the snowfield to Camp Muir I had never seen a mountain up close like that. Not so distant glaciers glistening, ice blue. Camp Muir sits at about 10,000 feet above sea level, in comparison to Paradise at

5,400 feet. Since Josh was in peak climbing season, physically his body was strong. I will be the first to admit he carried all the heavy items for our climb. Fortunately, Josh had some food stashed up at Camp Muir, as he had planned to take me up prior to leaving camp the day before.

We got up to Camp Muir mid-afternoon, set to go to bed and rest by 5pm, all to wake up in five hours with an alpine start, at 11pm to start our climb to the summit. I remember my legs were so sore and flexing to take another step took me a couple hours to retrain and trick my body into fully complying. Going across the Disappointment Cleaver in the middle of the night felt like an out of body experience. I could barely see where I was stepping, knowing if I stepped wrong it could be deadly to both of us. As the world grew lighter, it was only then did the idea of being literally perched on the edge of a mountain became my immediate reality.

Out of all of Josh's ten plus years climbing Mt. Rainier, he still states that that year was one of the most dangerous with multiple ladder crossings and an ever-changing route.

I thought it was awesome.

For me it was really interesting to actually be able to see him guide. Mt. Rainier is a pretty cool office. You really don't understand a mountain until you are on it, and even then, my knowledge of the hazards was very slim. I found beauty in overhanging ice wanting to watch the light hit the crystals, whereas Josh would see hazards and encourage us to move quickly. His proficiency in understanding the mountain made much more sense to me when I could see and physically understand what he was talking about. To no surprise, he was incredibly good at his job and exceptionally strong.

Just after sunrise, we summitted Mt. Rainier together around 7am. I remember thinking that the last push before the summit was a mental challenge. I have long maintained that climbing is having the skill of walking exceptionally slow uphill. It is slow and steady all the way. I hadn't thought about bringing headphones to listen to music or podcasts, so I had nothing to distract my thoughts.

I have a distinct memory of when I was growing up when my best friend and I were debating how to walk. Do you walk right-left or left-right? We decided to take a poll of people at the nearby grocery store as people were walking to and from their cars. We discovered that the majority of people are right-left walkers like she was.

I am left-right even though I am right-handed. In walking up the snowy mountainous fields, guides often kick steps into the snow to make it easier to forge a trail. Every single time I would start to walk I would have to retrain myself to walk right-left, which was unnatural to me, as the trail was of course in the opposite pattern.

For me, it is difficult to get to a physical and mental place walking slowly. Running is much different. Training my mind to walk slowly was hard. It confused my body because carrying a pack, at higher than normal altitude, rest-stepping slowly up the mountain physically was just as difficult as going on a long run.

We lucked out with gorgeous and clear views. From the summit, the panorama is beautiful, with clear views of Mt. Adams, Mt. Hood, Mt. Baker, Mt. Shuksan, Mt. Jefferson, the North Cascade Mountain Range and Mt. St. Helens, plus looking down across the landscape we had just climbed. I had never been that high up in my life by physically using my own legs. It was expansive and open. I felt as if I was on the top of the world.

Not many people can say that they peed at the top of Mt. Rainier in the ice caves located under the crater rim, but I did. One of Josh's favorite stories is telling people that when we got to the summit the first thing I stated was, "That's it?"

All I can say is that after that much work climbing a mountain, there should be a cookie stand located at the top.

We started our descent downhill which I very quickly realized I thoroughly disliked. All my mental preparation was getting to the summit. I somehow forgot that was only the halfway point. Going uphill was a challenge, but doable. Downhill was a whole other story. I would clench every single muscle in each step hoping that I would not slip and fall all the way down the mountain. I had to adjust my stride wearing crampons strapped to my mountaineering boots so they would not tear my pants that I had borrowed from another guide. Going back down the Disappointment Cleaver I was in delayed fear knowing I had climbed it in the near dark.

I was exceptionally slow and hungry. Someone had eaten the food Josh stashed and I was out of snacks. By the time we got to the parking lot both of us were fairly cranky. However, we did it. In what takes the average person and guided climb three days and two nights, we achieved in two days, one night. At that point Josh's summit count was in the high 70s, but climbing together was meaningful.

Later that night we went to a local outdoor concert at our favorite bar, downtown Olympia. I danced in a pretty flowery yellow dress with shin bang bruises up and down the front of my legs caused by wearing my mountaineering boots too tight. We ran into various friends that evening who asked me about the bruises. Each time I proudly stated, "I climbed Mt. Rainier today."

When Josh was in first grade, he was asked what he wanted to do when he grew up. He stated he wanted to climb Mt. Everest. Fast forward some years, and many trips later, Josh's dream opportunity is presented to him, the untenable Mt. Everest. He found out in Autumn of 2015.

I was not one who was overjoyed at this opportunity, but rather terrified. Feeling like the most unsupportive and selfish partner I could be, I begged him not to go. I cannot imagine how hard this was for Josh. He was about to accomplish the one thing that he had been dreaming about since he was seven years old, and he was with a partner who was seemingly against it happening.

In February, a month before Josh would leave for Nepal, we took a trip to Costa Rica. Close to our four year anniversary, there, on the beach at sunset, Josh proposed to me. We called my mom and shared the news to our friends on social media. Naturally, we had discussed our future together as a couple and we remained committed to each other. It was a happy day.

While we were in Costa Rica, we had engagement photos taken. It was fun, different and the photos turned out perfect. Many of them were taken on the water in the afternoon light and the colors strikingly popped. Neither of us knew what the future would hold, but in those moments, we were blissfully content.

In the couple of weeks after we returned home from our vacation, we hastily planned some of our wedding details. Most importantly, we picked a date and location. It seemed hectic and rushed trying to find time to visit locations in our price range in the limited time we had before Josh left. Apparently not many people plan weddings within six months. To me, it felt like eternity. I would have married him the next day.

The day before Josh left, he built me another bookshelf as a surprise. When I came home, there was a giant jar with "Paradise Falls" written on it, and a replica photo album titled, My Adventure Book, from the movie, Up. Next to the photo album Josh had put together photos and notes in envelopes for me to open every single day when he was gone. It was one of the sweetest, most thoughtful things anyone had ever done for me.

Most flights that he was scheduled on when he travelled for work would always be between two and four in the morning, and this was no exception. As always, we sleepily and stressfully made our way to the airport where I dropped him off. On my drive back, I was blinking back tears the whole way home.

During that time, we of course, were newly engaged. We had a date set for our wedding, five months later in August. Wedding planning came easy to me, and it was something to occupy my mind with when I let it. Letting it occupy my mind meant that I let myself believe that we would be getting married that August. Letting myself believe that Josh would be coming back home to me alive and well.

I honestly have no idea how I coped that first time. It all seems as if it was a blur, even though in the moment it felt as if time moved as slowly as possible. Every time Josh would contact me, he seemed strong and in excellent spirits. This of course, was a good thing overall.

I remember feeling as if it was a slap in the face.

Josh exerted large amounts of effort as best he could to make me feel loved and important. Yet, I still felt insignificant, and therefore resentful. Resentful not to Josh, but to the mountain. How in the world did a mountain hold such a grasp on my husband? Honestly, I still don't know. It tethered in what felt like an incomparable hold.

The hold that a mountain held over Josh in turn, paralyzed me. I felt incredibly alone.

The year prior to Josh's trip was the Nepali earthquake that killed over 9,000 people including climbers, trekkers, Sherpa and guides. This took place during Everest season, where many people had already made it to Everest Base Camp. Josh's coworkers told stories of performing CPR for hours at over 17,000 feet above sea level. Things like that were all I could think about.

I could not see past planning his funeral in my head, because after that I felt as if I couldn't bear to exist. If that happened life did not seem like anything to me, but empty.

Running felt as if it was my only solace from myself. I was never an athlete in school, never played sports, and even based on mandatory physical education classes very quickly realized I was not wanted on anyone's team. Yet, I found the patterns of running to be soothing to me.

It became a coping mechanism, something I could control. It kept my anxiety at bay, and I did not have to rely on anyone else. Not that I don't enjoy being on a team, but this was different. With that, much to the dismay of my active friends, I do not like running with other people. Every single run compounds the fact that all I need is myself, breath by breath, lungs filling with air. Running taught me that I was self-sustainable enough to survive my own self. In those days, weeks and months that Josh would be gone running gave me just a tiny bit of courage. Even if my worst nightmare would happen, maybe I would be able to get through it.

Quickly, I began to realize that "Mt. Everest worry" was different from any other type of worry. When Josh was on other mountains guiding, I did worry, but not to the extent that I did while he was in Nepal. After adjusting to him being gone, I would be able to maintain a much more balanced life, albeit quiet. This felt different. There was a repetitive obsession that I had and I could not seem to get out of it. I was convinced that something awful would happen.

Another side effect of this trip was that I lost my appetite. Food stopped being appealing to me. There is a twelve hour and forty-five-minute time difference between Washington State and Nepal. Our days and nights were flipped, and when Josh and I were able to communicate, it was always very early morning, or late at night for me. Because of that, I stopped sleeping. At one point I went to the doctor and was prescribed a sleeping aid but ended up only using it one night because I didn't want to accidentally sleep through Josh's call.

I was obsessive about keeping my phone with me at all times. I realized that I could place my phone in between the shower curtain and liner. I took my phone running with me. A missed text or phone call could mean the difference of not being able to communicate for days. The few times that that had happened I would mentally beat myself up, becoming my own worst enemy.

Re-imagining the real possibility of Josh not coming home gave me a false sense of control. I thought if I was hopeful in the climb going successfully, I was ill prepared and irresponsible.

What if he didn't make it home alive?

I did not have any faith in myself to be able to survive that tragic scenario without some sort of mental preparation. That mental preparation turned out to be constantly envisioning Josh's death and how I might feel because of it. In some twisted way, thinking about how I might feel if the worst possible thing could happen somehow gave me the tiniest shred of hope that if it happened, I might just survive it.

I would lay awake at night, closing my eyes to only stare into my brain. With my anxious and active brain, I would be trapped in a stark white, too small windowless room, with huge bookshelves lining one side. The shelves were dark, making it feel claustrophobic and smaller than it really was. My brain would watch myself quickly pace back and forth, the feeling of my breath shortening as I tiredly laid in bed. As far back as I can remember, this is how I have fallen asleep most nights.

During the climb, my mind pace quickened and my ability to shake myself out of it lessened when Josh was on that mountain. My biggest desire would be that I had to run. I never could actually run because it was the middle of the night. I desperately needed a true physical indication of why my heart would be beating so fast. The feeling of needing to catch my breath never actually disappeared.

Some nights it would take hours to fall asleep. Some nights I would not fall asleep at all. Some nights I would only fall asleep at sunrise only after fully exhausting myself.

This was a pattern that I only knew too well.

When I was finally able to sleep it was as if my body would reset itself, if only for just for the few sleepy moments I would have as I would just be waking up. It felt as if my entire body had finally slowed down. Once I would fully wake up that feeling evaporated and I would start the mental marathon all over again.

After a few weeks of feeling as if I was on a hamster wheel imagining Josh's death like some sort of voodoo monster, I decided to try and focus some of my energy into something positive. I decided to start the volunteer process to work with the Make-A-Wish Foundation, Alaska/Washington chapter.

Many kids that are part of the program have gone through unsurmountable medical issues that affect their daily life. Most of them cannot plan for the future, as the future is uncertain. Yet, a single wish might be something they can try and look forward to, despite whatever the future brings to them and their family. The idea that I could provide a little magic and happiness in these kids' lives before time played its awful tricks gave me some solace in what I was personally going through.

I can't say that it directly helped with my day to day anxiety but looking back it does lend a nice metaphor to what life felt like for me. Focusing on the negative and the endless what-if scenarios was something that I felt as if I could not break free from. I was trapped in my own mind, unable to escape myself. Taking myself out of my own situation and applying my energy elsewhere seemed to help my sanity. It distracted me from my own destructive thoughts and placed me in a situation where I was forced to see the good in this world.

Kids can uncannily see the truth in emotions displayed, feigning happiness does not work; you truly must emanate happiness. Thrusting myself into situations that often were medically hopeless, you still had to see the light that was sparked at the end of the tunnel that planning and creating a wish can create.

When Josh summitted Mt. Everest that year, he made me a sign which he subsequently brought back for me after he returned home. He had a friend take a photo of him holding it. It said how much he loved me, the date and location being on the top of Mt. Everest. As stressed as this entire expedition had made me, I am still exceptionally proud of him. It is an extraordinarily admirable feat, that most people do not even think of accomplishing.

When he was gone, Josh encouraged me to focus onto something positive, like planning our wedding. I had decided as part of the wedding decorations I wanted an antique teacup on each table for the reception. Finding pretty, unique and affordable teacups was not as easy as you may think. At that time, I was driving around a lot for my job and any hole in the wall shop that I saw, I would stop.

Another important thing that comes with wedding planning is the dress. I had thoughts of wedding dresses since I was a little kid, as many people do. I knew of a designer and had an idea of what style I wanted. I had found that the average couple takes at least a year to plan a wedding. That seemed very over the top to me. Five months did not stress me out, but everyone I interacted with was. I refused to start shopping for a dress until I knew Josh was okay. Which pushed out my wedding dress shopping until the last weekend in May, just under three months until we walked down the aisle.

I decided that our theme for our wedding would be based on *Beauty and the Beast*, a beloved favorite story of mine and one that Josh begrudgingly agreed to. Our table decorations would be old books and antique teacups I had collected, with a single rose in a vase, atop a mirrored centerpiece on each table. Our decor was subtle to the theme and only admirers of the story would appreciate the delicate nods.

I had discovered a designer who made wedding dresses based on Disney characters. I knew that was where I wanted to go. There were only a handful of the stores in the country, and luckily there was one about an hour away.

I planned a trip with my mom, aunt, and some close friends to go shopping with me. It was all very last minute, because I would not commit to going until Josh had summitted Mt. Everest, which he had done a couple days before the trip. I remember the relief and silliness that I had felt going into the wedding dress store.

It was as if getting married was finally real and truly happening. I had not let myself truly think that it was going to occur. All I could think about was the potential sad story I would tell for the rest of my life – I was engaged to the love of my life, who died climbing Mt. Everest, and I would just have this unused wedding dress forever hanging in my closet. That narrative would play over and over in my head.

When I found out he had summitted, was on his way back down, and subsequently then home, I snapped back into reality and the excitement of our impending wedding really hit.

When we got to the wedding dress store, I narrowed it down to two different dresses. One, was what I had planned on getting since I was a teenager, even though of course I had not seen it in person or tried it on until then. The other one was very unlike the one I had always planned on having. It was much more form fitting, a looser on the bottom, sweetheart neckline and beaded crystals cascading down from the top down. Everyone I was with was very unhelpful telling me I looked great in both. Finally, one of my oldest and best friends was honest and helpful. I picked the latter.

Josh's only request about my dress was that it did not have sleeves. The dress that I picked was the second option, based on Queen Elsa, from the movie, *Frozen*. It did not have sleeves, but the train attached to an ethereal, detachable cape which I threatened and scared him with up until he saw me walk down the aisle. In actuality, of course, it was exceptionally lovely, and "cape" did not give an accurate depiction.

It just so happened that the dress that I tried on was my size and there were no others in stock, and there wouldn't be for at least six months. The wedding dress salespeople were much more panicky about our three month countdown to the big day than I ever was. However, because this was apparently the only dress of this model that existed, and because it fit, I clearly was destined for it. I was able to walk out of the store with my wedding dress that day.

A few days after my fated meeting with my wedding dress, Josh returned. I picked him up from the airport skinny and tired. Climbing to the top of the world is hard work.

BEFORE

part III

Within that first week of Josh being back home we decided to climb Mt. Rainier together again, via the Emmons Glacier route. Josh told me that in the climbing world, many people climb Mt. Rainier to practice for climbing Mt. Everest. Its massive glaciers, crevasses and alpine terrain make it a great training ground.

This time in my preparation I had two days' notice, instead of one. Immediately, I loved that route so much more. You start the climb 1,000 feet lower, still in the trees on the Glacier Basin Trail. At the beginning, Mt. Rainier is hidden from view. When you finally see the first mountain views poking out of the tree line, you are still in the woody sub-alpine meadows, far below the snow. The true roots of the mountain show themselves.

The Emmons route is not maintained by the National Park Service or the mountain guides, making it a much more remote alpine environment. There is not a shoveled trail, no wands, anchors, or ropes lining this route. It was much more lone; less people climbing and one with the earth. All you see is the mountain at its raw nature.

The east side of Mt. Rainier is majestic. Looking up from our Base Camp at Camp Schurman, the ice and snow looked overwhelmingly large. The only other time

I had travelled by rope was the year prior, during our summit climb. I found that I remembered things that I had earmarked in my brain from the year before. It helped me adjust easily to this climbing trip. I could not believe we were going to climb up all of it. To the top.

Again.

Once we ascended the large section, I realized that the mountain is deceptive in its majesty. After, there's another bigger slope to attempt. Crossing the Emmons Glacier was impressive, especially for a non-climber like myself. The Emmons is the largest glacier in the lower 48 states. It is expansive and vast.

We summitted on June 6, 2016. On our way to the top of our last section of what's called the corridor, we climbed as the sun rose. I remember we took a break as the sun finally crowned the world into its gaze. A new day had officially begun. I had never seen this side of the mountain, let alone from that vantage point. It was breathtaking. I felt the dichotomy of feeling so unbelievably small, and very much part of the living world at the same moment.

We came down from the summit to rest after our success back at Camp Schurman. The next morning, we headed back home. This trip usually takes climbers four days, three nights. It took us three days, two nights. It was and still is, one of my favorite parts of Mt. Rainier. The days that we spent on the mountain and the rawness we were exposed to was what makes this mountain revered. I finally had a level of understanding of why Josh loved this specific mountain so much.

If getting past the trial of Mt. Everest was a nightmare, this was the dream.

J osh continued to guide on Mt. Rainier that Summer, but looking back so much of those three months leading up to our wedding ran together. I spent most days so unbelievably grateful for the simplicity of the act of planning our wedding. Most things came together easily, and there was a lot of celebrating and looking forward to the big day moments that we shared.

On the day of my bridal shower I was not in the greatest mood. Formal celebrations like having a bridal shower thrown seemed a little out of date. Being the center of everything, having to wear a sash and open gifts in front of people just isn't my thing, but I powered through. Josh was working in the office as Operations Manager that day and I remember calling him frustrated after. I decided I was going to drive out to Ashford later that afternoon, and Josh said we would do something he knew I would enjoy.

Later that day, Josh drove us into Mt. Rainier National Park where we went on a short, but steep hike up to a waterfall and enjoyed some beers. To date, it was the only time I had ever gone hiking with a full face of makeup on and I remember the mist from the waterfall made my eyeliner and mascara run down my face. In my mind that part of the day was my favorite part of my bridal shower, even though it had nothing to do with the actual official shower. It was just me and Josh in the middle of the woods which is my favorite way to spend any day.

Leading up to our wedding things had gone pretty smoothly. My stress level was much lower since Josh had returned home safely from Nepal. However, as uncomplicated as things had been, the day of our actual wedding had a few hiccups. Most notably was the rushing around finishing up last minute things. We had taken on the responsibility to organize, set up and take down all equipment and decorations. In theory, it was a great idea. In actuality, it added some additional stress the days leading up to the ceremony.

The morning of our wedding day one of Josh's coworkers and our friend asked if we needed anything. He was already in town, ready to help us set up, seven hours before our ceremony. His willingness and consideration to help was heartfelt and saved our sanity.

Our wedding day itself was filled with about a hundred of our family and friends, on the hottest day on record that year. We had chosen an old colonial house, outside for the ceremony and reception. I remember walking down the aisle and feeling the sweat trickle down my back all the way into the butt crack. The top of the aisle was the only shaded part of the entire yard. As I write this, I am hoping years later that our family and friends have forgiven us for almost melting into puddles because it was so unbelievably stifling.

Our good friend, who had originally introduced Josh and I many moons back married us. I wrote my vows the night before whilst taking a bath after our rehearsal dinner. It was not out of procrastination, but out of fear that my words would not be good enough.

Sure enough, they were.

I am a person that spends a lot of time attempting to hide emotion on an average day, hoping that people won't see through me. Most days I fail. Still, I fiercely guard my heart. Yet, in that moment, as I was about halfway through my vows I started to cry, wearing my heart on my sleeve. I guess it was not a surprise to anyone how much I loved Josh.

We had our reception catered by the local Taco Truck and the photos surrounding that are still some of my favorites. Leading up to the wedding I had worked hard at staying healthy and working out regularly and eating carne asada tacos on our wedding day was the perfect pay off. What I hadn't realized is that in all of the final fittings of my wedding dress to get it tailored, it never occurred to me to try and sit down in the dress, let alone lean forward over a plate and try to eat something.

Initially, I had a moment of pure joy. I had just gotten married; I was about to eat my favorite food at our wedding and finally reward myself with the most delicious tacos imaginable. Except, I found I could not sit down properly. I had to half lean backwards because the parts of me that stretched out so perfectly when I was standing seemed to have all squished together when I sat down, and my dress was too form fitted to handle the squish factor. True to form, a bride rarely ever gets a chance to eat during their wedding, and this was no exception. Josh helped me with a couple tacos, and I survived to celebrate into the night.

Our first dance was to the song "A Tale As Old As Time", and it was one of the first moments that day that it felt like Josh and I could just *be*, him and I. It was a sweet and heartfelt moment. We laughed in joyful disbelief that we were finally married and all these people around us were watching us. At the end of our dance, Josh hugged me. His embrace was tender and kind. I remember thinking how lucky I was.

Our reception was a huge celebratory party. Both Josh and I were exceptionally happy. All the hullabaloo leading up to the wedding was over and we could finally just celebrate. Our bartender mismanaged our alcoholic drink instructions, so we had a limited variety, but an unplanned open bar the entire night. In the mountain guiding world, there were a handful of legends at our wedding. Now looking back, even though life looks much different, our wedding was still one of my favorite and most fun days of my life.

Neither of us really relish having the spotlight on us and we both found the average wedding toasts to be boring. Instead, we both decided to ask one person from our respective honor to deliver two individual speeches. Mine, was my childhood best friend. She spoke of our friendship going all the way back to when we were six years old. It made me tear up. Josh picked one of his best friends as well. His speech was funny, kind and genial. He ended it by singing a song that both him and Josh had made up years ago about me.

For me, one of my most memorable moments from our wedding was toward the beginning of the reception. We had just signed our marriage license, and both Josh and I had our witnesses. His, one of his best friends, the one who had given the toast. After we signed, his friend came up to us stating that if either of us ever needed anything in the course of our lives, he would be there. There is a photo of this moment from afar documenting where we are all laughing about something that he had said to us.

He was insistent, passionate, and earnest in his speech to us.

It meant a lot to me.

Little did I know, that less than a year later, I would be calling upon him to help me bring Josh back to life.

Celebrating with our families and friends was amazing. It was one heck of a party. However, after we were congratulated off, driving away was one of the first moments that we had that were just us. Our wedding festivities were great, and the day before was filled with advanced reception set-up and our rehearsal dinner. Earlier in the week family from out of town arrived, and Josh also held his Bachelor party. Our week had been fun filled and busy, with the end goal of course, being our wedding. As we were driving away, in one of our first few moments of just us we decided to stop at a local bar before going home.

We stopped at the same bar that we had gone to the night we summitted Mt. Rainier for the first time together. Josh in his suit, me in my wedding dress. They were holding another outdoor concert and the bar owners brought us drinks on the house. We danced out on the patio until we went home, and Josh carried me "hot-dog style" because I could not bend in my wedding dress, through the threshold of our front door.

Within a week of getting married we put an offer down and closed on a cabin in the woods. It is located in Ashford, mountain guide central. The same place that for the first year or so of us being together, I swore I would never have property. The back deck of our cabin has a tree built in through the deck, looking over the river. It was, and still is idyllic. We bought the cabin as is, with all the furniture, kitchen supplies, etc. included. This was good and at times, also frustrating. We inherited the cabin's black bear collection, which I loved, even though excessive.

The Autumn following our wedding Josh was home for a few months. We were able to settle down back into our normal life focusing on our cabin. We looked forward to our honeymoon that November to Disney World in Florida. To me it was as if we passed all the tests that life wanted to hand to us. During that time, I remember thinking back to what I felt like just a half a year prior to that, a duality of anxiety and anticipation constantly at battle with each other. Josh going to Nepal, summitting Mt. Everest and returning home safely felt as if it was the luckiest thing that could have happened.

I was so incredibly thankful to the universe.

During our honeymoon we visited all the parks in Disney World and Universal Studios. I undeniably love Disney, and this was a dream for me. Animal Kingdom in Disney World was our favorite. At the time, one of the newer main attractions in the park was the Expedition Everest ride. I had seen it briefly running through a few days prior, as I had signed up for a charity half marathon running through all the parks as "something to do" during our honeymoon. Again, the irony is lost on me.

Walking through Animal Kingdom you see Mt. Everest looming in the background before you get to the Nepal area. Walking through, even Josh was impressed. The designers had garnished the area to be as traditionally Nepali as they could. After the main entrance in line for the ride, Josh described photos on the wall of real Sherpa he knew and had worked with. He rode on the Expedition Everest ride three times. I did not partake, as fast-moving journeys such as roller coasters terrify and panic me, even though we chose an amusement park for our trip.

Being in fake Nepal was strange to me. I thought that this was as close as I ever would get to "Mt. Everest." This felt safer to me and I was not as envious or terrified of it. The ride in front of me was real, but the mountain was imaginary. This utopia was the only way I wanted to ever see or think about Mt. Everest again.

And then that beautiful image was shattered.

Some time that Autumn Josh floated the idea of going back to Mt. Everest. He indicated that he was asked about it at work, and because he was so successful the year prior, professionally he was in line to return. It was as if the hypothetical shards that shattered were shot into my heart dissolving our perfect life. I was extremely hurt, upset and angry at pretty much anyone that was involved, including myself. Of course, I took it out on Josh. We both disagreed, fought and cried hard over the topic. He would go back and forth weighing the opportunity versus the toll it would take on me and our marriage.

The moment that the topic was suggested, I knew he would go back. John Muir stated, "The Mountains are Calling, and I Must Go." If I could assign a defining quote to describe my husband, that would be it. I knew Josh inside and out. This was not a question with an unknown answer. The mountains hold a power over him, one that even he doesn't totally understand.

Mountains and I have a contentious history. It was as if I was in this constant battle of tug of war with Mother Nature over my husband which I never would win. I just could not understand the loyalty that he had toward mountains, when it didn't feel as if he had the same loyalty toward me. This feeling was at the heart of all my anxiety. As much as Josh would try and comfort me, I always had that little voice in my head isolating me.

With every assurance that he had, Josh left for Nepal to climb to the summit of Mt. Everest for a second time. It is hard for me to go back to the muddy feelings of what I felt the first time around. I tried to block so many of my feelings out, numbing myself. As I write this I am still dancing upon the earthy subject, not wanting to dig deep. It is as if my shoes are glued to my feet and I can barely feel the earth below me. On the contrary, the second time around I remember and feel everything as if it was yesterday.

Knowing that he would go back was absolutely devastating to me. I was crushed. Even though I had survived the Spring prior, I still felt victim to it. This time around I knew the dark place that I had been, and I did not want to go back. It was so much worse knowing the mental dark hole you are on the edge of, slowly being pushed closer and closer not wanting to fall back in.

In my experience, that is what trauma does to the mind and body. I understand trauma; I work and study it in my social work profession. And yet, it still knowingly got the upper hand. Panic attacks are not necessarily caused by a trauma itself. When you go through a trauma there are side effects. Those side effects trigger the fear of mentally going back to that hidden place that your mind has buried away. True to trauma form, I was terrified of going through that again.

It never occurred to me to walk away. It was only within writing this that I wondered if someone reading this would ask the question. It would be easier to leave, right? Why would someone choose this life and go through it willingly?

Those questions nauseate me.

Even the thought of it leaves a distaste on my tongue. I am disdainful that it is even a question. I love Josh, and love withstands everything.

At my job we work with at-risk youth in the foster care system. With the participation of every youth that comes through our program, we create a safety plan. What to do if they are feeling depressed, anxious, suicidal, etc. This is important for success because it gives people the opportunity to think about what might be helpful to them in hard moments.

This time around I created a safety plan for myself. The day after Josh left, I signed up to run a half marathon. It was scheduled about seven weeks later, ideally about two weeks before he was due to return home. I had a previous relationship with a therapist from a couple years back and I requested to re-engage with her immediately. I made sure that at any given time I had something to look forward to, even if it was small.

On paper, I was fine; I set myself up for success.

Inside, I was a wreck.

I had this feeling that something bad was going to happen. At the time I wrestled with arguments in my head of whether I had convinced myself that something bad would happen, or if it was something that I just felt in my gut. I have always trusted my gut, and in the markers that the universe provided. I could not distinguish or delineate if this was my anxiety talking, or if it was something deep down.

Looking back and recalling the year before, I felt Josh successfully accomplishing his goal and returning safely home was by far the lucky stroke of the world. I just could not understand why you would want to test that good fortune. I remember talking about this in therapy. My therapist brought me back around to what was real, versus the crazy train of thoughts my mind would take me on.

Contrary to never abandoning my loyalty for Josh, I have had days where I think about leaving my job for something else. Something that would not cause as much heartache or secondary trauma. Again, I signed up for the nitty gritty parts of marriage, but a job does not have to be forever.

Recently I learned a valuable lesson. I found out a former client overdosed from drugs and died. She was maybe twenty years old. It was my job to call their former case manager who had moved on from that position, but still a good friend. As he burst into tears over the phone, I realized that the job itself will never leave me. I won't escape it.

In that moment of clarity, I shifted my perspective – I don't want to escape it.

The work I do will continue to be meaningful. The work that I have done will not be erased.

It reminded me of early on in our relationship when a coworker asked me why I stayed with Josh. This was before we were married, shared vows and promised our lives to one another. Still, the question disgusted me. Honestly, the idea of spending every single waking moment with the same person would drive me insane. If I wasn't so worried about something going wrong the time to myself would be much more enjoyable. Our relationship was not built on the amount of days or time we spent together, but rather on making the days and time we did spend together count.

I truly don't think many people understand that difference. I think it is easy to develop a routine and stay stagnant within it. The idleness takes over. The idea of making memories and having real conversations can fall to the wayside when every day is the same. Neither Josh nor I live our lives like that. We each value our independence and individuality. We need time apart with ourselves in order to be better together.

On this Everest expedition, Josh was guiding with one of his best friends, the person who signed our marriage certificate as the witness to our wedding. Before they left, he messaged me saying that everything would be fine, and he would take care of my dear. Remembering his promise to us on our wedding day, it comforted me knowing that someone that cared for Josh would be there in case anything happened.

Early on in Josh's trip, a friend invited me on an adventure. I was to show up at her house and we would "adventure" in her RV. I showed up with my overnight bag and snacks. I had no idea what to expect. I was instructed to enter the vehicle and pick a direction. This is how we would drive. At every light or crossroad, we would alternate who would choose the direction. Sometimes we kept driving straight, sometimes we would turn.

We ended up at a winery near Westport, WA. Hungry from all our decision making we stopped. We pretended we were fancy eating their cheese plates and sampling wine. We continued to drive and ended up at the ocean.

As far back as I can remember, I have loved the ocean. One time when I was probably about six or seven my mom's best friend was supposed to be watching me while my mom was working at a daylong conference. We were at the ocean and I remember stopping at the place where the water meets the sand. The tide was coming in, but I just stood there watching the water come back and forth to me. Even at such a young age, watching the waves crash felt therapeutic to me. As a little kid, I did not realize that since the tide was coming in, the sand I was standing on was getting more and more mushy. I had begun to sink. I almost drowned.

After the panicked moment of "the not drowning incident" we rushed around trying to get all the sand and salt to disappear. My mom's friend was not the most responsible and was stressed about what would happen if my mom found out. Back at the hotel, it was as if I had collected all the sand on the beach in my clothes, hair and rainboots. When my mom came back, she immediately knew that something had happened. Our hotel room had turned into a sandy pit. In the eyes of an adult, namely my mom, we had experienced a dramatic and scary day.

It is one of my favorite memories.

Ever since then, I have loved the ocean. After many trips to the ocean over the years, I was back. And it was different. We arrived at the edge of a storm, the Spring weather just on the cusp. We watched the waves turn large and ominous, collide into the beach and rocks. I felt as if I could fully breathe. Each time the waves would build and then subsequently crash down it was as if the wall inside me I had built was becoming slowly softer. Maybe it was a metaphor for the storms of life, rolling in, passing through, never staying.

Maybe I could get through this Everest season.

As the days commenced, I continued to spend a lot of my extra time running. Through running, I was training my body to endure. With endurance, I also gained resilience. Every single step of most runs I think to myself of how not fun it is. The physicality was tough, but it was never a barrier for me. Forcing myself to get dressed, lace up my shoes and walk out of the front door is always by far the hardest part of any run. I realize that I am the one who puts myself into the situation of running. I am very aware that I can take a break, walk, or simply turn around and go home at any point. But I never do. I run my set amount that I intend to. Every single time. I force my body and mind to endure and build resilience. I continue to teach myself that I can accomplish hard things.

Most of the time running gave me a physical outlet for my brain that constantly felt like it was the one running. The exhaustion that I felt from running made sense to me. I had just run five, ten, fifteen miles. I should be tired. Yet, most of the time my brain was running in an impossible loop which exhausted me mentally and emotionally and was much harder to grasp. Exhausting myself physically was much easier to deal with, as it gave me something to focus on. Through extreme physical activity, I had found a way to quiet my mind. When I was running, my thoughts would not jump around, but rather move through me in order to process their meaning.

While Josh was gone, I lost my appetite again and ate mainly small kale salads for lunch and that's about it. Even though sleep was never restful for me, I stopped drinking coffee and had green tea every morning. The extra caffeine in coffee would make focusing on anything throughout the day unbelievably difficult and put me on edge. If I was invited to happy hour, my limit was two drinks. I did not want to pass the point of giddiness to extreme sadness.

Like the year prior, I spent every night tossing and turning, and if I fell asleep out of exhaustion, it was not restful. I laid in bed every night as my thoughts jumped back and forth like a frog moving from lily pad to lily pad. I have fallen asleep many nights like this, whether or not Josh was on a mountain, but this time it was at a hyper level. My thoughts were illogical and nonsensical. I could not focus long enough on them to work through them, as my mind was frenetic and almost manic.

I ticked off the things I had to do – run, therapy, wait to hear from Josh, and the days slowly passed. I am not sure why, but after a few weeks I realized I had not shaved my legs. As the weather turned to a nice Pacific Northwest Spring, I continued to not shave. I have no idea what I would have done if Josh had not returned home. However, it was a small thing that I could control, so I held onto it.

Control played a much bigger part in my life then I was consciously aware of. So many things were happening that I could not hold any sway over. The few things that I could hold control over was my routine. Some days I would welcome distraction, such as going to the river with a friend. On days that I would defer out of pure weariness, I would get up from my bed and force myself to go for a run. After I came home, I would collapse into the couch, emotionally and physically exhausted. Running was, and still is my daily win.

During that time one of the television stations seemed to have the *Harry Potter* movies playing every Sunday. Growing up I read the books as they came out, and I was the same age as Harry Potter himself. As the books were published, every Summer I would beg my mom to take me to the bookstore on opening day only to spend the next few hours and days, however long it would take for me to read from beginning to end.

Oftentimes throughout the years I would re-read the books, treating them like a sacred text. The themes and struggles made me feel less alone and made me strive to be great. On the days that Josh was gone, and I only made it out to the couch, again the story was a source of comfort. The plot never surprised me because I knew it so well. I could re-watch the movies or re-read the books and just zone out. It alleviated my overall stress because unlike my real life, I knew exactly what would happen next.

I had envisioned Josh's funeral over and over in my head, not in sadness, but in a feeling of preparation. I did not want to think about what type of flowers to put on his grave, but I felt as if I should be prepared just in case. I had even exerted control over the worst possible scenario. As morbid and horrible as the scenario is, the control comforted me. If my nightmare actually happened, I felt having a plan would offer a safety net for me to fall back on. I didn't realize that this type of control was not supporting me in any way, but rather constricting me like a snake tightening its grip on my heart, distancing myself from a very real and alive Josh.

I started volunteering with a local music group, a set and scheduled day each week. It was for an eight-week program which meant that it was the bulk amount of time that Josh was scheduled to be gone. I had participated in many of these eight-week sessions over the years. I ticked off each week as it occurred. It was something that I could count on that had an end goal. We would watch and chart progress as the weeks went on, marking growth. This session I also kept track of my own betterment, the goal being not to completely drive myself crazy.

Before Josh had left, he had added another stack of envelopes for me to open daily and add to our adventure book that he had given me the year prior. As much as I loved them, it was a little painful. There were days that I would let stack up and I would open multiple envelopes on a day that was not so hard.

Despite it being hard, I loved the thoughtfulness that Josh had put into this project for me. Many of the photographs were from our engagement photo shoot and snapshots from our wedding. Some days seeing the sweet memories balanced with my own tortuous brain was too much. I felt as if our life together was too good to be true. Some gloomy days the envelopes would unintentionally become a cruel reminder of how much I really had to lose.

Even though I was frustrated and worried about Josh being back on Mt. Everest I rarely felt sadness. Even though my anxiety was crippling, it never made me feel sad. I think a lot of people pair worry and sadness together, but not me. I never felt sorry for myself, or that I should be pitied. I did not cry, nor did I feel sorrow. I happily chose my life. I was simply worried.

Similar to the year before, contact with Josh was variable. Not being able to count on when I would hear from Josh was difficult for me. Depending on where he was on the trek to Base Camp, I would hear from him frequently or infrequently. Like the year before, I continued to be obsessive with my phone, never disconnecting or taking a break. Once the team arrived at Base Camp and started their rotations to the high camps, the ability to communicate changed.

Base Camp on Mt. Everest sits at about 17,000 to 17,500 feet above sea level, depending on where you are situated. When climbing at high altitude the body must adjust. At higher altitudes the amount of air pressure reduces and breathing limits the amount of oxygen molecules. By staying in one spot for a while, the body starts to acclimatize and produce more red blood cells to transport their way through the body to create deeper breathing.

If you ascend in altitude too quickly you can suffer from acute mountain sickness, high-altitude cerebral edema, and/or high-altitude pulmonary edema. To combat this on peaks like Mt. Everest, climbers go to higher camps to let their bodies adjust, and then come back down to Base Camp to rest, giving their body a chance to develop the red blood cells. In a sense, climbers zigzag up and down the mountain.

Performing well at high altitude is not something that you can really train for. Your body either adapts well or adapts poorly. Furthermore, being physically in shape does not change the likelihood for experiencing altitude sickness. Many people and climbing guides have the desire to conquer higher peaks such as Mt. Everest, but cannot due to their body's reaction to altitude.

A few years back on a personal trip, Josh, along with some coworkers attempted to summit Denali in Alaska. One of his good friends was also on the trip. He was a fellow mountain guide who Josh boasted was one of the strongest people he knew and preferred to co-guide with on Mt. Rainier. However, when they reached about 17,500 feet on Denali, his strength failed him.

Josh watched one of his friends turn into a limp noodle, experiencing high altitude sickness. As much desire as the group wanted to continue their climb, and as strong as this person was at 14,411 feet, that all came to a halt. Just under 3,000 feet shy of hitting the summit of Denali, they were forced to turn around and descend back down the mountain.

Much to my guilt-ridden dismay, Josh of course, performs excellent at altitude. He was a collegiate swimmer; his lungs were used to breathing in and exhaling out in tough conditions. His grandfather and father were also avid recreational climbers, climbing it seemed was truly a part of him. I am not sure why those facts never comforted me. Looking back, it should have eased my worry, as not only was Josh never anything but successful in the mountains, but climbing was also in his blood. I'm sure that this is something that my therapist tried to get my stubborn brain to absorb, but my anxiety that something would go wrong far outweighed a clear mind.

A little over a year prior the movie *Everest* had premiered, based on Jon Krakauer's book, *Into Thin Air*. It was about a famous expedition from 1996 where eight climbers had died. Josh had read the book and seen the movie and enjoyed it. It seemed as if everyone in the entire world would ask me about it, especially when Josh went back to Mt. Everest for a second time.

No one seemed to understand that this movie was the last thing that I ever wanted to watch. Josh shared that production of the movie was done very well, the mountain and deadly scenes were exceptionally accurate to the environment. I still refuse to watch the movie. I do not believe that I need a movie to replicate its scenes over and over in my head, haunting me. I did not want to make this real-life tragic event a drama for entertainment. I had my own nightmares to contend with.

It was getting closer and closer to the summit rotation. Josh and his best friend would message me photos of themselves goofing around in their spare time at Base

Camp, just waiting for their bodies to acclimatize properly. I learned the year prior that actual days spent climbing Mt. Everest is only about three weeks, whereas the full length of the expedition takes two and a half months. Most of that extra time is spent waiting for your body to acclimatize. Time, it seemed, was not just an opponent of mine, but all were awaiting its final bid.

Josh reportedly maintained feeling healthy and ready for the final sequence up to the summit, and back down again. I was ready for it as well, knowing that it meant this would be the first step in him starting the journey back home. I had no logical reason to believe that Josh would be anything but successful. Yet, the chain of events that happened over the series of the next few days changed the course of both of our lives.

The dates are different, but because of the time difference, it just so happened that the day that Josh summitted Mt. Everest for the second time, was also the same day I ran my half marathon. It made me happy to think that we both accomplished something that we were proud of on the same day. I raced in the morning, happily cutting twelve minutes off my previous half marathon on our honeymoon just six months prior.

That morning the sun was shining, and I was hot. I ran quickly, ignoring the sweat that was pouring into my eyeballs, blinding me. I continued to pump my legs and my arms as if all the monstrous fears of my head were chasing me. I felt like that on every run, but this was different. The monsters had become corporeal, growing legs and towering over me. I ran in an attempt to escape them, hoping for that feeling of exhaustion at the end of a long run, keeping the creatures at bay.

Later that day on May 21, 2017, from the highest point on earth, Josh phoned me from the summit of Mt. Everest. He told me he had made it and held up another sign of him at the top for me just like last year and would send me the photo when he could. He conveyed to me that he was okay, he loved me, and they would be heading back down to camp soon.

I was so excited. He had made it. Again! The amount of people that make it to the summit of Mt. Everest is very few and far in between. Josh had just made it twice, in back to back years. As terrified, resentful and worried as I had been, I was also extremely proud. It was and is quite the achievement.

I did not hear from Josh until very briefly the next morning. I remember him sounding exhausted and worn out. I didn't think anything of it, assuming that he was naturally depleted due to summitting the world's highest peak a mere twelve hours before. He told me that something had happened, but he was okay, and good news is that he would be home sooner than expected, within about a week or so.

I, of course, was ecstatic. I am not sure if that is all my brain would let me hear or not. Whatever had happened could not have been that bad. As wild as my imagination had gotten, I never imagined something terrible might happen AND he would come home alive. My scenarios always ended deadly.

That unforgettable phone call took place early on a Monday morning, and I coincidentally had therapy scheduled that same day. Honestly, I did not think anything that serious had happened to Josh. He seemed tired over the phone, but spiritedly good. He assured me that he would be coming home in one piece, no broken bones. I thought that he was rightfully fatigued, finding that climbing to the top of the world probably was not a walk in the park like it had been the year before.

While Josh was gone, I had somehow built new channels in the rabbit hole of my mind. My brain had spiraled my true self deeper and deeper inside. No one really knew the turmoil of what was going through my head. I checked the boxes, went to work, and did what I needed to do. Most people in my life had no idea of what my inner discourse was to myself. It had twisted any sort of positivity into villainous creatures plaguing me. Now that Josh would be on his way home it was as if I had finally found the way out from the burrow. I could start to think clearly again without shadows darkening my thoughts.

During therapy I remember feeling accomplished. I spoke about what Josh had mentioned to me and his demeanor over the phone. Even if my therapist felt as if something serious had happened, she didn't let on. We scheduled another appointment the next week where I had the freedom to cancel if I felt good about it. Contrary to running a race the day prior, this felt like the finish line. We made it through another Mt. Everest season.

Little did I know that everything leading up to this was the deep breath before the plunge.

DURING

part I

Josh and I had spoken regularly as he had started the journey home. In what seemed like a stroke of luck, he told me he would not have to spend the three additional days walking out of Base Camp. His client had volunteered to spend the additional cost for both of them to fly directly out of the Khumbu Valley. They flew back to Kathmandu and waited to schedule a flight home. To me, everything seemed to go smoothly and in a timely manner. I was overjoyed that Josh would be home within the week.

I spent those initial days in between while Josh was travelling to remember how to feel. When I stepped out into the sunshine I finally could feel and absorb its warmth. I went for a couple runs fully enjoying the waterfront views without my own demons on my tail. I cleaned our house to get it back to the "Josh standard", as he is much tidier than me. The hollow feeling in my core started to fill.

Josh and his best friend both flew into Seattle. It was a beautiful, warm Spring day. I was wearing a new dress I had bought for the occasion, and turquoise wedges that matched perfectly. The morning before picking him up from the airport I thoroughly misjudged the amount of time it takes to shave one's legs after neglecting that task for two and half months. I was late for work but had no worries in my head. I was so excited that it was Josh's coming home day. Despite forgetting why I never walk in heels to begin with, I felt as if I was walking on air.

At the airport, seeing him for the first time I noticed he was particularly skinny. At the time I did not think he looked as skinny as he had been after coming home from other trips, but still, he had thinned. Now, looking back at photos from those first few weeks of him being home he looked sickly. Both of them seemed very relieved and happy to have made the long journey home. They sang the song they had made up about me all through the airport, mirroring the moment from our wedding that Summer before.

We parted ways after the boys collected their massive bags of gear. We have an entire room dedicated to Josh's mountain gear at our house. The number of things that they travel with still amazes me. They embraced together and then enveloped me into their hug as well.

Nothing felt out of place. It was a sweet moment and I was glad to be included.

On the way back, I had planned for us to stop and grab some lunch, but Josh just wanted to get home. Travelling for around sixteen hours after coming off a mountain for two and a half months is not something I could totally relate to. Though, I understood how soothing and comforting home can be. We got home and ate whatever random scraps of food I had left in the refrigerator. I recalled I probably should have gone grocery shopping, but prior to him being home, the thought had not occurred to me. I still had not really eaten a substantial meal the entire time he had been away. After his extensive travelling, all he ultimately wanted to do was take a nap, finally in our bed.

Later that day after we rested, we just laid in bed chatting. It always is a nice moment after Josh returned home from a climb to finally be able to hold a real conversation. Communicating from a mountain is not actual real communication. There is usually a delay or overlap in dialogue, almost every statement is followed by the other person saying, "What?", and then we would repeat the whole cycle. Anything significant or detailed lost its meaning.

I had spent so much time worrying and worst-case scenario planning in my head the fact that Josh was truly home felt surreal to me. Yet, under the surface of our conversation there were stories unspoken. I had not yet learned what had happened that Josh wanted to share with me. In those first few hours of him blissfully being home, tragedy was looming.

Laying in the safety of our bed, Josh started to tell me his tale. What he hadn't shared with me was that prior to their summit rotation he was not feeling well. Not awful, but not awesome either. Josh was conscientious that every event during their final push to the summit affected each other, causing a chain reaction. Overall, getting up to the summit itself was the first obstacle. For him not being at full health, it was not as easy as it was last year, but still doable. For his client on the other hand it was extremely difficult, and Josh was in charge.

The year before Josh had been designated a one-on-one client. However, early into their trip, the client decided to go back home, not ready for the physical and mental demands that it takes to climb to the highest point on earth. Instead, Josh was adopted into the standard climbing group, serving as an additional guide for an already staffed group of clients. Since he was "the extra", splitting the work between the other guides made things easier overall. Josh was successful, strong and thrived within the team.

For this year's expedition, Josh was asked again to guide a client one-on-one. Not having to worry about multiple people or a team of climbers, just one person. This was part of his assurance to me leading into his return to Nepal. He stated that it is much easier to guide like this because simply put, it is just one person versus a whole group of people to have to manage.

Each Western guide also has a Sherpa guide with them and their client, or clients. They are living maps of the mountain. The person that travelled with them this year was on his eleventh or twelfth summit attempt. Josh said he and their Sherpa got on well, despite him not speaking any English.

As the course of the trip unfolded Josh expressed to me that his client probably would not be his close friend in the real world. Though, he said that their professional relationship was fine. Like many people's profession, Josh would do his job and then go home. Sometimes he became authentic friends with the clients he guided, but that was not an expectation.

He stated his client seemed physically in shape and paid additional cost for a one-on-one guide. In 2016, attempting the summit of Mt. Everest was around $60,000 U.S. dollars, being part of a standard group. This does not count any extra gear you might have to purchase, plane flights, additional oxygen, or helicopter flights, to say nothing of paying additionally for a guide to yourself. Climbing mountains is expensive.

So, on their summit day, Josh was not feeling well. As they got higher and higher to the summit, his former Army Ranger, cross-fitting client was seemingly gutted, creating a less than ideal situation. Mt. Everest is of course, the highest place you can get to on earth... the entire world... our planet. There is a reverence, as well as a usual fair trepidation for most anyone who chooses to attempt going to the summit.

As a whole, mountains in general can be foreboding, unpredictable, unforgiving and restless. Even in the best of all scenarios, even without warning something could instantly change. With reverence, there is great power. With trepidation, there is disquiet. If reverence and trepidation are missing, you are only sharply left with ego.

Walking up to the summit most people are aware of the stories that climbers tell of seeing dead bodies. Every year as people from all over the world attempt their summit news articles are released about the dead bodies, reminding the world for a brief two-week period of what you are facing as you climb to the top of the world.

This is absolutely the case that Josh attested to. For me, I cannot even comprehend wrapping my head around how that would make me feel. To a certain extent I can imagine it and I am profoundly horrified. The professional side of my brain looks at the situation from a psychological aspect.

How does the trauma of seeing fellow climbers, dead bodies frozen in their journey, unable to go on affect your own brain, knowing that you have narrowly stepped on and/or seen those who could not continue?

Humanly, does walking past these fellow people guilt and taint your journey and ability to truly achieve your own dream, knowing they died in their own pursuit?

Does it make it worth it?

Does succeeding in the attempt inadvertently put out of one's mind the journey it took to get there?

I ask these questions because I believe that they are important.

No journey is complete without sacrifice.

Knowing what or who you are willing to sacrifice in order to achieve a dream or goal can say a lot about a person. I think that many people are blinded in the pursuit of their dreams, not meaning to cause wreckage amidst the wake of succession. Asking forgiveness later is usually easier than preemptively trying to imagine any conflict or hurt that might be caused. Josh was willing to sacrifice the toll it would take on me returning a second time, not aware of the toll it might take on him. He never fully can understand what it was like for me before, during or after, nor can I understand what his fated experience was like for him.

The first hurdle in the summit rotation is making it to Camp One to your first break. There you have the ability to set your pack down and rest for a short while. Camp One is just after the Khumbu Icefall, at about 20,000 feet above sea level.

Even just 3,000 feet out of Base Camp Josh realized getting his client to the summit would not be an easy task. After their break, Josh carried all of his own gear, plus his client's gear up to Camp Two, situated at 21,000 feet. They rested there for one night. Eating and hydrating especially at altitude can make or break a person's success. Josh's adult client refused to eat, and Josh ended up waiting on him, directly handing him food to eat and water to drink.

In consultation with the expedition leader, the guides decided the client would have to make it to Camp Three the next day within six hours, otherwise forgoing his prospect to go to the summit. Again, Josh carried all of his own gear, plus his client's. He was told there was a lot riding on his client's success – money and the company's reputation.

They made it in five hours and forty-five minutes.

They rested at Camp Three. Josh cooked, coddled and cared for his client, neglecting his own health, and still not feeling well. There at 24,500 feet, Josh set his client's oxygen at full level, whereas he set his own on a lower level.

The next day on the way to Camp Four, Josh turned his client's oxygen up to four liters per minute, his own set to one liter per minute. His thinking being that they could switch once they got to camp. Josh was giving his client the best chance of success. Camp Four sits at 26,000 feet, and is otherwise known as the South Col. They got there and slept for about five hours.

On May 20, 2017 they left for the summit around 8:30pm.

Seeing the dead bodies once again, was part of the job. At about 26,500 feet on the Triangular Face they saw a Sherpa guide who had clearly died the night before. Not being able to set aside and separate your feelings to compartmentalize them in the moment can cause a deadly misstep. Josh explained that they had to continue up the mountain, his client not able to process, the mental game affecting the physical.

Hitting what is called the Balcony at 27,000 feet, Josh swapped oxygen bottles with his client. At this point, Josh was not able to utilize any breaks that they might have to slow down or catch his own breath. He was constantly taking care of his client, with no rest himself. Josh's expedition leader explained that he had to drag them both up the mountain, the client's failure to summit was now not an option.

Yet, at what cost?

In the end, is it just about the money?

Or is it about the accomplishment?

Do you sell a part of your soul, human decency left in question in the quest for greed or status?

Mountain Guiding can be lucrative if you plan your trips accordingly. With that, it is also a self-seeking career, constantly beating out your fellow coworkers for the chance to guide on that one elusive mountain. The industry itself is very small and can be very cutthroat. The average client pays exorbitant amounts of money for yet another dinner party talking point, and this was no exception. In comparison, the average guide usually only guides for the love of the mountains themselves, not for the acclaim of doing so. As the old adage goes, if you can't do, teach. It's like pulling teeth attempting to get Josh to share about his mountain achievements with people.

Never in a million years would it occur to me that you really could pay your way to the top of the world.

As they went up the south east ridge, they saw another nearly unconscious Sherpa guide in his early twenties come tumbling down the slope, with his harness barely attached. The client wanted to help, but if that happened, they would all die there. It was a harsh reality to put their lives above the single life of another. However, that is the journey that Mt. Everest defaults you to. Josh tied Sherpa off to a nearby fixed line, hoping that someone would rescue him, never hearing of his outcome.

About thirty minutes later, they saw an Indian climber clinging to the rock face, the client of the fallen Sherpa. Josh realized that those two had dangerously been out and at high altitude for over twenty-four hours. Josh encouraged him to descend, later finding out that he had died in the attempt.

They kept climbing to the top of the world.

When they reached the summit, the client had pre-paid for an additional oxygen bottle on summit day. Mountain guides do not have that option. Fated with good weather, they spent about two hours at the summit of Mt. Everest. Taking in the views, letting it sink in that they had finally made it.

Though, their journey had just started.

What was a difficult ascent up to the summit, quickly turned into the easy part. Descending the south summit, Josh abruptly realized that his client was in mountain guide terms, "Shitting the bed." The amount of time it took for them to continue downhill intensified, all factors involved turning to treacherous. The client was barely functional from the summit back down to the South Col. Josh and their Sherpa held him over their shoulders, carrying him most of the way. They saw another dead body at the Balcony. The client was functional enough to understand death could easily be imminent.

The group was not able to rescue the person, but the person's soul gave motivation for them to continue. Josh was in communication with the expedition leader, trying to coordinate staying the night at the South Col in order for them all to gather some strength. They were informed that that would not be possible because of a ninety mile an hour windstorm that was due to come in that night.

They had to make it all the way back down to Camp Two in order to survive, descending eight thousand vertical feet.

Josh radioed Everest ER who was situated at Base Camp and whose job it was to be prepared to consult those with medical emergencies on the mountain. Josh was instructed to administer his client dexamethasone, nifedipine, and epinephrine. Dexamethasone is a fast-acting steroid to combat cerebral edema. Nifedipine is used to lessen the effects of pulmonary edema. Epinephrine stimulates the fight, flight, or freeze response, giving a person the ability to move.

The group left all their gear, sleeping bags, pads, and extra clothing at the South Col. All they continued to travel with was the clothes on their backs, one oxygen bottle each, one water bottle each and just enough snacks to make it through the next few hours. They started heading downhill, the client was unstable and slow. At this point Camp Three had already been dismantled without food or fuel, and the possibility of maybe an empty, lone tent. Along with the weather warning, they were forced to head down to Camp Two, five thousand feet lower than they were at.

Josh called for aid.

His coworker that was on a different team who had summitted after them approached Josh, his client and their Sherpa. His coworker's group was on their way back down, but still above them. Hearing Josh on the radio, he had headed down the mountain to help and met them at the Yellow Band, at 25,500 feet, still above Camp Three.

At this point, the client collapsed, eyes rolling into the back of his head, unresponsive and experiencing cerebral edema. He had 38% oxygen saturation. Since he was on oxygen, he should have been around a 95% saturation rate. Josh checked their bottles, masks and regulators, all properly working. His body had simply stopped processing oxygen.

Josh called Everest ER again, and even though it was technically too early to re-administer medication, they advised him to do it anyway in hopes to save his life. Forty-five minutes later, he still had no response.

They radioed to their expedition leader that they needed more help. Sherpa that were situated at Camp Two refused to help, angry at the company's expedition leader for their own reasons. It became very real that they might all die on this mountain. The lead climbing Sherpa, the Sirdar, found out that it was Josh who needed assistance. Josh, who treated everyone with kindness and genuinely cared for the Nepalese people had someone in his corner. The Sirdar organized a group of eight other Sherpa from various other companies to head up the mountain and rescue them.

At the Yellow Band, Josh and his coworker built a platform in the snow and watched people descend from their successful summits.

No one offered to help.

Josh, his coworker and their Sherpa had given the client all of their own personal oxygen tanks, all three guides without oxygen of their own. After about four hours, the client started coming to, no cognitive abilities, but the ability to sort of move. The three of them carried him by rope, needing to continue to descend because of the impending storm. As the sun went down, the air turned very cold. They had left their cold weather gear at the South Col, carrying as minimal weight as possible. With no warmth from the sun, no oxygen, water or food the possibility of not surviving was threatening. Slowly, the group resumed their descent.

About four hundred feet above Camp Three Josh collapsed, the will to continue slowly abandoning his psyche. His coworker and Sherpa took care of the client whose will was also continuing to withdraw.

In and out of consciousness, delirium, and the strength to properly stand, Josh took himself down to Camp Three alone. Every bit of energy he had to stay on the fixed line was utilized, willing himself to not fall down the mountain. When he got to the abandoned camp, he found a mostly empty tent, crawled in and collapsed in a heap ready to die.

Josh radioed down to the expedition leader, telling him his last words to pass along to me. He said, "Tell Marisha I'm sorry, and I love her." At this point my husband accepted death as his fate. I am told his best friend had followed the day's account, others having to hold him back at Camp Two, ready to run up the mountain to save Josh and bring him back home to me.

I believe that this is when our souls acted as one. We were intertwined as husband and wife, two partners who actively chose each other in love. Love, I believe really does make the world go around. In many hard moments together and apart, I feel as if both of our hearts beat together keeping our souls alive.

Josh was essentially dead for two to three hours, clinging onto just a shred of life. The Sherpa rescue group finally got to the client. The expedition leader radioed to Josh's coworker to leave the client in the hands of the Sherpa and find Josh. He raced down the mountain to Camp Three. In this life or death moment, he realized Josh had curled up to die next to bottles of oxygen tanks, regulators and masks.

Josh had not been able to cognitively disseminate them to save his own life.

His coworker instantly hooked one up and unzipped his coats. He laid on Josh giving him what light and warmth he had, trying to share body heat and bringing Josh's hypothermic body back to life.

Once the Sherpa rescue group came down to them, four helped the client, four helped the guides. His coworker was able to walk, and Josh was drug back down the mountain, draped over the shoulders of the Sherpa, fully assisted the entire 3,500 feet back to Camp Two. Josh was pumped with the same cocktail of drugs that just hours before he had administered to the client.

They arrived around 2am, thirty hours after leaving the South Col to head to the summit. On average, it should not have taken them no more than sixteen hours.

Josh remembered waking up in a tent the next day, remembering only bits and pieces of the ordeal. His best friend was not there, as that day was his scheduled summit rotation. At one point, Josh ventured into the group dining tent where he heard his client boasting victoriously of his summit, "crushing it" in triumph. Everyone who was there had heard what happened in the wake of the radio calls.

Josh recalls merely shaking his head and walking away nauseated at the thought.

In Josh's first letter for me to open when he was gone, he spent a majority of it promising that he would come back home. It was only during the telling of his story that when he passed along his last words to me that he started to cry. To this day I have only maybe seen him cry three times.

Yet, he had kept his promise to me.

Despite being a little broken, he was home.

Even after hearing Josh tell his story, I had not truly understood the full depth of what had happened and how those chain of events would affect everything to come. I was not aware how sick he was going into summit rotation. Nor did I understand the things at play out of Josh's control, like the Sherpa initially refusing to help and how much money and greed can fuel the industry.

Since that first time, Josh has retold the story more times when I have been around and each time new details emerge. At first, I thought that he was trying to protect me, knowing that my biggest fear had indeed happened. In time I realized that protecting me might be true, but it is also coupled with his ability not to fully remember. Josh's brain also wanted to protect him from this traumatic event, small otherwise hidden details that can creep out over time. Since processing, we both have wrestled with those memories.

I understood that everything that had happened to Josh was a hugely significant event, and I respected the magnitude of it. I knew on some level that I was over my head in helping him, or myself for that matter. I remember that the next day we went on a long walk through our neighborhood together. Josh promised me he would never go back to Mt. Everest. I did not prompt him, nor ask him about the possibility of returning.

I know exactly what I was wearing, where we wandered and how the sun felt on my face. I was finally back to holding Josh's hand. It felt like it was a dream. I did not understand how he had almost died the week before and now was walking right next to me. How could both of those statements be true? I asked him if he would be willing to come with me to my next therapy appointment, as it was coincidentally scheduled in a few days. Josh not being one to seek out therapy, agreed.

That first weekend that he was home we decided to go up to our cabin. We had a mountain guide friend who needed a place to stay and had been living there while Josh was in Nepal. At the time, he was still there. Instead, we pitched a tent and slept out on the back deck. It overlooks Big Creek, which in the Summer months trickles down with ease and calm. In the Winter months, depending on the rainfall and the snow melt, it thunders down much more like a river; loud and ominous. There is a tree that the deck has been built around, sticking up through the planks on the far edge. Whether it is Winter, and we are watching the snow gently fall imbuing tranquility to the roaring water, or in the Summer having morning coffee listening to the birds sing and the trees sway, it is home for us.

Water maintains the circle of life, a natural cycle showing the world all things come back to us. Falling asleep outdoors, listening to the water ebb and flow was a perfect way to commemorate our first weekend together of Josh being back home and alive.

The day after that first therapy session was when everything that had happened hit me like a ton of bricks. Josh had been home only a few days and we were trying to settle into "our normal." Him adjusting to not being on a mountain anymore, and me, adjusting to living with someone again. It was the typical dance that we both were familiar with after having spent some time apart. Already within that first year of our marriage, January through that current June Josh had only been home non-consecutively fourteen nights.

Again, the average person did not understand our life.

It was a challenge that both of us were used to and we learned to adapt.

That Tuesday for whatever reason, we were both irritable. I decided to go on my weekly solo kayak to gain some solitude. Stroke by stroke I started to feel better. Once I paddled across the bay of the Puget Sound, I was able to have a prime view of sailboat races. I felt as if it was my lucky day. I noticed that the sun turned bright orange in the sky; there must have been a fire near. The high clouds turned into a smokey layer, masking the sun into a bright orange orb. When I am on the water it is as if time suspends itself. The ticking of a clock turns to seagulls cawing and the waves mark the passing of time.

I always am in a better headspace when I can take time to think, while also doing something to minimally distract me. I process best while I am active, i.e. mostly running and kayaking. The adrenaline and frustration ease their way through me, leading me to address situations with a much clearer mind. What I didn't know was that this minor disagreement that I cannot even remember would be the least of my worries.

This is where my story begins.

DURING

part II

I had been gone kayaking for just under two hours. I decided to paddle back and head home a bit early, upset with myself that I had gotten frustrated earlier. At the time, our apartment was very open and spacious. Walking in the front door you immediately were in a large living room and kitchen combo, with bedrooms on either side of the floor plan. Josh was not in our bedroom or bathroom, and I hurried to look outside to see if his car was still parked, which it was. Thankful that he had not left, I realized that he must be in our other bedroom, which we only used for storage of all Josh's mountain gear, holiday decorations, etc.

Immediately something was wrong. Josh was curled up in a ball on the floor, incoherent and dry sobbing without any tears. There was a half empty bottle of vodka next to him, leftover from our wedding. I had seen people have emotional mental breakdowns before, but never to this extent, let alone the person that I was married to. Separating yourself professionally in order to maintain that line of still being competent is one thing. At that moment I still felt I was capable of handling this. I started to console Josh, attempting to calm him down a little bit. I wanted to call 911 because he was so mentally gone. He begged me not to… and I didn't. I remember tricking him into drinking some water by telling him it was more vodka.

I had come home in need of having to use the bathroom, and that need had grown more insistent. I felt exceptionally guilty even leaving Josh for a few minutes. What I did not realize is that what happened next would leave me with a feeling of culpability that even on my worst days I still grapple with. I came back into our spare bedroom with Josh nowhere to be found. Turning around in circles, I realized our front door was partially open. I ran outside still barefoot, dressed in my bathing suit top and shorts. He was standing in the middle of our parking lot, yet the look on his face showed me that he was mentally very far away.

The minute Josh saw me he took off running through our parking lot. He headed toward the entrance where our apartment complex was situated. It was in a nice neighborhood with houses surrounding the apartment buildings. The air had turned muggy and compressed, the smoke in the sky had trapped all the heat and made the air feel claustrophobic.

On that warm Summer evening, the house next to us had a circular sprinkler, the kind that make the "ctch-ctch-ctch" noise as it sprays water. He stood next to the sprinkler and the look on his face intensified. I realized as I was talking to him, he had no idea where he was, or who I was. I didn't know what to do, but just begged him to come back inside and come home. After a few minutes of him fully disoriented, he was able to recognize that it was me who was talking to him.

As fast as it happened, the recognition vanished just as quickly.

Again, he took off running back into the maze of our apartment complex, now heading to the upper parking lot. There was another house lining the back side of the far apartment building. The lower part of their yard was an unkempt dirt, rocky hill with various pokey weeds, the owner of the house and the apartment complex both refusing to maintain the yard work. Josh ran up the side of that hill with ease, not noticing the blackberry thorns, or bothered by the rocks and gravel that were slashing my still barefoot feet. I followed him, trying to keep up to his pace. He cut through the homeowner's yard, ending up on the street side in front of the apartment building.

I begged him to stop, eliciting what I hoped was calm, even though at this point I had started crying. I tried not to shout, or scare him off again, but my tears still fell. I think for a few seconds he knew who I was, because he just kept saying over and over, "I don't deserve to live. I should die."

Josh begged me with all his being to let him die. He would not let me get close enough to touch him, so there was about six feet in between us as we stood in the bike lane. We were on a main street in the residential neighborhood and a car came down the hill every five minutes or so. Every time I would watch Josh gauge where the car was in relation to where we were standing. The math angles and the calculation of speed working in his head. My husband lunged in front of the cars as they drove by, trying to end his life. Every time he lunged, I lunged; grabbing him to nearly miss every time. I would then step back, and the process would repeat in a cyclical nightmare I could not seem to get out of.

I do not know how long we were on the road like that. It feels like forever and yesterday at the same time. He finally agreed to come home. We walked through the front door and Josh collapsed on the ground. I laid next to him, terrified of what would happen next. He was insistent that he needed to drive downtown and get a cheeseburger. Even after this awful night his desire to want a cheeseburger gave me hope that the real Josh was in there somewhere. Knowing that him operating a car was not an option, the next best thing was that we go together, which he refused.

In the moment, I hated the idea of leaving him, but I finally convinced him that I would leave and get a cheeseburger for him. That ten-minute round-trip drive was the longest ten minutes of my entire life. I sneakily took Josh's car keys along with my own, knowing that if he tried to leave again at least he would only be on foot.

When I walked back through the front door, he was still thankfully laying on the living room floor. He then ate half his cheeseburger and it seemed fully exhausted himself. He finally had fallen asleep. I stuffed a couch cushion under his head, grabbed a blanket and laid next to him the whole night. I did not sleep a wink. The next morning in a groggy state, Josh prodded me asking me why we were on our living room floor.

He was not able to cognitively remember anything that happened the night before.

The next day was when the vastness of everything that happened sunk in. I took the day off from work, stating that I was sick. I secretly called upon Josh's best friend who had vowed to be there for us at our wedding. I knew Josh's life rested in himself and others, not me. He called me back promising to encourage Josh to go to therapy, let me stand by him and said he would check on Josh consistently. I am forever grateful, knowing that he could have been the difference between Josh choosing to stay alive, fighting for life and love, or leaving this earth forever.

We had therapy again later that week, where I asked if I could go for the beginning. I shared only bits and pieces of the story, knowing how precarious Josh's mental health was. The therapist knew me well enough to read between the lines and asked for twice-a-week sessions for a while from Josh. In those next weeks they created a safety plan and what to do if certain feelings and memories arose.

That night when he ran out of the house it was because our windows were open and, in the distance, he heard the house around the corner's sprinkler system start. The "ctch-ctch-ctch" sound reminding him of the constant stream of helicopters coming in and out of Everest Base Camp. It was about two years later that I heard those exact same helicopters, my mind vividly remembering this memory and our story coming full circle.

I was concerned about what would happen when I left for long workdays unable to stop home at lunch, or the grocery store, wanting to have my own eyes on Josh at all times. We developed a check in system that slowly lessened over time. I focused all my energy on helping Josh in any way possible, trying to ease his pain. Surviving a traumatic event is one thing, living with the pain of surviving is a whole other battle.

The owners of the company Josh was still working for expected him to be in full Summer guiding mode on Mt. Rainier the next week. A week of "vacation" after almost losing your life, attempting to commit suicide due to survivor guilt, and then expected to return to yet another mountain seemed like a recipe for disaster. Josh knew on some level he was not doing okay but standing up for yourself at your lowest low can be just another hurdle. His argument was that since he was not at a mentally stable point, clients were at risk. Josh was able to advocate to push out his Rainier season a few weeks, to the beginning of July.

This begs the question – What is the cost of a human life? Someone who dedicated eight years of service, almost dying in the process should hold some merit. Yet, the value of Josh's life diminished before his very own eyes. He advocated for the rest of his life, asking for payment for therapy to heal and move forward. Is success guaranteed? No, but just like a mountain adventure, the best chances of success can indeed be bought. Josh was asking for the chance to continue to live, success being life, asking for reassurance that his life did in fact matter. In the end, the company agreed to pay for only three sessions of therapy.

During that first month I minimally went to therapy alone, but rather we went together. I mostly gave up the later part of my sessions so Josh could have even more time, billed under my name. I still went to work; few people in our lives knew what had happened. I remember being productive at work, getting things done and robotically checking the boxes. Looking back, I have no idea how I did that. After a couple weeks passed, I started to run again. Not far, always close to home, but a couple runs a week. I am not sure if they helped, the guilt I felt spending time dedicated to myself canceled out any positive feelings a run would elicit.

I ignored and pushed away any thoughts of the traumatic events that I had just gone through and centered solely on Josh. For better or worse, I cannot imagine a better metaphor of what marriage vows stand for. Real love is hard. That Summer Josh started to push me away, angry at himself, the world and taking out invisible frustrations on me. After trauma the little things become big things. I had to think about every single word I would say, and how I would say it; holding my breath hoping that my precious chosen words would not set him off.

Almost dying is hard.

Watching someone trying to die is also hard.

Trying to wrap one's head around both of those at the same time is unthinkable, but that was our life, day by day.

I was furious and heartbroken at everything that had led up to this point. I soon turned to what had always comforted me most – books and research. There was nothing specific about mountain guides or climbing, but there were studies on military personnel and post-traumatic stress disorder. PTSD is something that I have faced every day at work in family and youth clients. Facing it in your own home, in your partner and within yourself is a whole other barrier. I read countless studies of veterans returning only to realize the war hauntingly followed them home.

There were a few studies that I read that spoke about how dogs, specifically puppies can help. They offer unconditional love, force their owner to stay in the moment by playing, feeding, or taking them outside, and helping to re-train a trauma brain. I asked Josh during a therapy appointment how he would feel about adopting a dog, seeing if there was buy-in. He was somewhat apprehensive to the idea; cost, apartment rules weighing into the decision, but he agreed. I was overjoyed. I had spent weeks guilt ridden and useless in Josh's healing, but finally I had a task. I held onto it, re-reading the studies over and over, highlighting passages, knowing that this had to help. However, accomplishing it proved to be less than seamless.

Our apartment manager denied our request, stating that there were no dogs allowed on the property. Josh accepted that, however, I was not discouraged. I collected professional letters from our therapist and Josh's doctor stating that this would be for a medical need. Federal Disability Laws covers the state of Washington and emotional support animals cannot be denied. In contrast, it is the same as not offering a designated handicapped parking space for those who need to utilize it.

The owner of our apartment complex still denied our request. I was outraged. Everything that I had read about State and Federal Disability Laws confirmed that denying our request was in fact, illegal. Fueled with fire in my veins I contacted the Washington Housing Authority who acted as a proxy going between us and the apartment complex. I was correct – what they were trying to do *was* illegal. The last thing that I wanted to be doing was initiating a legal battle, but it seemed that was the road in which we were on. After weeks of back and forth, weeks wasted on not having a puppy for Josh's immediate support, the apartment complex's lawyer let us know that they had conceded, though with terms.

Infuriated that it had taken an additional six weeks for them to realize they would not have won the battle in court; we still came out on top. We agreed to their terms – the dog would have to be less than sixty pounds, hypoallergenic, and we would have to submit shot records. Weeks earlier when I first had this great idea, I had reached out to a labradoodle breeder about forty minutes away. They were family owned, had an extensive application packet and seemed as if they really cared about if their puppies would have a good home.

I re-contacted them. I found out that the original puppy that Josh had liked had already been claimed, but there were two more still available. Asking for photos and descriptions of their four-week-old personalities, we chose the "happy and silly" one. They were hosting adoptive family six-week visits, in two weeks. The next day I filled out the deposit online, emailed Josh the receipt telling him there's no backing out now.

The first time we met our sweet Ellie pup Josh did not know what to do. He was nervous around most animals, not having grown up around many. Ellie spent most of that visit curled up in my lap, tricking us that she was a calm, lazy puppy. The puppies eight-week mark hit coincidently on our wedding anniversary, forever cementing in our love by bringing her home on our first year as a married couple. Josh held her as I drove home and continued to hold her the rest of the day. I reflect on those first few days of having her because it has shown me every day since I was absolutely right in our decision to get a puppy.

Ellie saved Josh's life and in turn, she saved mine as well.

A few weeks before having a puppy, Josh was finally supposed to go back to minimally guiding on Mt. Rainier. He had been able to push out his return till August, something that he was nervous about, but inclined to. I was not overjoyed with Josh going back to guiding, but Mt. Rainier had always felt safe to me. In all honesty, the distance and time away from each other while Josh was on mountains never really bothered me. I would miss him of course, but the worry that something terrible might happen far overtook any other emotion. My ideal was when Josh was on Mt. Rainier, because it always felt as if it was in our backyard. In reality, a mountain is still a mountain. But it was close to home, on a clear day you could see it from our front porch, and I could drive to it within a couple of hours. I always thought to myself that if something ever happened to Josh on Mt. Rainier, I would be able to collect his body easily. It never occurred to me how morbid that sounded, but that was an average glance into my brain.

I didn't want to lose my Mt. Rainier summit succession from the past two years, so Josh, our therapist and I had decided that his first climb back would be just him and I. That year we climbed the Kautz route, a significantly more difficult climb than the Disappointment Cleaver or Emmons Glacier. As the past two years had been fairly easy for me, this was harder. This made me feel like all the stories of everyone who holds those esteemed Mt. Rainier climbs in such a high regard were in fact true.

We started the climb at Paradise on the Skyline Trail, which is one of my favorite day hikes. After an hour or so we veered off the dirt hiking trail down into the climbing trail onto the glacial terrain. This was definitely not a day hike anymore. We were back on the Nisqually

Glacier surrounded by icy blue landscape and crevasses all around us. After climbing what felt like forever, we moved along to the Wilson Glacier which had joined with the Nisqually. The first night we camped around 9,500 feet at "The Castle" and got ready to ascend the ice chute the next day.

The ice chute sits at about 11,000 feet above sea level with the angles of climbing at 35-50 degrees. The second night we had planned to climb up the several hundred feet of the chute, ascend the next five hundred feet to the summit and sleep on the top of the mountain. Except, when we started going through the chute due to the way the snow had formed, every single step was a third, to halfway as tall as my body.

Every single step.

We were walking on exposed glacial ice and I used my ice axe as leverage to heave myself out of each step. Carrying a weighted backpack, balancing with boots and crampons on, and looking back at angles upwards of fifty degrees and stepping up blocks of ice that were half the size of me was exhausting. Even though we had only ascended a few hundred feet, I was spent. We slept at about 13,200 feet for a few hours instead of on the summit.

Josh built us a makeshift camp on the side of the mountain. It had turned incredibly windy and cold. He moved huge, heavy rocks to create a barrier from the wind to offer us some protection. To this day, I have no idea how he lifted those boulders with such ease. Josh was back on a mountain that was more home to him then our actual home and he seemed to be doing just fine.

We left for the summit around 3am, achieving both of our goals. I remember how windy it was, the mental challenge of just going over a thousand feet had seemed. Yet, we made it to the top. Coming down I was tired and quiet. I wanted to know what Josh was thinking, but he was also quiet, and I did not want to upset him on his return back to the mountains. We came home and continued on. Josh likes to comment that in all the photos on that trip I was smiling, when in reality during the climb I was pretty cranky. Sometimes photos don't tell a thousand words. You might not really have any idea of what a person might be going through based on their appearance.

Josh started to periodically guide back on Mt. Rainier. He requested only the standard Disappointment Cleaver route and not to be lead guide. He did not want to have to make major decisions on the mountain, rather just follow directions. As the month of August evolved, he asked to work in the office more. His mind and energy to guide was dwindling and he did not want to be doing this until the end of the season through September 30th.

I went back to spending the weekends in Ashford if Josh was working. One weekend I was sitting in the office hanging out with Josh. His coworker who had saved his life on Everest, that had given him oxygen to bring him back to life walked in through the door. He had just gotten off a difficult Mt. Rainier climb and was tired, smelly, and sweaty. I ran across the room to him, wrapped my arms around him and immediately started bawling. I didn't care who was around us, still not many people knew what had happened. He was soothing and the kindness he conveyed in that moment I will never forget. Before the incident he and Josh got along well, but didn't necessarily stay in contact outside of guiding season. Now we are forever tied to him.

I am eternally grateful.

The owners of the company gave Josh grief, treating his request to continue to be mentally healthy as a hassle. Josh found out at the beginning of September that his name was taken off the Argentina and Mexico trips for later that Winter, both of which we counted on monetarily and was already scheduled to guide. This was the start of a mini rockfall. No one had told him about the change, and he had consecutively been lead guide on those trips for the past five years.

To this day I do not comprehend the motivation behind how that company works. Valuing employees who work in such high stakes environments seems like such common sense to me. Taking away a person's work in what seemed to be out of spite is out of my realm of understanding. Refusing to be a part of the healing process, taking no responsibility of causation and having to fight for only three therapy sessions is an insult. Since then, we have heard other stories from former and current coworkers who had their own brushes with death. Some experiences paralleled Josh's, where others the company used money as a form of bribery.

Again, what is the cost of a human life?

Are some lives worth more than others?

Do cost and value signify the same thing?

In mid-September Josh while working in the office, he was asked to cover additional Mt. Rainier trips through that month. This seemed to be his breaking point. He had made it extremely clear that being on the mountain was not benefiting his health.

Josh quit on the spot.

It was an explosion that people who were around still talk of, becoming the stuff of legend. He gave up his ambitions and career, because his dream had betrayed him. Josh was scheduled to climb the next day, coincidentally with his best friend. He fulfilled his duty and they both came home after the climb to tell me about the epic blowout. We celebrated by going out downtown, Josh finally feeling a semblance of freedom.

That night we ran into a friend who managed the local rock climbing gym and was looking for a new head route setter. Josh was hired in the moment and we all celebrated with another round of beers.

The next day after Josh had quit, I signed up to run a full marathon in less than two months. I knew that I needed something that would hold my sanity if Josh was going to be home every day for the inevitable future. Running had always given me that and training for a full marathon forced me to focus due to the time and dedication it required. It seemed as if things were finally looking up.

Josh started working at the local rock climbing gym and had a very regular schedule. Something neither of us were used to. It was a challenge for both of us, but in time we found a balance. We started to make plans to remodel our cabin within the next ten months. I trained for my marathon, running upwards of twenty-two miles a week.

The marathon itself was in Seattle, two days after Thanksgiving. I had only told one other person besides Josh about it, plus our friends whose house we were staying at. It is not that I didn't think that I could do it, I just never wanted the pressure or acclaim of it before the event itself. Running for me had never been about other people, it was only about me and my relationship to the run itself.

The night before the race Ellie kept us up whining the whole night, scared of being in a new place. Without a good night's sleep running 26.2 miles in the moment was hard, but achievable. It was a typical Autumn Pacific Northwest day and drizzly with rain showers. It was just enough moisture to cool down my overexerted and overheated body. I finished in just under four hours and twenty-eight minutes. I was satisfied with myself. I felt good and strong.

The training for the marathon took its toll on me. Having to run fifteen miles on any given day was mentally difficult, as well as the time it takes to do that. However, that was the point. Even though that was what was most challenging for me, I am very aware that running is what kept me mentally stable during that adjustment period. That same night after running the marathon we went to a concert. It was not the greatest planning, adding in walking around downtown Seattle finding a restaurant and parking was the last thing I wanted to do. Despite being fidgety in the small, hard concert seats because my hips kept going numb, the concert itself was awesome.

The next two months after Josh resigned, five other senior mountain guides quit as well. One started up his own company that today is incredibly successful. The rockfall that Josh started when he left felt scary and isolated. It took a while for the news to spread and for Josh to finally not feel so alone. His intent was not to create change, but change it seemed was unavoidable and contagious. Many other guides over the course of their career had their own unique near misses with death that might have been avoided if the value of a human life outweighed a dollar sign.

We spent the next ten months remodeling our cabin and de-bearing it from the former owners inherited style. Remodeling something with your significant other is the ultimate test of patience. And most of the time both of us failed. Patience is not a strong suit of mine, nor Josh's. Both of us work exceptionally well in crisis mode, but in day to day work we become incredibly nitpicky with each other. Despite that, it gave Josh something to focus on and complete. We had worked for months to finally feel as if we were not chasing our own demons. As each room was finished, we were able to see visible changes and we felt proud.

On President's Day Weekend 2018 coming home from the cabin, we hit black ice and totaled our car. Josh being the slowest driver on the planet, already was going twenty-five miles under the speed limit, but black ice takes no prisoners. We both were shaken, but physically okay. Ellie was in her crate in the backseat wailing the saddest doggy cry we had ever heard. Since she was so fluffy it was hard to tell what was exactly wrong. We were able to pull her out of the car and her front right leg flopped in a way that no leg should ever move.

We were stranded on the side of a remote road near Mt. Rainier in the middle of Winter and I was in my pajamas. We had minimal cell phone service and few cars passed by that early in the morning. Our beloved doggy was broken, and it felt hopeless especially as the snow started to fall. We called 911 who never showed up, even hours later. Thankfully or not, finally a car came driving by who stopped. We realized it was one of the owners of Josh's former company, and they had not spoken since Josh's blowout. He let us sit in his car until Triple AAA arrived hours later. We were thankful for the warmth. Another former coworker and friend of Josh's who was working nearby was able to drive us back home, directly to an emergency veterinary clinic.

The doctors performed X-rays, telling us it was likely that Ellie's leg would have to be amputated. It was our decision to try and save it or not. The difference between saving it or not was about $1,000 at an already high amount we could not afford. I kept imagining her sweet front leg just laying on an operating table after they sawed it off, thrown in some garbage can. That thought still makes me tear up.

We had to try.

Since it was President's Day no one was open, and she would need a very skilled surgeon. We brought our broken eight-month-old puppy home and had the second longest night of my life. We both were sore, and I was unable to move my right shoulder and neck. We laid on the living room floor with her as she whimpered the whole night, all of us barely getting any rest.

We were able to make an appointment for Ellie with a specialized orthopedic surgeon in a couple days. We are not ones to seek out charity, but a good friend set up a Go-Fund-Me campaign that significantly helped our cause. It was unexpected and very kind. The surgeon performed an emergency procedure, saving her leg with two plates, nineteen screws and a metal rod. Due to the stress, she stopped growing, even though she was supposed to grow about an additional twenty pounds.

After she was medically healed, we were thankful to discover water physiotherapy to help her regain some range of movement and motion. To this day her leg still is not the same, utilized as a pseudo-tripod, minimal muscle development and she just does not trust that it will hold her. Josh was distraught with grief, blaming himself because he had been in the driver's seat. He could not wrap his head around hurting his beloved puppy, the one who brought him back to life after he came back home, cheating death.

Less than a month later we were working on our cabin and Josh more or less sawed through his finger with a table saw. Having just removed our first-aid kit for whatever reason, we wrapped Josh's finger with paper towels and duct tape, driving forty minutes to the nearest hospital. He had hit an artery and blood was spraying out of his finger like a squirt gun. The doctors cauterized the arteries to make it through the rest of the weekend. That Monday Josh had to establish and schedule a check-up with a primary care doctor before any hand specialist would evaluate.

Two days later he was finally able to see a hand surgeon that casted his hand and arm, hoping to not have to operate. Josh got a hot pink cast to match Ellie's cast, as it seemed my entire family had broken itself. With extensive physical therapy, Josh luckily never had to have surgery. It is a little mangled and he has lost some forever feeling, but overall, he is okay.

Continuing remodeling our cabin with a one-handed Josh and a dog that was not able to use all four legs was just another obstacle that we had to hurdle.

The last day of June we finally were done. We created our own small business for travelers to book our home as a vacation rental while visiting Mt. Rainier National Park. We threw a party with our family and friends to celebrate. The morning of our celebration we still were completing the finishing touches and screwing the kitchen shelves into the wall. After all our literal blood, sweat and tears we had transformed our cabin into our sweet piece of paradise.

Within those ten months of renovation, Josh and I missed many family occasions and friend events. We had spent any moment that we weren't home or at our jobs working on the cabin. Our second home was Home Depot. The most time-consuming project was redoing the trim. Our cabin had trim lining the upper, lower and corner part of the walls and windows. We decided to sand and re-stain all of it. Six five-foot pieces would take me on average an hour to stain. Our chalet windows alone had twenty-eight pieces. I will never redo trim again. We spent every possible second remodeling.

I spent most of that Summer hiking as much as possible with my friends. We explored areas of the Pacific Northwest that were remote and beautiful. Many of our hikes would offer magnificent views that you could only see from hiking to the end vantage point. We spent many hours exploring the forest on our own terms, laying by found waterfalls and creeks and enjoying our suspended time in the woods. We discovered the soul of the world and we bonded over life, love and adventure.

Josh's coworker and friend who also quit around the same time had started his own very successful mountain guiding company. Soon after, he asked Josh to do some Operations work for him. He also scheduled one Mt. Rainier climb with funds going toward The Tiger of the

Snows Fund charity. He asked Josh to lead the climb, which he agreed. The Tiger of the Snows Fund gives access to education for many children whose Sherpa parents have died on Mt. Everest. It is something that Josh and I both support wholeheartedly.

Leading the charity climb, Josh worked with other guides from various companies who asked if Josh was interested in guiding again. It had been almost a year since he had left the guiding world. We talked about it and he finally had gotten to a point where he missed it a little bit. Josh started working for another guiding organization, different than before. In the hiring paperwork Josh was surprised to find out about how they promote strong mental health if someone has an adverse experience, encouraged therapy, communication and valued their guiding staff. He was still able to do Operations work for his friend who started his own company, work minimally at the rock climbing gym, and guide a little bit on Mt. Rainier.

It had taken over a year, with what felt like one thing after another happening, but life finally seemed more stable than it had been in a long time.

That September all guiding companies started their "Everest talks" – who would be guiding and setting in place the next Spring's expedition. No one had asked

Josh to go back, but he of course knew this had started, especially because he was doing the Operation's work for his friend. I remember him casually mentioning Everest the next Spring and it was like someone had pulled the pin in my mental grenade. I was hurt, angry and scared that this could even come back up again. Josh in turn dropped the subject even in general conversation, ceasing any mentions of the mountain to me.

Soon after that conversation I had dinner with my group of girlfriends. They knew bits and pieces of what had happened, and I shared my recent thoughts on the topic. I knew deep down that Josh was destined to go back to Nepal, if only to retrieve the part of himself he had left behind. When I started verbalizing my thoughts, and not reacting out of fear I realized what needed to happen. It was as if the puppet strings of my life presented me the next steps to come. I was scared, but I respected the symbolism.

J osh had to go back to Mt. Everest.

And I would go with him.

DURING

part III

On October 1, 2018 I gathered up the courage to send a message to Josh's friend who had started his own mountain guiding company. I tentatively asked what the feasibility of both of us going to Mt. Everest would be. I requested that this conversation remain between the two of us. I was nervous about what he would say, thinking my ask would be silly, unrealistic or unachievable. Here I was asking this world renowned six-time Mt. Everest summiteer for an enormous favor. In the mountain guiding world, this guy is famous. He wrote back quickly with positive enthusiasm and thoughtfulness. Knowing Josh's story, he said that he would be glad to have us both, saying that it would be good for both Josh and me. This generosity and willingness to help us survive the ordeals that we had been through changed our lives.

By mid-November it was set. Four months later in March of 2019, both Josh and I would be heading to Everest Base Camp. Josh, leading the trekking group in and out, not climbing any higher than that. I would be joining the trekking group with Josh, spending every day together on this journey. At this point, Josh had left the climbing gym and was doing full Operations work for his friend, as well as guiding on Aconcagua in Argentina again in February.

We kept the news to ourselves for the first month or so. I needed to let it sink in and try and adjust to the idea that this was going to happen. Again, like running my marathon, I did not want this journey to become about other people. It was about me and Josh. I asked for new hiking boots for Christmas, nervous of telling my family about our impending adventure.

Prior to our trip I wanted to be as emotionally prepared as possible. Similar to preparing myself every day for Josh's death, this was the opposite. I wanted to prepare for both of our successes. Knowing that the sights and sounds that Josh may have blocked out would be at the forefront of his mind being back in a place that nearly killed him, I asked him to go to therapy again for a little bit to prepare. I myself also started to re-attend, with my same therapist from before. Both our therapists knew of each other and worked together to ensure that we were on the same page.

Preceding our trip to Nepal, we arranged to go to Southern Thailand, to the very same beach Josh had gone to the day after our first meeting. In January our plane tickets were bought and the reality of it started to sink in. I finally had told my family and was slowly working things out at my job. It was hard to wrap my head around leaving home and not attending work for five and a half weeks. I had never taken a vacation longer than two weeks and here we were planning an adventure with a couple backpacks, no guarantee of cell phone service, or even showers. Doing something incredibly out of my realm of thought and comfort zone was an adjustment. It took me a long time to admit to myself that it was really happening.

A little less than a week before our car's totaling anniversary, I was driving home from our cabin after spending the weekend with girlfriends. Josh was already in Argentina, set to start climbing the next day. Two and a half blocks from home another car ran a red light and hit me and Ellie, now totaling my car in the process. The person stayed just long enough to see me make it out of the intersection and then left. Again, here I was ironically almost a year later in the same situation with a totaled car in my pajamas on the side of the road. Both of us were shaken, but physically okay. I remember Ellie had this low, guttural growl at the base of each breath. Out of anger, not fear, my hands kept shaking. I had to use talk-to-text to send Josh a message, hoping he would see it with the time difference and debatable cell service.

Josh saw the message, calling me in disbelief of what had happened. He kept telling me he wanted me to go to the hospital, which I refused. Incidentally forgetting that I had to convince him to go to the hospital when his own finger was its own spray can of blood. Driving my car, the two and a half blocks to get home was terrifying. The accident had caused it to drag fully on the ground, scraping metal against asphalt, two tires rapidly losing air. I pulled it into the first parking spot at our apartment building and it promptly died, never starting again. Josh messaged his best friend who was in Montana at the time. I had to talk him out of driving to Washington just to come check on me. That night he surprised me by ordering delivery Indian food to me which I happily ate while taking a bath, discovering that Styrofoam take out boxes float on water.

The next day into week and a half Washington had the worst snowstorm it had ever seen, upwards of twenty-four inches in just a few hours. Schools, work, gyms, etc. were closed, everyone hunkering down. At that point since I was car-less, anywhere I wanted to go I had to walk. My car had become a sad snow mound, becoming one with the ground. It took longer than usual for a tow truck to agree to pull it away due to the weather. I cleaned my car of all my personal belongings in my snow boots. I found the highlighted studies that I had kept so close about how dogs help people cope with PTSD symptoms in a folder in my back seat. I brushed the snow that had fallen inside as I opened each car door, secretly thankful that Josh was not there to lecture me for all the random junk I kept in my car.

Josh came back home after a successful expedition in Argentina and we were just under a month out from our trip to Thailand and Nepal. I habitually attended physical therapy and massage therapy, as all the work I had done after the first car accident set my body back after the second. I was nervous about having to carry a weighted backpack every day and learned stretches and techniques that I could utilize myself, without hands on care to minimize my day to day aches.

We spent quality time at home with our beloved fur babies and hiking trails in preparation of our trip. As fortune would have it, all three of my girlfriends happened to be going to Thailand, separately within the same month and a half period. Two of them came home a couple days before Josh and I were supposed to leave, teasing the warm sun and culture so close to my grasp.

The day before we left for our trip was my last therapy appointment. I remember stressing out, not thinking that I was emotionally ready for this journey. My therapist aptly declared that I was ready, and she was going to give me the gift of time, ending our session after only fifteen minutes. I would have more time to pack and do all the last-minute things I needed to accomplish. She reminded me to write, one of my coping mechanisms that we had discussed.

Writing historically helped me process feelings and emotions, especially complicated ones. It is significant that during all previous Mt. Everest experiences I did not journal at all. My therapist left me with a poem, reciting it from memory, a metaphor of unknown things to come. I thought a lot about the poem on our flights. It steadied my thoughts as the countdown to our five-week adventure of a lifetime was about to begin.

Up until this point, the longest I have ever spent away from home was about two and a half weeks, spending time at my best friend's house during the Summer as we grew up. The farthest I had ever traveled in mileage was Florida for our honeymoon. The only other countries I had been to were Mexico and Costa Rica, also with Josh. After thirty-one hours of traveling we finally made it to our destination. We flew from Seattle to Taiwan, to Bangkok, Thailand to Krabi, Thailand and then long boating the last twenty minutes from Krabi to TonSai Beach. A fourteen-hour advanced time difference than home, we grabbed our backpacks, jumped off the boat, waded through the water to the beach, finding the same place Josh had stayed at six years before.

*M*arch 25, 2019

Well, we're in Thailand. It's even more beautiful than I could have imagined. I can't believe that six years ago Josh left this to come home to me. Apparently, it's a lot different then what it was like when he was here. There's a huge concrete wall dividing "old TonSai" with new TonSai. There are tons of graffiti on it, words and poems. One of which was coincidentally the exact poem that my therapist recited to me before we left during my last session. I saw it the first morning that we were here. Took it as a sign that this is truly exactly where I'm meant to be, with my dear. It's truly the most beautiful place I've ever been.

I cannot believe that places like this exist in the world, let alone that I am lucky enough to be here. Never in my lifetime would I have guessed I'd land in a place like this.

Though, I miss home. Immensely. Especially Ellie and Mushu. There are cats here I keep trying to befriend, and they remind me of home. To get here you must take a longtail boat, which is incredible and amazing. I love everything about the water and the jungle. Days are in about the low nineties, with the Andaman Sea about eighty degrees, which suits me just fine.

After we arrived, that night we crashed in our bed, exhausted from travel. The smell and dirt of various airports and planes clung to my skin. There were bugs that made their way inside our bungalow, crawling all over us, but I slept like a rock. Josh woke me up early the next morning to walk down to the beach, saying that we could take a nap later. We sleepily made our way down to the beach holding hands. Our walk was about six minutes, already warm with the early sun hitting the biggest rocky cliffs I had ever seen. It seemed as if we were the only ones up this early. As tired as I was, I felt as if I was finally awake, my heart recognizing itself in my surroundings. The water was gently coming to the beach, touching our toes. Every photo I had ever seen of this exact place, even the ones Josh took years prior did not compare to the beauty that was right in front of me. I was awestruck.

We stretched our legs along the beach and Josh pointed out the massive cliffs along the beach and water. The cliffs were at least 1,000 feet high and he pointed out the climbing routes he had climbed when he was here before. After a bit, we went back to where we were staying and monkeys followed us down the path, which felt unreal. Walking along, there was a concrete wall separating the beach from the inhabited jungle part. The wall puzzled Josh, as it had not been there on his previous trip. As striking and displaced as this man-made object seemed to be, split between the beach and jungle, it was intriguing. Each section of the concrete slabs had artwork painted on it, pictures, poems and phrases integrated with each other.

As we strolled along, I tried to read and absorb what was created on the wall as much as possible. We came upon a section that was simple. A heart in the corner of the slab, and part of a palm tree on the edge. The handwriting that it had been painted in struck me, black and artistic script. There was no title, nor an author. I started to read the eight-line poem and almost fell over in shock. Josh must have seen the look on my face and asked me if I was okay.

Half a world away the poem that my therapist had recited to me on the eve of this journey was in writing right in front of me.

In life I always have stuck to the mantra that I have to follow what feels right. Sometimes it is little things, like the mention of a movie in conversation and then it just happens to be on television that same night. Other times, it's bigger events, like seeing Josh for the first time and just knowing somehow that the entire world conspired for us to meet. So many moments are ironies, paradoxical moments that make me feel as if I am on the right path. Josh thinks it is strange, but to me has always been comforting. I have always trusted in the universe.

This was one of those moments.

Everything that we had gone through and prepared for made this moment of seeing this poem before my very eyes to be true.

Later that trip Josh did some research to find that TonSai Beach was to be developed to become more Western style, i.e. with modern resort buildings and structures. Old TonSai was built more traditionally in a rustic manner, using the jungle as resources, roofs made of palm leaves, and walls of palm trees. The concrete wall was an actual symbol dividing the old from the new. On the beach side there was already a more Western style hotel built, not simple hostels or bungalows. The wall saddened Josh, all the beach bars and restaurants of the past had been moved into the jungle, behind the wall, hidden from immediate view. Though I could see Josh's upset, this was the only TonSai that I knew.

I recognize that if and when we go back it will be completely different. This in particular saddens me more than most other changes that might happen. Nothing quite matched those first feelings I had on that beach. Yet again, the universe reminded me that the world keeps spinning, time keeps ticking and the only moments we can count on are what is right in front of us.

M*arch 26, 2019*

I cannot get over how beautiful this place is. Josh has taken me hiking through the jungle the past two days. I finally am feeling better. Mentally. Spiritually. Emotionally. Physically. This is definitely the type of environment that I thrive in. It's hot. Jungle hot, and hot on the water, both of which I love. I wish the animals were here. They would be too hot… and miserable, but then I'd have all that I need. Minus a real bathroom. I do miss that. And our bed.

I am getting nervous for Nepal… we only have two more nights here.

We decided to go on a hike up to Railay Beach Lookout Point. The hike was only a couple miles, but it was a steep climb. Even mid-morning it was already hot out and the trail was dusty. I felt as if my skin was going to melt off with the heat. Once we got up to the viewpoint, you could see the entirety of the arcs of

Railay and TonSai beaches, surrounded by jungle and sea. The hike was indeed worth it. It was an absolutely gorgeous vantage point.

Most of the days we hiked in the jungle in the mornings and then laid on the beach. Listening to the waves gently hit the sand shushed all the nervous thoughts I had away. We spent our afternoons talking and relaxing before our great adventure. Everything about Thailand was idyllic and perfect.

The food in Thailand was delicious. Thai cuisine is my favorite overall and eating real Thai food in Thailand was incredible. Every Pad Thai dish had chicken, huge shrimp, and all the vegetables you could imagine. Tom Yum soup was made with coconut milk found from the trees in our backyard jungle. Absolutely everything was fresh, picked from the sea, or gardened from the local villagers. Even the size of chopsticks were smaller than American chopsticks, and easily fit into my hands.

I am not sure why I did not mention this in my journal entries, but I got a bad case of food poisoning in Thailand. The only thing that I had ingested that Josh had not was a delicious picked from the beach mango smoothie, blended with untreated ice cubes. We had been sticking to bottled water to be safe, and my desire for the best smoothie ever tricked me to forget that ice cubes were made of water.

We had decided to go kayaking, one of my favorite pastimes, on the Andaman Sea. Josh is the only person I ever go kayaking with, and that is only when we are kayaking in other countries. Like running, I generally do not like kayaking with other people. I enjoy having time to appreciate nature directly surrounding me and giving time to reflect over what thoughts or worries are going through my head.

However, on this trip I realized I was not feeling well about halfway in. I was paddling in my dream setting, the warmest waters I have ever felt, viewing the most perfect setting I had ever seen. Our views did not seem real; they were so different then what I was used to at home. I told Josh I was not feeling great but wanted to continue. I remember watching colorful fish swim around our kayak and then promptly puked all over them. That is when Josh deemed that we should head back to shore. I was set on paddling through the sickness, but for the first time in any of our kayaking trips, Josh decided to paddle, and his strokes held more weight.

I spent the rest of that day sleeping, only waking up to a quick thunderstorm, with lightning lighting up the dark sky like a firework display. Looking back, it makes me sad that I lost the rest of that day lying in bed while our time living on the beach was so limited. The feelings that I experienced the night we first set foot on the beach are incomparable to any place I'd ever, and still have been.

March 27, 2019

We upgraded our stay yesterday to a private, clean and very nice bungalow. Definitely the nicest place we have ever stayed. We woke up where Josh served me coffee in bed, just like at home. We used our special key card to enter into Old TonSai, walking the length of the graffitied wall in what looks to be a dying village. We started our morning hike going further and further into the jungle, past abandoned homes and huts, the remnants of what felt like the world and new TonSai has forgotten about. We hiked through the jungle from TonSai Beach up and over to Railay Beach. The sounds of nature permeated my ears, with the locusts buzzing, monkeys cackling and the rustle of a slight breeze through the jungle leaves.

We came through and decided to explore a diamond cave, a glittering cavern with curves and edges. When we got to Railay we decided to have breakfast. We tried going to a local spot we found the day before, but it was closed. We ended up at the Railay Beach

Resort, which sounds just as it is. There was a buffet filled with food, waiters clean shaven, all wearing the same uniform. It was surreal eating at a place like that when TonSai is struggling to stay alive. It makes me very grateful to have the life I do.

Later in the day we decided to take a longtail boat to explore three of the surrounding islands. The first was extremely populated, but the second was so quiet and serene. It felt like only us on the island. The third was a good mix, but I however felt home on the sea. It's amazing to me how at home I feel on the sea, and in this place. I miss home – but this part of the world is a part of my soul. I am the happiest version of me surrounded with sun, sea and sand. Yet, being so close to the jungle is inevitable. Hearing the jungley sounds and walking through these trees awake a part of me I didn't realize was there.

TonSai beach was alluring, and overall few tourists inhabited there, most being rock climbers to climb the huge cliffs overlooking the beach. The beach itself was a bit rocky, but there was a short walk through the water and over a hill to get to Railay Beach. Railay was full of white sand and without rock. We hiked there every day, spending our time there. I would spend the afternoons listening and watching the soft waves ebb and flow making their way to and from the beach.

The water was strikingly unlike the volatile ocean at home, but rather tranquil. Yet, both bodies of water felt like two sides of the same coin to me. The vastness and power of each gave me a sense of peace unlike anything else.

The restaurants on Railay Beach were all outside and more westernized, as well as hotels with more leisured amenities. We were able to eat lunch at various restaurants, have afternoon drinks, and they had a small store that carried sunscreen and other limited items.

There was also a much longer back way to walk through the jungle to Railay Beach. We did that in the mornings getting some exercise before it got too hot outside. Hiking through the jungle felt as if I was listening to the background of a nature soundtrack. It felt surreal to me that the sounds of what I was hearing were surrounding me in real life. It reminded me of Rudyard Kipling's *The Jungle Book*, and I was sure Kaa would pop out of the draping trees, whisking me away forever. Josh assured me that there were not any snakes, but I never looked it up to confirm, as I am sure he was just trying to not cause me panic.

Seeing other parts of the surrounding islands was just as dreamlike as it was being on both TonSai and Railay Beach. One mellow afternoon we decided to take a private longtail boat tour of some of the surrounding islands. I absolutely loved being on a longtail boat. They could move fast, so the wind flies through your hair. The boats sit close to the water and you can lean over to touch the surf at any point, cooling yourself down from the hot Thai sun.

The boats themselves are long, narrow with pointed tips, and sit down close by the water. Most boats repurpose automobile engine motors for transport. The engines are mounted on the end of a long pole that can rotate 180 degrees in the water to steer. The propeller is mounted on the shaft directly, therefore not needing a transmission or any other gears. When the pole and engine is lifted out of the water, the boat is essentially in a "neutral" gear. I never saw any female boat drivers, but if I ever have the opportunity to learn, I think it would be my dream job.

One island we sailed past was called Chicken Island, where the trees and cliffs had formed to look like a chicken, Mother Nature I'm sure giggling to herself. Another island we were able to wade into the water where the most colorful rainbow fish were feeding, swimming around our feet like this interaction was completely normal. The last island we visited was very linear, and we ventured down past where anyone else was. We found this huge swing made from driftwood that we swung on under this gigantic tree, shading us as the water came in under our toes.

On our last night on TonSai, we ate dinner at our favorite outdoor restaurant on the beach. Above us, base jumpers were diving off the cliff above us, soaring down to the water and opening their parachutes just in time to glide gracefully into the sunset. We watched the magnificent colors of the sun change and fade, with the tide slowly edging its way closer to us, one last time. I wanted to stay in that moment forever.

March 28, 2019

Well, we left TonSai today. By far the saddest I have ever been leaving a place. We took our last longtail ride into Ao Nang and taxied to Krabi. We visited the Tiger Cave Temple, overlooking all you can see. To get to it, you climb a set of staircases with 1.5 feet stairs, totaling 1,260... all in 96-degree heat with 81% humidity. My phone tells me it feels like 110 DEGREES! This felt harder than any mountain I've ever climbed. The temple itself was beautiful, and the walk up gave lots to think about.

As a woman, knees and shoulders had to be covered, and I wore a scarf over my dress, making it feel even hotter. Most people were serene and respectful, but also the opposite. For not being a person that identifies with religion, I still value being respectful.

Being back in the city is strikingly loud. Thousands of people, cars, roads and stimulation. Within minutes I already missed TonSai and the slow steady pace of the villagers. The birds chirping away and the steady beat of the waves against the sand. I'm nervous for the next part of our adventure. Nothing will ever be the same as TonSai, even TonSai.

But Nepal will be absolutely different. We fly to Bangkok today and Kathmandu in the morning. Life is about to drastically change. And I do not want to forget Thailand. TonSai, a town of 150 people has my soul.

Despite being halfway across the world on a tiny piece of land, surrounded by so few people, far from my beloved animals, our cabin and the woods I had never felt as home as I did on TonSai Beach. I can't pinpoint it. I never would have guessed that this little section of the world would resonate so strongly with me. I knew it would have an emotional connection, as going there mirrored Josh's trip years prior. However, it is as if I found part of myself that I never even realized was missing.

Edging back into society was hard. The world is very loud. When I was in high school, I participated in a three-day group silent retreat. I loved it. We had writing prompts and things to think about throughout, but everything was so still. Contrary to spending most of my days with an inner monologue of worries, stresses and what-if's I strangely found peace in the total solitude. I was able to quiet my mind from mentally pacing around. It felt as if I finally could just coast.

The silent retreat was on the edge of a peninsula in Washington, in a huge mansion, surrounded by trees, property and water. Any noises that one would try and seek out were met with the noises of nature, the water trickling, birds chirping and the rain falling. After it was over, driving back home I felt abundantly overwhelmed. The average sounds of the world hurting my ears. I remember hearing a garbage truck squeal with squeaky wheels, clunking the garbage cans noisily. My peaceful shield of the world I had just created started to chip away. I never thought I would have that sense of quiet serenity again. TonSai Beach was that place and even more.

Visiting and touring the Tiger Cave Temple was an amazing experience. The temple itself is remotely located within a valley of trees and countryside, with a large golden Buddha statue at the top that you can see from miles away. The climb up and back down the stairs was difficult for both of us, as still to this day, was the hottest we have ever been. The stairs were about sixteen inches high, and about six inches wide. They were not flat, but uneven and you had to watch your footing as they were not all equal.

When we completed the 1,260-stair climb, we finally were right in front of the large golden Buddha statue. It was even larger than you could imagine. We ventured around the other temple buildings, exploring the little balconies and prayer spots and enjoying the beautiful views of the forest below and the Andaman Sea in the distance. That was the last view I had of the serene water. Being so far up, the air was quiet and subdued, but fragrant with incense. It was a reverent way to spend some of our last few hours in the remote places of Thailand.

*M*arch 29, 2019

No tree in sight…

Landed in Bangkok last night around dinner time. Automatically hated it. Our hotel was less than ten miles from the airport and took two hours to get to with traffic! The amount of people and things were staggering. In comparison, Seattle has about 800,000 people, whereas Bangkok ~ 8 million. So absolutely different from TonSai. The smog in the city is disgusting from all the pollution. Visibility is less than 25 miles at best, and my lungs hurt terribly. All I want to do is cry, but I can't. I need release. My eye twitch is back, and it hasn't been since January.

We just boarded the plane to Kathmandu. I am looking forward to seeing some things, but all I want to do is relax and sleep. I have barely gotten a good night's sleep. I miss the animals so.

I know I need to channel my inner Michelle Obama for this trip, but I just don't want to. I don't want to be around anyone, only the animals. I cannot imagine what I'm going to feel like in a month. I feel like my soul is already screaming with the amount of stimulation. People are exhausting. I keep trying to imagine what my therapist would tell me… something about visualization and next steps of adventure and journey, I suppose. I really don't want to, though.

Josh keeps telling me the Himalayas will make me feel small… nowhere else on earth are mountains that big. That may be true, but I'm not sure I will feel that way. Being as low as possible on the water has always made me feel the smallest.

It's funny to think about – a month ago I was afraid to start writing again. Now it feels like it's the only thing keeping me sane.

Going back to those thoughts strikingly made me realize how nervous I really was about the next part of our trip. Landing in Bangkok and travelling to our hotel was one of the most panic inducing moments of my life. During that taxi ride, I used every focusing technique I could think of. I tried to slow my breath so I would not have a panic attack, closing my eyes and imagining the tide of the Andaman Sea.

Before we left for our trip, I had downloaded episodes of podcasts I listen to, as well as recently bought Audible so I would not carry the weight of books on our trip. For me, reading has always been about the story. It was something to distract me from my own anxious thoughts, and to just disconnect. Like running forces me to focus on the inhaling and exhaling of breathing, reading forces me to focus on the words on the page, line by line, back and forth.

Up until this point I appreciated the distraction that fiction lends to. Something totally different, and not true. I love the fantastical nature that stories imbue. I spend much of my social work life listening and reading other people's real-life stories of hardship. Unless strongly recommended, I tend to choose stories to read that do not have a basis in reality.

Growing up, the first election that I was able to vote in was for President Obama. I was ecstatic that he won, following his campaign, enamored by his speeches and promise of hope. Hope, of all things. Hope for a better America. The romantically simple idea that we can hope to be better than we once were was idyllic. America was founded with great ideals, but most do not realize what was lost with the proponents of those ideals. We still have a long way to go. I was proud to support the Obama's as a family. Recently, Michelle Obama had come out with her book, *Becoming* and I downloaded it to listen. I could not think of anything more inspirational to listen to. Additionally, it was about twenty hours long and it would take up a lot of time to listen, which was a bonus.

I started the beginning right before we left for our trip. I wanted a bit of a hook prior to dedicating so much time to listening to her book. Michelle Obama narrates the audio version of the book herself. She starts out her memoir long before their family held such stature as the first family. I was surprised to learn that she was not overjoyed at the job of being a "political wife." She describes it as going through a lot of motions, smiling even if you don't want to, and always being gracious despite what you might be feeling inside.

Her honest candor paralleled strongly to the feelings that I had heading into being a part of a trekking group, as well as the looming feelings that I knew being on Mt. Everest would create.

I was nervous about interacting with such a group of likeminded people, and their common goal of going to Mt. Everest. This was never my dream. I was nervous about interacting with other mountain guides who also committed their careers to the mountains like Josh had. What if Josh realized that the mountains were still calling to him? What if he realized that the mountains meant more to him than me? What if none of those things happened, but I still stayed so wrapped up in my nervousness that I could not interact with others without seeming like a crazy person? Like Michelle Obama, I had to be able to hold it together and smile.

DURING

part IV

March 30, 2019

Landed in Kathmandu, Nepal yesterday. From the plane Josh pointed out the entire Himalayan range, including Mt. Everest to me. They all looked like pointy clouds, but to Josh much more. One of the first things we saw on our cab ride to the hotel was a smokestack formed by the burning of bodies. We learned that in Hindu culture it is very respectful.

So far Kathmandu is smokey, busy, people/motorbike and car filled, but very poor. Nothing like Bangkok… but, pretty. Today we went to the Monkey Temple which was much different than the temple we visited in Thailand. Much less ornate, but still beautiful. Minus one of the monkeys trying to eat me.

Getting off the plane and heading into the airport in Kathmandu was unlike any airport I had ever been to. In America airports are like shopping malls. They are bright and shiny, filled with pretty things and people bustling around to get to the next destination. There is usually a sense of something better to be attained, whether it is a vacation or work trip, people in airports seem to have a goal. The airport in Kathmandu was small and run-down compared to American standards. The people were hurried, scurrying about like squirrels who just dropped their stash of nuts.

There is a large mural painted on one of the walls, a Welcome to Nepal sign of peace flags, the countryside and mountains above. Josh was insistent that I had to take a photograph with the mural. At the moment I wasn't overjoyed, the feeling of the plane, forced air and wearing sweatpants was not ideal. I also had realized very quickly as we flew in and saw the Himalayan range that being in Nepal was very, very real.

It was as if we were just happy in Thailand and now suddenly, we were in Nepal. I felt that it all happened too quickly. I did not think that I was ready for any of it. I had spent so much energy fighting, cursing and resenting this mountain and country. I never thought that I would be in this place. I was just barreling down in a plane looking at the real Mt. Everest and now abruptly landing in Nepal standing in front of a welcoming sign smiling for a photograph. I was nervous and intimidated, but I knew what this meant for Josh. I grinned and took the photograph.

The scene outside of the airport was surreal. The hurried people anywhere else did not compare to the bustling that was occurring outside in the parking lot. We met one of the Sherpa who worked for Josh's friend's guiding company and he provided hospitality for travelers. He was younger, impeccably dressed in a smart suit and fun tie. He exuded warmth and was easy to have a conversation with. I immediately liked him. He put me at ease by asking us questions and sharing facts about Nepal as we drove through the city.

We drove along the Bagmati River, passing by the Pashupatinath Temple and saw smoke. We learned about the ritual of burning the dead on pyres and what it represents in Hindu culture. The Pashupatinath Temple is a World Heritage Site and one of Nepal's most sacred places. The smoke smelled unlike anything I had ever smelled before. We found out that it is an important ceremony that releases the soul from its physical form. Nepal is split between two cultures and lies on the border between Tibet and India. The religion of people is either Hindu from India, or Buddhist from Tibet, more specifically Tibetan Buddhism, which is different from Thailand Buddhism. I liked learning about the traditions as well as learning about the Nepalese culture as we drove.

Our hotel was named The Yak and Yeti. When we got there, Josh explained that it was one of the nicest hotels in town. This said a lot, as Kathmandu itself is very, very poor. I felt sheepish driving up to a place that was gated, its emblem on the side of the building designed in shiny gold.

There was a version of the Yak and Yeti in Disney World. On our honeymoon, Josh had told me stories of the hotel, transporting himself away from fake Nepal to his memory of real Nepal. And now I was experiencing the same type of transportation, yet in reverse. I realized I really was in Nepal and this was really happening. A moment repeating itself with variance and truth. I start to absorb the world around me, taking in all the people, places, smells and sights.

Josh wanted to take me to one of the Himalayan temples, named the Monkey Temple, Swayambhunath. There were monkeys in Thailand, but this was unbelievable. There were hundreds of monkeys at this temple. Absolutely everywhere. It was incredibly overwhelming. We went to the temple on a misty, rainy day. The air itself was smoggy due to pollution, but with the rain it seemed cleaner. The monkeys themselves ran around, climbing the buildings of the temple, swinging from the trees surrounding. We watched the bigger monkeys interact in comparison to the smaller ones. Natural hierarchies were evident in the animal kingdom.

At one point, Josh wanted a photo of me with a monkey. I had taken a great shot of him earlier with a monkey and he wanted to reciprocate. When we were in Costa Rica, we went to this wild Capuchin monkey sanctuary where monkeys would jump down from the trees and land on your shoulders, head or arms. I loved it. They were black and white, small and had hugely soft tails. I fed them bananas and enjoyed every second. Josh is adamant that one of those monkeys bit him, but there was no blood and I was suspicious. If anything, I think it might have just been a little nip.

However, in this moment in Nepal the monkeys were quite different. They were huge in stature and teeth. The best word I can think of to describe them as is fierce. In this photographic moment, I remember there was a leaf that had fallen on the ground and I wanted to keep that as my marker. The monkey was sitting on a ledge, about eye level with me, and Josh kept encouraging me to get closer. I did not have the greatest feeling about this, and a split second later this monkey almost ate my face off. I had never been so panic stricken in my entire life. I wish I could erase that moment of terror from my memory, but it just so happens that Josh snapped the photo at that exact moment, freezing the frame forever. After that I was much more skittish of any monkey we encountered.

*A*pril 1, 2019

Kathmandu is busy – people, cars, bikes going through life as fast as possible. The only reason I can surmise is for survival.

The city itself is dust and dirt filled, the latter does not bother me. I do however miss clean air and water. There are stray, street doggies all around and I just want to take them all home. We visited another temple yesterday, which was pretty to see.

All the guides arrived yesterday and went to dinner, myself included. All seem like lovely, fun people. It's nice to interact with other real people for a bit.

It thundered and lightened a bit last night and it felt like the world was ending. It was amazing. Today it is finally clearer, and the air isn't wrought with thick smoke… the rain cleaned. The other day the sun set by 4pm, only about two-thirds through the sky shrouding the city in early darkness.

The smog and people are so overwhelming. I miss home and Thailand where I felt as if I could breathe emotionally and physically. Driving around yesterday felt like people overload. Josh keeps wanting this to be a positive and perfect experience and I just feel like I want to get through it. I don't know why he loves this city so much. At home he is a perfectionist, so very clean and orderly. Completely different from Nepal.

We visited a different temple, farther away from where we were staying. At Boudhanath Temple there are huge buildings in the center of a circular square, in the middle of the city. There is one large stupa that dominates the skyline of Kathmandu. Stupas themselves are dome shaped structures that are Buddhist shrines, many used as a place of meditation. There are steps that lead toward the top of the temple, prayer flags coming down, angular and blowing in the wind. There were elderly monks around the temples surrounded by incense, meditating and praying, sitting in various nooks and crannies. I had never seen anyone with so many wrinkles look so beautiful.

What was striking to me was how you could tell most of the wrinkles were formed from laugh lines and smiling. It contrasts so much with American culture of always trying to stay and look as young as possible. A symbol of age somehow being negative, yet here it was a sign of wealth. Not in the material, but in the wealth of living a happy life. I often think of the monks at Boudhanath when I am feeling overwhelmed by my own physicality. Painting a smile on my lips and contouring away the laugh lines away does not actually imbue happiness. Being happy imbues happiness.

After leaving Boudhanath, we arrived back at the Yak and Yeti. The energy of the hotel had changed. Clients and other mountain guides had started to arrive. The lobby was filled with people's climbing and trekking bags. Josh immediately recognized two people in line waiting, other mountain guides from Ecuador and Argentina. I was used to the reunion of mountain guides. They embraced as old friends like no time had passed between them, and for about ten seconds I felt invisible. Those ten seconds confirming all the worst thoughts in my head, thinking that this is how the rest of the trip would be. And then to my surprise, the two other guides embraced me as well, a natural extinguisher of the flames my demons had created. I felt as if we were immediate friends. That feeling has continued to this day.

Later that night there was a guide dinner at an outdoor restaurant nearby. The whole guiding team was finally here. I was invited to dinner, as well. I only knew one other person there; rather, I had met them and had a handful of conversations a couple years prior. Out of all the experiences I had with being the wife of a mountain guide and being thrust in various situations with other guides, still despite not knowing anybody I had never felt more part of the group until this moment.

Situations like this are usually my nightmare. I tend to like having a good background and gauge of a person before I engage in conversation with new people. I make index cards for my mind to reference back to in order to have the best outcome of conversation. In general, the idea of small talk gives me inclination to run far, far away. It is not that I am anxious about saying the right thing or feeling a certain way. I honestly am indifferent to the "how are you's, weather and baseball" pleasantries. I would pretty much do anything to avoid it and therefore I am perceived as awkward in new social situations.

Most people that get to know me find this out quickly. I do not placate during conversations, nor do I appease trivial chatter. I prefer and demand real conversations of meaning, heart and mind. And so here I was in Nepal, at a restaurant at a huge table of people. I had not met almost all the entire group before me. Much to my surprise there was minimal small talk, but rather the sharing of stories. It was one of the few occasions in my life I can say I felt genuinely included.

*A*pril 2, 2019

Tomorrow we leave Kathmandu and take a small plane to Lukla. No helicopter, thank god. I am excited to get out of the city. Last night was another sleepless night – our hotel has armored guards with AK-47s during the day, but a night they leave and close a wrought iron gate. Once that happens, it's like the city pulsates with madness; bass music, and people screaming into the night.

Just as the city was, I was wrought with nervous energy. That night we had our whole team dinner including all the mountain guides, and clients who were trekking and climbing. I stressed out about what to wear, I only had one sundress that I brought, and what if I didn't look right? That day my entire left side of my forehead had decided to peel, the decisions of not wearing enough sunscreen in Thailand coming back to haunt me.

I had not brought much makeup on this trip, only Chapstick and mascara. I created a "foundation" out of some sort of dipping sauce I had stashed away from lunch that day mixed in with liquid hand sanitizer. I usually have a side part in my hair, and I changed the part so my hair would be inclined to cover the side of my face that was peeling off. I messaged a friend panicking about this situation, knowing Josh would think I was a crazy person who mashed up food to use as face foundation, as well as not following his diligent sunscreen application schedule he had adhered to in Thailand. She was kind, assuring me that it would be fine, we would be in a restaurant and everything would smell of food anyway.

As ridiculous as the situation seemed, it provided a nice distraction from our impending departure the next day. Against all odds, I was ready for it. We had been in Kathmandu for four nights; Josh helped to get the team set and ready, and the guides got a chance to meet the team and get organized. We had time to explore the city and wander into Tahmel which was located within walking distance.

Tahmel is a walking, cyclist and/or wagon only part of Kathmandu. It is filled with shops built upon shops, exploding out over each other. A tourist spot in a sense, as it is a one stop shop for anything you might need or want. Anything meaning – restaurants, hotels, hostels, massage, clothing, mountain or climbing gear, and nightlife. The best cheesecake and bruschetta I have ever had in my entire life is in Tahmel. I bought a new face buff with the design pattern of the trekking map to Everest Base Camp and convinced Josh that I needed cheesecake any chance I got.

One thing I could not quite get used to was the ten-minute walk to Tahmel. In Nepal there are no crosswalks, few stoplights (and those are rarely abided by), no guarantee of a general direction of traffic and countless motorbikes zipping in between the cars all without a speed limit. Walking in Nepal you had to use every sense you had, constantly on edge and each step the difference of getting hit by some sort of vehicle or not. It was chaotically terrifying.

I was also looking forward to moving past the subtle racism that was initiated against me. I was born in India and adopted at four months old. I'm as American as they come in speaking and habits, but not in looks. Nepal and India have a sordid history, rivals at best. They used to be a part of the same country, but split, a bad breakup for the history books. There is an inherent distrust and dislike of Indians by most Nepalese. And me, walking down the street in a tank top and shorts, blatantly disregarding the female culture at hand, in Indian skin, holding hands with a white man garnered many disgusted looks. To say the least, I was very much anticipating a change in scenery and reaction.

This experience intrigues me in many ways. Growing up in Washington State, and the lifestyle that I was raised in surrounded me with white people. In Thailand and Nepal, I was surrounded by people who looked more like me than anyone I had ever been around. At first it startled me, but after more days passed, I grew comforted. Despite the rivalry between India and Nepal, it made me feel a sense of belonging to see others similar to me in looks.

Our dinner with the entire team kicked off the days to come. Everyone was excited, even though most were not sure of what this journey would hold. Everyone there represented all different walks of life, as well as called home to eleven different countries. I had fun hanging out with Josh and the rest of the guides. We sampled different fancy appetizers and drank lots of beer and champagne. Thankfully, no one said anything about my "makeup."

As a collective group, it seemed as if this party was a preemptive celebration. We had not trekked or climbed anything; no goals had yet been achieved. It is only in reflection that I realize that this was the one and only time the full group as a whole would be able to celebrate together, as our trekking group's trip was much shorter than the climbers.

April 3, 2019

Took a prop plane to Lukla and trekked to Phakding today. Prop plane was terrifying, and I hated every second of it.

So far, the trek was fine, pretty views here and there, but interacting with the clients is hard for me.

I also feel like an imposter hiking in the footsteps of Sherpa who have continued to walk this trail for years on end. I don't know the history of Mt. Everest as a legend but would like to learn. Hiking in the perfect gear, boots, poles etc. while Sherpa often in bare feet, carrying at least 50-100-pound loads on their back amazes me.

Just like in Kathmandu, the Nepali people at the airport seem to dislike me for how I look. In comparison, the Sherpa who are trekking with us are so incredibly kind and genuine and take me for who I am.

I had never been in such a small prop plane in my entire life. It was so scary and loud. The propellers were deafening, even when using ear plugs. The width of the plane fit people four seats across and maybe twenty people in total. Josh held my hand the entire time. One of the other guides was in front of me and kept turning back and giving me a thumbs up sign. Everyone seemed to be excited, loving this moment. All I could think about was that we were in a tiny object hurtling through the air.

We flew into Lukla which is the most dangerous airport in the world. It is situated on the side of a cliff with a straight drop, the runway under 2,000 feet long, a little bit over 9,000 feet above sea level. These factors make it incredibly difficult to have a successful landing and takeoff without injury. The pilots themselves have to be much more skilled to avoid such missteps. I was incredibly relieved when we landed.

We met the Sherpa who would be travelling with us on the trek to Base Camp. They were friendly, kind and incredibly polite. I learned that contrary to Western misinformation, it is offensive to call someone who is not of Sherpa descent, a Sherpa. Sherpa does not mean "to carry", but rather is an ethnic group. Like any other place, their jobs are whatever is needed in the Khumbu Valley such as guides, porters, cooks, yak drivers, etc.

We trekked into Phakding which was a bit forested at first and then opened into greener and more expansive hills. We followed the path of the Dudh Kosi River and it reminded me of hiking in the Pacific Northwest. Yet, home felt so far away from where we were. I quickly learned the term "Nepali flat", meaning up and down, up and down. It was really happening. We were officially on the trek to Everest Base Camp. I wondered to myself if I had made it. Or was making it to actual Base Camp making it? Or maybe finally returning home was making it?

Donkeys and yaks carried loads back and forth, as well as the start of tea houses. We started to see the many boulders, stupas and prayer wheels painted and inscribed with Buddhist prayers, protecting people during their journey higher. Most much bigger than me, a solid reminder that everyone that has traveled here has been blessed. Josh explained to me as you pass a prayer wheel it is tradition to spin it, initiating the protection of what the wheel can offer you.

As far back as I can remember, every year for Christmas my mom gives me candy lifesavers in my stocking. I am honestly not a sweets person, but I do love the tradition of lifesavers. It takes me a long time to eat through the candies themselves. This year, I brought the whole package of them to Nepal with me. I broke out the first roll on that first day of trekking. It warmed my dry throat and acted as a form of a lozenge. It sounds silly, but having a flavored, small treat that reminded me of home was nice while we were hiking.

Right before we got to the tea house we were staying in, there was the first rope bridge to cross. The diameter of the bridges could fit two people walking next to each other, but it was safer if you walked quickly in a single file line, as often there would be porter Sherpa or animals crossing in the other direction carrying large loads. The bridges are high up, rickety and a single rope on the side to help keep your balance. Since bridges connect two parts of land, often divided over water or canyon they were windy; you had to balance to keep your footing stable. Surprisingly, I loved the bridges. The views they offered of the landscape were gorgeous and picturesque. As the bridges themselves were suspended, we were suspended in the moment as we crossed.

*A*pril 4, 2019

Hiked up to Namche today. About 3,000 feet of elevation gain.

The team seems to have settled down a lot, not buzzing around frantically which is good. I went into this not wanting, or searching to make friends, but I may end up with some.

Tomorrow Josh and I go on our private Mt. Everest viewing hike which I am nervous for. I think he's doing well so far, his soul at peace. Mine is okay, I miss home and Thailand so very much.

Namche Bazaar is shaped like a crescent moon, situated on the slope of the hills, hidden from view. It is the largest village to encounter on the trek to Everest Base Camp. As you come around the corner emerging from the trees, suddenly you are in Namche, hundreds of buildings, hotels and shops coming into striking view. You are at the bottom of the hill and walking up the main street you see a man-made river flowing down the side, with huge prayer wheels spinning as the water flowed through. People touched the water, absorbing its blessings as they passed.

It feels strange to have been so isolated, surrounded by just trees, mountains and nature and suddenly you are back in civilization, Nepali style. You can buy almost anything you need in Namche, as it is filled with so much. It is packed with people, dogs, donkeys and yaks. The dirt trail had turned to mostly cobblestone, each step carved carefully by hand.

On those first few days of trekking, I realized that the Khumbu Valley was filled with stray village dogs. Hindu legend tells a story of someone voyaging through the land who loses his family but adopts a loyal dog who joins the journey and protects him. Because of this and many more legends surrounding the animal, dogs are revered. The Nepalese celebrate Kukur Tihar, the day of the dog every year.

Josh had very strict rules about petting or feeding the dogs, so we would not expose ourselves to any diseases that the dogs might have. I ignored him every time and would pet all the doggy's that I would see. Channeling Michelle Obama had its perks. Later after returning home and creating our scrapbook, I realized I could create a whole separate album of all the dog photos I took.

Outside of the tea house we were staying in, there was a clearing with a sign stating, "Yak Parking Only", which made our group giggle. The entire group of us trekked in together, staggered by teams A, B, and C. Josh led group C, mostly trekkers, but some climbers were a part of it as well. As a team we trekked and ate meals together. The nervous energy that the group had exhibited toward the beginning had seemed to ease.

The conversations turned from the sole excitement of Mt. Everest to life and family. It was hard for me to relate to a lot of the clients. Trekking to Base Camp or climbing Mt. Everest were lifelong dreams of theirs. They were rightly excited and jubilant that this was finally happening for them. I started out the trip in disbelief, mentally pinching myself to remind me of the reality. This never had been a bucket list item for me. It was difficult for me to understand and relate to the rapturous euphoria I was surrounded by.

In Namche there was the ability for limited internet access, and I messaged one of my best friends a very long run on sentence. I told her how I didn't feel like I could connect to anyone and everyone was so different than me. Because of the time difference, I did not receive a message back until the next day. In response to my drawn out and complaining message all she wrote me back were the words "Michelle Obama" in upper case letters about ten times, not so subtly reminding me to take a breath, smile and keep putting one foot in front of another.

I was at the point of the book where Michelle Obama told her story of growing up. She spoke about her parents, her brother and her education. She talked about life on the South Side of Chicago in the seventies, and how her guidance counselor did not think she was "Princeton material." She had an intrinsic belief in herself, continuing to persevere through hard things. In listening to her words, I started to absorb them. No one had told me that I couldn't accomplish this. I had to believe in myself and had to believe that I could accomplish this journey to Everest Base Camp.

*A*pril 5, 2019

Namche is nice. A bit excessive in the amount of "Western money making" stores, but the history of the village is incredible. It used to be the main trade route betwixt Nepal and Tibet hundreds of years ago. All the buildings are made from hand, carved or chiseled stone into perfect rectangular objects.

This morning Josh took me on a special walk, just he and I to view Mt. Everest for the first time. It's so far away from where we are at, but still big. It is hard to tell the scale because we are already so high up. We also hiked up to Everest Hotel with the group later, but the clouds came in and made Everest views unavailable.

Josh gave me a specially made necklace right before we saw the mountain… a carved rock that naturally looks like the summit top, also taken from the summit of Mt. Everest from Josh's last expedition there. So very special to me.

I am not sure what I think about seeing it for the first time. A lot of the surrounding area reminds me of Paradise at Mt. Rainier. I think it is just having the representation of what Everest means that I'm still trying to work out. Surprisingly, I've had a really fun day with Josh; we've been making a "Tips for Tip-Top Trekking" video for his best friend. It has been fun just goofing around with my dear.

Since we were staying two nights in Namche to acclimatize, Josh and I had some time to relax and just be together. As much as Josh loves to climb, he is not a fan of hiking, or trekking, unless the goal of the trek is to get to a climb. Going into your local REI store or being in the wilderness field for a job yourself, mountain guides are often asked pretty common and obvious questions. Professionally, Josh kindly answers, but internally it can be a mental slap to the forehead. So, we decided to create a mockumentary video of our trekking tips such as: do not trek and text, taking the hard route and never losing your glamour.

Our video turned into a fun distraction for the both of us. Our friends and family enjoyed it, as it showcased the views of our trip so far. We took video clips of each other and laughed when we had to redo a take. Josh pieced it all together as we spent time at a cafe in Namche, where I discovered my new favorite drink, hot chocolate mixed with rum and topped with whipped cream.

On our second day in Namche our group was scheduled for an acclimatization hike just above the city, about 1,000 feet higher than we were staying. The hike would offer the first possible views of Mt. Everest. Knowing the trip schedule, I had been nervous about this hike for months. In therapy we decided that if it was possible, Josh and I would do a sort of pre-hike before we went as a group together. Neither of us could predict our feelings of seeing Mt. Everest would create.

Josh and I were able to make that happen, so we woke up early before breakfast and hiked up. Namche was quiet, the city hadn't quite awakened yet. It was just Josh and I, both alone in our thoughts on this brisk morning. As we rounded the corner and Mt. Everest came to view, we saw a Sherpa asking for donations. He startled me out of my own brain, jolting me back in the moment.

Josh donated and then he turned and asked me to look at him. He pulled out a small box for me to open, the necklace placed delicately inside. He explained to me the meaning and reinforced the fact that he came home to give this to me. The Everest rock was wrapped in wire, a piece of the wild trapped in my grasp, hanging as a pendant suspended forever. For the rest of the trip I kept the necklace close to me, reminding myself of the love that binds us.

Seeing Mt. Everest for the first time wasn't what I thought it would be like. It almost felt anticlimactic finally seeing it in person. Since we were already so high up, the scale of Mt. Everest just felt like another mountain, not the highest peak in the world. Being at Paradise, Mt. Rainier felt more impressive to me. Since it was so far away, we could only see Mt. Everest's peak, not the whole of the mountain itself. It did not feel enormous, or jaw-droppingly grand to me. It sat elusive, situated in the background with other peaks in the foreground.

Later that day when we went up to the Everest View Hotel as a trekking group, Mt. Everest was not visible. It was obscured by clouds and fog that rolled in since that morning. Yet, the clouds parted perfectly when Josh and I arrived at our viewpoint earlier that day. It felt as if they had briefly parted just so Josh and I could have that moment together.

April 6, 2019

We left Namche this morning and trekked to Deboche. It was pouring rain the entire time and much of the trek was under tree cover. It reminded me of home, and the first half of the day made me very homesick. The second half was very muddy, which was not fun.

The Sherpa still amaze me, carrying their loads just as heavy as before, with plastic over the items, never once wincing, speaking or making those on the trail aware of their presence, only by footsteps. They remind me of silent warriors.

I'm getting on with most of the team and meeting nice people. It has surprised me finding common ground. The tea house we are staying in the next two nights is called Rivendell, like in The Lord of the Rings *books! It is the nicest spot so far.*

There are so many dogs in Nepal, all which remind me of Ellie. I miss the animals so, so, so much. We saw a perfect view of Ama Dablam and the summit of Mt. Everest today. It still looks like a picture in a book, yet I'm viewing it with my own eyes. It is hard to wrap my head around the reality of it. Nothing in me wants to climb it, though.

Tomorrow is our Puja ceremony, with monks blessing us for the trek or climb. Josh has always loved that part and I am looking forward to experiencing it.

About twenty minutes after we left our tea house in Namche it started pouring down rain. We all bought umbrellas from one of the shops, starting the long, slow walk to Deboche. Mine was rainbow colored. Being from Washington, the rain is very familiar. As much as I love the sun, I also love curling up with a nice book and drinking a cup of tea, cozy inside while listening to the rain fall. Walking in the pouring down rain, carrying a pack is a whole other rain experience.

We also saw the first views of Ama Dablam. It is just over 22,000 feet and strikingly stunning. Its peak is pointy and prominent in the skyline. It has long ridges coming down from the top and a huge hanging glacier on the forefront. Ama Dablam means "mother's necklace", as the hanging glacier looks like a pendant hanging from a person's neck. It was strange to me, feeling the weight of this mountain in our views. This felt impressive, unlike the brief Mt. Everest view we had the day prior. We would continue to see Ama Dablam dominating the skyline most days on the rest of the trek.

The first part of the day was fun. The rain offered a change in our outlook of the scenery. It also reminded me of home. Seeing Ama Dablam was impressive. At lunch we stopped at a very small, cramped tea house to escape the rain. We were all soaking wet, drenched from the rain and sweating from walking uphill. I had hot, spicy soup for lunch warming me from the inside out. My clothes had started to dry out enough that they were not dripping with water, but just a constant dampness. My skin was hot from the sweat and coupled with the dampness my entire body felt clammy. As we left, we took a team photo in the pouring rain with our umbrellas over us.

The second half of the day was miserable.

Just after college I flew to San Diego, California and road tripped back to Seattle, Washington. Early in the trip I developed an infection. I called my doctor describing my symptoms and she prescribed me antibiotics to pick up at a random Safeway outside Santa Monica. Unfortunately, I ended up finding out I was allergic to the antibiotics, as they were sulfa drugs. The medication caused my head to be in excruciating pain, as if it was in a vice. Those few days were a blur of some of the most pain I have ever experienced to this day.

On the misery scale, that afternoon resuming the trek in the rain falls just under the California trip. I started to get really cold, the cold where you cannot seem to warm up, and my body just wanted to freeze. Every step I tensed, as the last section to Deboche was walking downhill, and because of the rain it was a complete mudslide. Walking under the cover of trees seems nice in theory, but it made the rain droplets larger and inconsistent. At some point that afternoon I had also started my period. Because there isn't such a thing as bathrooms, or rest stops along the way, toward the end of the day I could not tell if my clothes were just so soaked with rain that water was trickling down my legs, or if it was blood dripping. Come to find out, it was a combination, forever staining one of my four pairs of wool socks I had brought on the trip pink.

Looking back, that day was when I started to let my guard down. One, at that point I didn't have anything to lose. Two, every single one of us on the team were walking on the same trail, step by step in the pouring rain. Granted, I felt as if I was the only one in misery, but we all were wet and tired. Even though I did not feel as I identified with the group, it started to not matter to me that we all came from such different backgrounds. We all were part of the same journey.

The opportunity to shower only happened every three or four days, yet that is all I wanted. We got to our tea house greeted by a warm fire and a pot of lemon ginger tea; our team's favorite. Contrary to most of the tea houses that were older than dirt, Rivendell had just been built. The room Josh and I stayed in had only had one other guest ever and each bed had real sheets with a bed warmer underneath. I had yet to discover anything as glorious as a bed warmer, but this was the best reward I could imagine after such a wearisome day.

April 7, 2019

We hiked up to Tengboche today for the blessing ceremony. The blessing was in a monastery, where monks chanted, and the High Llama blessed everyone individually. It was definitely a very unique and special circumstance.

I was happy to wake up rested and for once, warm. That morning I remember there was enough internet service that I tried to call my mom. For whatever reason she did not answer, and I remember thinking how much I missed home. Every night before we went to bed our Sherpa guides would fill our water bottles with boiling water so we could stuff them in our sleeping bags to keep warm. I would sleep in my long johns, wool socks, hiking pants, a long sleeve shirt and one of my puffy jackets. I would cover my face with my buff and pull my beanie down low on my face. Most nights I would sleep well, my body tired from altitude gains and spending most of the day trekking. Every morning I would wake up freezing, the idea of leaving the cocoon of my sleeping bag a barrier that often would make me late for morning tea.

When we hiked to Tengboche it was working our way backwards a bit. We were staying two nights in Deboche. Tengboche was located higher, about forty-five minutes behind us, giving us the day to acclimatize. The monastery itself was the most extravagant temple I had seen in Nepal so far. Thailand temples were very colorful with flashy metals, but Nepali temples tended to be simple. Here, there were decorative tapestries lining the walls and brass vases filled with flowers.

We all took our boots off and quietly went into the monastery, sitting cross legged, lining the temple. The monks marched in, sang and spread incense as they chanted before us. Each person was invited to come up and receive a Khata, a scarf, with a blessing directly from the High Llama. Josh had received a scarf and red string necklace from each trip to Nepal, granting him safety and protection. I never quite understood the meaning and symbolism until I had experienced it myself.

April 8, 2019

We trekked to Pheriche today. Absolutely beautiful day. Clear, crisp and the views were amazing. One of the places we stopped for a break we met one of the Sherpa who rescued Josh. I immediately broke down in tears and gave him a hug. Could not stop crying for twenty minutes, which was unexpected. The amount of gratitude that I have for the people who rescued Josh is incredible. It is strange to be so overcome with emotion. It's few and far between that it has ever happened to me.

There really is something magnificent about being in the mountains. All you have is what is in your pack, who's around you, and the air in your lungs. Josh is so at peace in this arena of his life, much more so than at home.

Josh told me later he hadn't remembered who had saved him, but when he saw Namgyal today, he instantly remembered. Trauma is a funny thing. The brain only wants to survive and tricks you into hiding certain things. Secondary trauma is just as interesting. Every time Josh tells the story new details emerge. It was only just until recently that I had learned none of the Sherpa wanted to go up and rescue him because of their hatred of the company Josh worked for.

That thought kills me.

When I started crying, it was in front of all the clients and the overload was unreal. I have never had such an outpouring of emotion, except when I saw [Josh's coworker] *who saved him after they returned home two years ago.*

So, it was at about 13,000 feet above sea level that all the grief that had become a part of me, my inner thoughts, and initiated in every step that I took turned to liquid. It poured uncontrollably out of my eyes, my heart and every piece of me.

Two years ago my tough, steadfast and accomplished husband came home a shell of a man, not realizing how seeing the balance of the fragility of your own life can affect you. The event itself was traumatic at best, yet he came home alive, albeit suffering. I of course started to live a life shrouded in secondary trauma. The grief and anger of reliving his story and the continuation of both of our sorrow over and over was exhausting. This cycle became a part of my everyday life.

Along the trek we had met many individuals, guides and Sherpa that Josh had worked with over the years. At about 13,000 feet between Dingboche and Pheriche is when we were introduced to a young Sherpa, maybe in his late teens, early twenties. It was then in that moment of recognition that Josh realized that this person had saved his life. He communicated this to me about three minutes after the interaction, but the Sherpa had gone elsewhere. I frantically felt an innate need for him to come back.

And he did.

Just like my husband, he came back.

I ran to him, overcome with tears and inordinate gratitude and enveloped him into a hug. With the waterfall of tears and my emotional upheaval all I could utter were the words, "Thank you." He hugged me back, looked over to Josh and he knew.

I never thought I would have willingly traveled to this place in person, let alone emotionally. This place that took so many months away from our marriage, and eventually, very nearly my husband's life. Nevertheless, we planned to go to Mt. Everest together. Together we were trekking to Everest Base Camp sitting at 17,500 feet above sea level. We had prepared with lots of love, therapy and journaling. We knew each other's trigger words, coping mechanisms and what to do if we noticed the other person was not doing okay.

Never in my wildest dreams did I imagine the possibility of meeting one of the individuals who saved Josh's life. My therapist did not prepare me for that.

And yet, that is what ended up saving me.

Not the months of therapy, not our family and friends, not even adopting our beloved labradoodle. Coincidentally at that same break, I had just met a dog who I had deemed "Khumbu Ellie." I gave her some of my snacks and clean water from my water bottle. She was sweet, wiggly and just felt as if it channeled our happy puppy at home. I needed that reminder.

Meeting the person who saved Josh alleviated me from the grief cage I had put myself in. This moment on the opposite side of the world in the Khumbu Valley was what healed me and brought me back to myself.

I was able to carry on with the trek to Everest Base Camp, each step not with anguish, but conviction. My soul finally felt at peace.

Everything that we had been through had prepared me for this journey.

Being a witness to grief I was able to finally find meaning in our story.

April 9, 2019

Today we hiked to 15,000 feet which is my personal high point, which is pretty cool. I'm really enjoying trekking about with Josh, surprisingly. I miss home and the animals, but that's it.

Currently, I am sitting in the tea house in Pheriche, the wind is blowing, snow is falling from the sky and I'm warm inside with a fire going, drinking tea with rum. It is idyllic being here at 13,800 feet.

The day before we hiked to Pheriche. There were little Sherpa children on the side of the trail. So very poor, and yet the happiest smiles I had ever seen. They were both smudged with dirt, one wearing a too big t-shirt and underwear playing with a large barrel. I remember them staring as we strode past. Westerners with our heavy packs, dirty, but all mostly new hiking attire. I felt ashamed for desperately wanting a hot shower, knowing the privilege and luxury that I had.

Since we had left Namche, the trek itself became more and more remote. We were not surrounded by as many other groups or people, but mainly yaks and porter Sherpa carrying loads to Base Camp. The yaks themselves are hugely impressive animals. They are over 1,000 pounds and their horns are 30 to 40 inches in length alone. It was like something out of a dream walking along with these majestic creatures, hearing their bells chime as they roamed past, with the gentle breeze blowing past and the mountains in the distance. The peace in those moments are something that I now long for.

We could see Pheriche in the distance about a half a mile away and I started to run to it. I missed running, and for once we were on flat ground. It felt good to move fast, even with my pack on my back. I was surprised to feel out of breath at about a quarter mile. I remember Josh not overly excited about my mini run, reminding me we were at altitude.

Pheriche was by far our favorite tea house. It was more expansive, in the sense that we did not feel cramped at tables trying to find somewhere to sit. All the tea houses served basically the same things, but this tea house was the most delicious. Most served variations of fried rice, soup, spaghetti, orange "chicken" (made with yak), French fries, popcorn, momos and Dal Bhat, mainly rice with lentil soup or curry, and fried Mars or Snickers bars. My diet had become milk tea and momos with jam for breakfast, soup and French fries for lunch, and usually fried rice or orange chicken for dinner. I would have to find someone to share a fried Mars bar with for dessert because Josh would happily devour all of his in its entirety.

Between mealtimes we all would sit in the dining area, as it was the only place in the tea houses that had a fire to keep warm. As a team, we would chat, play cards, and journal. Josh brought the card game version of Monopoly which is much quicker than the board game version and minimally results in the usual tears and resentment. We taught many of our Sherpa guides how to play, and as they played their hands beating us every time they would apologize profusely. It was silly, fun and so normal despite being on a mountain.

We spent two nights in Pheriche. On the second day we went for an acclimatization hike up the hills behind us. That afternoon I hit my elevation high point. The highest I had ever climbed to was Mt. Rainier. After hitting my high point, every step forward I would mentally chant the mantra, "New high point, new high point." It made me smile thinking that with every step came a new accomplishment.

April 10, 2019

Josh had a hard day today. We hiked up to Lobuche Base Camp, around 15,500 feet. To get there, you pass through the dead climber's memorial. It was amazing to see so many pyramids of rocks from all sorts of religions, countries and cultures.

I asked Josh to make a memorial, which he did. Hopefully it puts the piece of him at rest that he left on this mountain. The backdrop views of the memorial are Ama Dablam and an entire Himalayan range. I think it is a beautiful place for those souls.

As we walked out, much farther behind the group, we ran into ANDY SERKIS who played Gollum from The Lord of the Rings *movies. Literally one of the coolest moments of my entire life. With the background of the Himalaya behind us. I am still absolutely star struck. I cannot believe this happened!!!!*

Just as I like to prepare myself with mental flashcards when I meet new people, I wanted to know all the stops for our trek. In preparation for our trip Josh gave me an itinerary with the various places that we would stop along the way. In theory it was nice, but the villages and tea houses did not mean anything to me but words. He didn't necessarily tell me about what each stop looked like, felt like, or what to expect. The itinerary also was not set in stone because anything could happen and the trip itself had built in contingency days. The end goal of course being, Everest Base Camp.

Since the climber's memorial was just something we passed through and did not make camp, it was not on the itinerary. With my limited knowledge of Mt. Everest, only exposing myself to the few facts I needed to know, I had no idea this was coming. It was also one of our longer days of trekking. That afternoon we stopped for a tea break at another tea house. The next section of the day we would ascend a gradually long hill, the top of which we could see from the tea house. There were flags blowing in the wind and the surrounding area was picturesque with the mountains surrounding us.

We were outside sitting as a team and I remember Josh just wandered away. The team itself was bothered by other random independent trekkers, not attached to a company who asked questions and sat too close. Staying healthy was important and the idea of sharing germs with someone could endanger the success of the group as a whole. After a while I realized Josh had not come back. I found him on the sidelines, up and away from the group and unsteady.

I discovered that Josh had not told me about the climber's memorial because he had forgotten about it. Again, the mind protects itself from the memory. As all my emotions had come raining down upon me two days prior, this moment was the equivalent for Josh. His journal was packed away in his pack, but I encouraged him to take some time to type some thoughts out on his phone. We were trekking in with another one of the guides and we asked him to take the group up, and we would follow behind.

As we climbed closer and closer to the entrance of the memorial Josh got more and more emotionally distressed. He is not one to show emotion, a constant point of contention between us. In comparison, I over think and over emote as much as possible. At one point he grabbed my hand and just squeezed. I am not sure he even realized how hard he was squeezing, but I held on.

We got to the top off the hill and looked back. The entrance had hundreds of colorful lung dar peace flags stretched across rock structures. We were on a large hill in the middle of a huge expansive valley. On this clear and beautiful day, the Himalayan mountains were especially striking, surrounding us in dignified stature. The light and shadows hit Ama Dablam highlighting its edges. Everyone there was quiet in respect, the wind the only voice to hear. The memorial itself was huge. Some notable climbers who had died had headstones taller than me. They were engraved with names and well known mountain quotes about the nobility of dying while doing something you love.

In all our conversations over the years Josh always expressed that he never wanted to die in the mountains. As much as he loved them, and at times as much as I was convinced that he loved them more than me, he had a reverence for them. A respect for their majesty and their wildness. Blinded by reverence, he walked the danger line so closely that it became blurred and all consuming.

So here we were, walking through the climber's memorial on Mt. Everest. The first section had some of the larger monuments, but those decreased. Most of the effigies were not elaborate, or named, but rather small stacks of gathered, flat stones about twelve inches high. These had no plaques, their dedications unknown. Hundreds of people, many from Sherpa families died in the ascent to their dreams, bodies unfound and unnamed, lost to the mountain forever.

I watched Josh process being in a place to pay homage to fellow climbers and Sherpa who had lost their lives. I realized something that I never had before. I had spent so much of my energy and time worried and resentful toward mountains, Mt. Everest in particular. "Everest" had become a trigger word for me, and I tried very hard to make it invisible and nonexistent. After Josh came home the second time and hearing his tale, all the resentment compounded upon itself, growing into a nightmarish creature, haunting me every day.

I encouraged Josh to build his own rock structure for the part of him that he lost on that fated day. In the slow motion like moments of watching him choose the perfect rocks to create his own memorial I realized that even if Josh had died, Mt. Everest could never be invisible to me. I would never be able to escape that mountain. What brought me to this place was in fact my love for Josh.

It occurred to me that if Josh had never come home from that trip, I still would have to walk this trek alone and without him, building my own tribute for my husband.

We both were emotionally exhausted, lost in our own thoughts. Our trekking group had already left, continuing the journey to Lobuche Base Camp. It was time for us to move on. We were at the far end of the memorial, seeing fewer rock structures around us. Suddenly Josh heard a voice and turned to me and said, "That was Gollum."

Thrown off by his statement, especially following what we had just gone through, I just stared at Josh. He repeated himself and it clicked. I looked around hastily. I am the BIGGEST *Lord of the Rings* fan. I was obsessed with the story, and especially Peter Jackson's film interpretation. I watched the extended movie versions and all the appendices over and over. My final history thesis paper in high school was about the advances in movie technology that Jackson utilized, specifically in the creation of motion capture and the character, Gollum. In an instant I recognized Andy Serkis' profile and gait. I immediately left Josh and ran to catch up to Serkis.

It did not occur to me to plan out something cool, or intelligent to say, but I did realize I couldn't just run and sneak up on a person. As I got closer, I slowed my pace into a more casual stride. I started to walk an arm's length distance away from him, confirming that this was exactly who I thought it was. He turned to me and all I said was, "You're Andy Serkis."

Matter of factly, he responded, "Why yes I am!"

Here I was in the most amazing location, equal to the mountainous film locations in New Zealand, surrounded by the Himalayan range talking with Andy freakin' Serkis. Josh caught up to us and volunteered to take our photograph. Serkis was kind, friendly and gracious. Our interaction was only about four minutes, but even when I think of it now, I cannot help but smile uncontrollably. A stark contrast to the rest of our entire day, but a light to me in a dark place.

April 11, 2019

Josh is sick. He barely slept last night and was shivering and feverish the whole night. I felt terrible. He took antibiotics and is still pretty miserable today. I went with the team on an acclimatization hike a little bit above 16,800 feet. The altitude wasn't terrible, but the terrain reminded me of the cleaver on Mt. Rainier. So far there has not been a day that has been harder than climbing the Kautz route on Mt. Rainier. It is nice to trek and acclimatize slowly.

The Sherpa and our expedition leader quarantined Josh so I had to move in a tent all by myself today. It's strange to be in a tent in the mountains without him. Because he has been sick, I have been hanging out with the other team members. It is cool seeing so many achieve their goal of getting to Everest Base Camp and/or going higher.

Before the trip in Kathmandu, that wasn't something I cared about at all. But, going through this journey with the group has turned out to be pretty fun.

Lobuche Mountain is about 20,000 feet high at its peak. Many climbing companies utilize it for its acclimatization for clients prior to climbing Mt. Everest, as well as a bit of a "tester climb" to see how people do. Our group stayed at Lobuche Base Camp around 15,500 feet, our first night that we had slept in tents. The only other nights I had slept in a tent on a mountain was on Mt. Rainier at significantly lower altitude. This was a whole other level.

We had gotten to the parts of the trek that were so significantly remote, tea houses and villages dwindled in isolation. We only had ourselves in surrounding, as well as herds of yaks. The huge peaks surrounded us, caked with snow, ice and prestige. Much to my surprise, Josh was right – the Himalayan mountains *did* make me feel small. That smallness gave me a sense of peace, as if there was something bigger in this world.

The team had nervous energy. The day before three of our trekking group members had to turn back and spend an additional night in Pheriche due to altitude sickness. After we got to Lobuche Base Camp and had a chance to have our afternoon tea, Josh started to feel sick. The clients were worried, Josh was our leader. He stayed in our tent, did not come to dinner and I brought him toast and hot tea. The first night at Lobuche he woke me up by violently shaking most of the night. I gave him my water bottle filled with hot water and felt his forehead which was blistering hot.

The next day Josh took antibiotics that started to help a bit, but the side effect was a skin rash because he is allergic. The rest of our trekking group joined us and into the evening things started to feel a little more normal again. The Sherpa guides assembled another tent for me in order to keep Josh's germs in a tent by himself. It was strange not having him beside me for those next two nights, especially knowing that it was because he was so sick.

We have contemplated how Josh got sick in the first place. He was overly careful about touching things and we all hand sanitized numerous times a day. Josh narrowed it down to another team member in a different group who had gotten sick just prior to the start of the trip. In my opinion I think that it was the combination of that person's germs, as well as the emotional stress of the day prior. Josh rarely gets sick with the average cold. When he gets sick it tends to be because of the underlying pressure he puts on himself. Usually when whatever he is worried about is complete or passes, he magically is not sick anymore.

I think the emotional scars he had guarded so deeply after he almost died were slowly skiving off, lessening the hurt. He was trying to be whole again. Healing is not easy. It is messy, hard and unfortunately not linear. He had misplaced the memories surrounding the climber's memorial. Just like accidently hitting your arm in the doorway, simultaneously on the same spot you already have an injury takes the body by surprise. Josh was not consciously aware of the wound, but his body remembered.

Since Josh was quarantined in his tent I started to bond with the team, without him. For some reason, I felt as if I was under less pressure. I began to seek out conversations, ask questions and get to know the rest of our team as people. We went on an acclimatization hike together, heading up Lobuche Peak. It felt a bit haphazardly planned, but it was a fun distraction for the afternoon.

April 12, 2019

We move up to Gorak Shep tomorrow. It is the last village, as well as the highest village on earth.

Josh mentioned at our team meeting tonight about keeping the goal in sight, which is Everest Base Camp. I feel like it's finally setting in, a way I had not thought of before. The goal was always to emotionally get through it, but somehow, I forgot to think about the amazing experience itself: Everest Base Camp. Something I never in a million years would ever have guessed I would ever go to.

So far, the altitude hasn't affected me terribly. Minor headache and dry nose in the mornings, but besides that I am doing quite well.

One of the things I have learned on this trip is that the world is quite small. Silly, but you can get almost anywhere on a plane flight and more often than not, six degrees of separation is real.

Our group decided to stay an extra unplanned night at Lobuche Base Camp. It gave our team members who had stayed in Pheriche an extra night to acclimatize, as well as giving Josh the opportunity to move from feeling like death toward the land of the living. Coincidentally, many people on our trip started to take Diamox which serves like a crutch for the body and helps combat altitude sickness. I never felt like I needed it, but since it was a sulfa drug, I could never take it, due to my own allergy. Though, the altitude never seemed to bother me. It was nice to stay an additional night at camp, just our group. Most of the climbers had gone on their summit attempt of Lobuche.

We hiked to Lobuche Village to stretch our legs. It is about the same elevation of Lobuche Base Camp and the hike itself is Nepali flat and winds around the river. It was nice to just meanderingly walk without having to wear a heavy pack and without a time constraint. We had lunch in a tea house as a team and were able to access the internet. Josh and I received a message from his best friend, informing us that he would be moving to our hometown when we got back to attend school and transition to becoming a helicopter pilot. Our days and thoughts were so enmeshed with Mt. Everest, it was nice to think about something having to do with home. I began to realize that we were more than halfway completed with our journey.

The rest of our time at Lobuche Base Camp we were able to relax and mainly think. For the first time during this journey I realized how amazing everything was. No, it was not my dream, and no, it was not on my bucket list. However, those facts do not take away from how grateful I was to be experiencing something so very remarkable. I started to let my guard down even more, opening myself up to the people I was surrounded by and the mountain itself. Much to the resistance of my mindset going into this trip, I startlingly cared deeply for everyone on this journey. It was not just my journey anymore; it had become a collective.

April 14, 2019

Last night we stayed in Gorak Shep, the highest village on earth. It means "dead crow" in Sherpa. The village itself was gross, but I surprisingly slept well. One of the clients had to be helicoptered out due to altitude sickness, which was stressful for Josh.

Today we got to Everest Base Camp. Initially, at the entrance I was shocked we made it to this place. [Josh's former company's] camp is near the entrance, where ours was toward the back. The walk from the entrance to the back was pretty miserable. I thought it would be pretty, but to me it seems rocky, dirty and wet. Camp is impressive, but I want to go home. I miss Ellie and Mushu and Thailand. I don't like being in a place where Josh almost died. It feels very unsettling to me.

When we arrived, it was so cold, and it was snowing. I'm pretty sure being unbelievably cold adds to my misery. I miss being hot.

The night we spent in Gorak Shep was very uncomfortable. The village and tea house themselves were very old, and for being the last village before the top of the world, it had limited supplies. I had gotten used to sweating most of the day, showering every few days and rotating the changing of my limited sports bras, pairs of underwear and socks every other day. I had not seen myself in a mirror the entire trip and having a permanent level of grime on me was my new reality. However, Gorak Shep was *dirty*.

Josh panicked about the cleanliness of our teahouse and we all tried not to touch anything, using our sleeves or napkins. That night he and I somehow shared a twin bed together, laying one sleeping bag down to create a barrier layer in between the mattress and the sleeping bag we slept in. We laid in bed that night listening to an episode of one of my favorite podcasts, *Armchair Expert with Dax Shepard*. It was an episode that made both of us laugh hysterically. Despite being in a very remote and desolate place trying to keep quiet because the walls were literally just boards, has become a fond memory for us.

The next morning was stressful as Josh had to coordinate a rescue for the sick client. Again, no one can predict the body's response to altitude, and it can come on incredibly quickly. Leaving a once in a lifetime opportunity is a difficult choice, and Josh advocated for the client to have proper medical treatment. We found out later this person made it back to Kathmandu by helicopter and was admitted to surgery where doctors found other contributing factors. He would have been dead within hours. Josh saved his life.

That morning, we as a group left without Josh so he could deal with the medical situation. I did not like trekking without him. I thought to myself, what if we got to Base Camp and he still was dealing with this situation? I could not imagine finally getting to our destination after all we had been through, without having him there. Fortunately, later he caught up to us and my worries were forgotten.

On our last leg to Everest Base Camp we navigated rocky, sandy and uneven terrain. We started to round corners and see in the distance hundreds of small yellow tents. Eleven days of trekking, 8,500 feet of elevation gain and forty miles. We had made it.

The threshold of Everest Base Camp was noted by painted rocks, decorated with prayer flags and a line of people with various levels of ecstasy waiting to take photograph proof of this moment. We stood in line as well, me in equal disbelief. Everyone around me was so incredibly joyous and I did not feel that. I felt as if I was a ghost of myself, watching my body from afar, going through the motions and smiling for the photos.

The Sherpa guides greeted us with hot Tang and gingersnap cookies. It was a welcome surprise. As the snow started to fall, we started making our way to camp, passing other companies' campsites and Everest ER. Ours was on the far end, overlooking the Khumbu icefall. To most people's surprise you are not able actually see the summit of Mt. Everest from Base Camp, other parts of the mountain block it, making the climb to the top even more mysterious.

Our camp itself was incredibly luxurious. We had a basic tent, complete with two brand new twin mattresses for each of us, never slept on. Some clients had paid extra for executive suites, complete tents with the ability to stand, heaters, and a working station. However, our little tent was just right for us. The dining tents were huge, six feet long tables inside, tablecloths, fake flowers on the table and the fancy little olives that Josh and I only would ever have at Thanksgiving. Those little thoughtful touches made me happy, but I still felt a sense of disquiet.

April 15, 2019

We woke up at Everest Base Camp to a decent day. Not as cold, windy or snowy as our arrival was yesterday. It was a bit clearer and sunny. We hiked partway up the viewpoint above Everest Base Camp. We couldn't see much, but it was fun to be above EBC and see the expanse. We stopped by [Josh's former company] *and* [the expedition leader] *was there. I ended up calling him a pompous asshole.*

We also met the Sherpa who organized the group to rescue Josh. Immediately I started crying again, and all the way back to our camp. I don't really like being here… I want to be anywhere else. I can appreciate the majesty of the mountains, but it isn't my thing.

Tomorrow we start the forty-mile trek back out, our first destination Pheriche.

Since it was a nicer day, we woke up to the sound of helicopters utilizing their chances with the weather, transporting supplies and travelers. I was instantly transported to the memory of Josh running out of the house two years ago, trying to escape the torment of his own brain. It felt like yesterday, constantly replaying in my head. I could not stop thinking about everything that had brought us here, all the trials we had faced. I noticed how overwhelming this experience was. All I wanted to do was run, but I was frozen in my mind and in this place.

Josh distracted me by suggesting that he and I start to create another mockumentary video, "Excellent Expertise to Elevate Your Everest Experience." Again, it was fun being able to goof around together, not taking things so seriously. In one clip of the video Josh is deciding to take in the view. The camera pans from the upper mountain down to Josh who is featured drinking coffee in his boxer shorts.

Seeing the camp of Josh's former company and the expedition leader that nearly led him to his death was strange. He was pleasant, yet completely unaware of the damage he had created. The lack of accountability he displayed was sickening to me. I still cannot understand the simplicity of not valuing a human life. So, I called him a pompous asshole. I have absolutely no remorse about it.

And it felt great.

Meeting the Sherpa Sirdar that organized the crew of people that saved Josh's life was unreal, but in a much different way. It was also much different than meeting the person who was in Pheriche a few days before. It was not the same upheaval that I had experienced, but I still was emotional. In the few days that we had travelled

I had grown, learning more about the journey as a whole and what brought us to this place. Despite my growing homesickness, I knew that this is where we were supposed to be. This was an odyssey, and it required effort.

The hike above Base Camp lent perspective to me. I was able to put one foot in front of another. Focusing again on every step as my new high point. We descended just into the Khumbu Icefall. I am not sure why, but I had not thought about how icy it would be. Every step was carefully placed, and we were trepidatious of hidden soft spots. Our viewpoint had become huge seracs, large stalagmite type ice towers surrounding us. Like walking under the stalactite like icicles on Mt. Rainier, I thought it was pretty neat.

Our Base Camp accommodations only grew in the few days that we were there. The kitchen was industrial sized, with huge pots and pans, complete with an espresso machine. The greatest shower I have ever taken was at 17,500 feet. It was a proper shower, with smooth stones "tiling" the ground, absorbing the water. It was unexpectedly hot water, the first hot shower I had the entire trek. There was a proper standing area to change clothes and I finally remembered what it felt like to be clean. I remember changing and switching my long johns that morning and when I took them off in our tent a cloud of my dead skin enveloped our entire tent. I told Josh it was dust from my boots. This shower was needed.

In the days after we left, the "big house" was assembled. It was 33 x 20 feet high tent, luxurious with carpeted floors, cozy chairs and the fancy espresso machine. The group of clients and guides heading to the summit used this as a group living room of sorts, lounging, hosting yoga sessions and dance parties. Following their accounts having fun after we started the trek to leave, and then back at home made me smile.

April 16, 2019

We walked out of Base Camp today. The day started out beautiful and was crystal clear. We walked down to Pheriche, back to our favorite tea house. When we got there, Josh told the team about his near-death experience. It's the third time I have heard it on our trip. It's strange to have left Base Camp. As much as it was an emotional experience, it is odd to be 3,500 feet lower in altitude.

Physically, I feel amazing. It is the first time in a long time I have felt as if Josh and I will be alright. As miserable as I have been at times, I am glad to experience this with my dear.

Last night we had our last full team dinner. Everyone went around and said a memorable moment. I, of course, started crying. Thinking of everything.

Someone mentioned that not everyone goes into the mountains, it takes a special type of person to do... which is true.

Somewhere at Everest Base Camp I had lost my wedding ring. Nothing major, both Josh and I wear silicone bands most of the time, and definitely while traveling. However, I don't like to wear jewelry when I sleep. I would always stuff my wedding ring in one of my zipped coat pockets, and my gloves on the other side. It would make it easy every morning when I would wake up to put on my ring and gloves while I was still in my sleeping bag. When we got to Base Camp however, it was snowy and colder. And I switched to wearing my heavier down jacket and one of the pockets did not zip properly, so I stuffed my ring and gloves in the same pocket. I assume that one morning when I pulled out my gloves, my ring flew out as well, lost on Mt. Everest.

On the morning that we left there was anxious energy surrounding us. Our team of trekkers would be leaving, separating from the climbers on our team, as well as the big group as a whole. We would be leaving our new friends, seemingly forever. There was no guarantee that we would see them again, as our daily lives did not intersect. The truth also being the mountain might hold them captive forever.

The feelings set in that along with some of the clients, I might not see the kind and wonderful Sherpa guides that travelled with us, along with the other mountain guides ever again. Many of these people had become our friends and became part of my story. We walked alongside each other becoming a part of each other's stories. We bonded over what it takes to complete the journey. The journey itself is admirable, friends and family proud of our accomplishment, but it's the little things that get you there and who you get there with.

Most notably was the dirt, lack of bathrooms, toilet paper and showers that we all experienced together. One stop we were directed to the "bathroom." It was an outhouse of sorts, a wooden wall dividing the view, a hole dug in the ground and a yak guarding it. This experience was shared between some of us and it is only from being a part of it that the ridiculousness of the situation can truly be understood. Josh never warned me about what the bathrooms would be like and how gross they would be. Boys have the privilege to pee outside, and it never occurred to him that I might have wanted to mentally prepare myself for that part of the trip.

Our team bonded with one of the Sherpa that adapted to our slow and steady pace. We, as a team learned that our favorite tea was lemon ginger, made with real lemons and real ginger. On the days that we trekked and got to a new location we would celebrate with an afternoon snack of shared tea, French fries and popcorn. We celebrated birthdays, new high points and life anniversaries together. I realized how lucky I was to experience this with my partner. Far from home, away from our friends and family, Josh and I made it to Everest Base Camp together, with a group of strangers accomplishing a once in a lifetime opportunity.

Some steps I struggled, wishing I was anywhere but there.

Some steps I leaned on Josh, thankful to have the support of my dear.

Some steps I stood in awe of my surroundings and the beauty of the world before me.

Step by step, I had made it.

And now, we were leaving. As unsettled as I had felt being in actual Base Camp, I recognized that I was living through one of the defining moments of my life. I was looking forward to leaving, happy to have made it.

Anxious to start the next leg of the journey. And glum knowing that this moment was almost over. I was sad after I lost my wedding ring, but it is nice to know that a little piece of me will always remain there.

Later that day I saw a porter Sherpa heading to Base Camp carrying a full size, four-burner kitchen stove on his back. I cannot imagine the literal strength that it takes to be able to do that. I also started to notice different things that I had not seen on the journey up. For instance, many buildings had been reconstructed after the 2015 earthquake hit Nepal. I noticed the newer, lighter and cleaner cobblestones on structures designating the literal shift that had occurred during the rebuilding process.

As we were coming down one of the hills, we started to see Pheriche in the distance. It's an interesting phenomenon living at a higher altitude and then quickly descending 3,500 feet within a few hours. I felt great. I felt lighter than air and ran a good chunk of the distance. Each step that I ran I felt suspended, my lungs filling up, grateful for the absorption of the extra oxygen.

*A*pril 18, 2019

Yesterday we hiked from Pheriche back to Namche. It hailed, snowed, rained for about three hours. Definitely not one of the most fun days... We somehow had to go to a different tea house than what was scheduled last night. We had to walk through a construction zone. Both Josh and I were in terrible moods.

However, later we ended up finding this pretty cool, natural bar that was all cobblestone and dirt. The owner talked to us for a while about the history of Namche, being the only village that can be seen by walking directly to it. Historically, the Nepalese viewed it as God's hidden jewel. He also automatically knew I was from India, and which part of the country.

Today we hiked from Namche to Lukla. It was very rainy and hailing, but not like yesterday.

I still can't believe that I did it. Everest Base Camp!

Josh said that in the past three days we have walked for a total of about 55 hours and 40 miles.

Going from Pheriche back down to Namche Bazaar was a slog. It was so unbelievably wet. On many parts of the trail there was so much rain you had to find the smaller pools of water to step in. Since we were descending in elevation, many parts we were walking in a river of water, gushing down the path. Since there had been so much rain, the water itself could not absorb into the ground quickly enough. Some sections we waded through got our boots, pants and lower legs soaking wet.

It got to the point where I could feel the pools of water at the bottom of my boots, my socks squeaking with friction as I took each step. I stopped using my umbrella because all the liquid was not just falling from the sky, it was falling sideways, zig-zagging its way down our backs, and up our sleeves. The wind forced the rain everywhere engulfing us as its own. I tried really hard, but I just could not imagine Michelle Obama in this type of situation.

Overall, our team tended to have a slower pace, meandering, enjoying the views and taking in the scenery. That day however, we marched along mostly in silence as quickly as possible, just wanting to get to our dry destination. We were wet with sweat, rain and a few tears from some. When we got to Namche, the excitement we had of finally being in the highest and most populated elevated city evaporated.

The tea house we were supposed to be staying at either misplaced or lost our reservation. Here we were a group eight people in peak Everest Base Camp trekking season needing a place to stay. We were drenched, frustrated and in disbelief that after such a long and arduous day we had nowhere to stay. Somehow, I held it together enough not to cry, knowing that if I did, I probably would just become one with the water, dissolving in my own pool of tears.

The Sherpa guides that were travelling with us were resourceful and networked. They identified a different tea house across Namche that we could stay at. At this point more rain and an additional half hour of walking was tolerable, we just wanted to get there. What we did not anticipate was the challenge of getting to our new location.

Instead of walking down, around and back up on the cobblestone pathways through Namche, our guides decided to cut across the village. Again, Namche is built on the slope of the arc of the mountain. Going down and around would have been much easier, but longer. Instead, we were in the still, pouring down rain and uneven ground trying to continue to balance a heavy pack.

We traversed Namche, travelling across the slope of the city. We went under what was an unmarked construction zone. Since we were not on the man-made cobblestone path, the trail was recently dug up dirt, crumbly and not packed down. It was unsteady to walk on. At one point still carrying our packs, we had to jump the distance across broken wooden planks. Parts of the earth dug up, large holes to avoid falling into, trapping yourself in a mud pit for all eternity.

We finally made it to our stop frustrated, but all in one piece. Our tea house was full of heirlooms and climbing relics from past expeditions, sharing history with its travelers. It distracted us from our thoughts of misery and the harrowing day we just experienced.

Later, Josh and I needed some time away from the big group, just he and I. He had never been to that part of Namche before and we decided to explore. We found this bar that had a very Portland-esque vibe, but in Nepal. The building itself was newer and more modern, appealing to Western taste. There were no floors, but just the earth beneath the tables and bar stools. Josh and I sat at the bar, had some beers and chatted with our bartender, the owner. It felt unusually similar to our daily life at home, something we had not done in over a month.

In this seemingly "real life" moment, I realized that somewhere along the way I had leaned in. Not showering every day, and walking to any sort of destination, carrying all the things I might need in a day on my back, no cars, technology, mirrors or makeup had become my normal. I had leaned into the adventure. Everything that I had worried about, stressed about and pressured myself with had evaporated.

I don't know where and when this had happened, all I knew is that it had.

That thought stuck with me for the rest of the trip. It continued to teach me about myself. I realized my ability to adapt. I realized my strength to make it through hard things. I realized sometimes I need to stop listening to the voices in my head and just keep putting one foot in front of the other, surprising myself with each step that is indeed sound.

*A*pril 20, 2019

Yesterday was such a long day. We had to be up at 5am and at the airport across the trail from our tea house. We flew for about 10 minutes and then a five-and-a-half-hour bus ride back to Kathmandu. It was crazy being so forced to reintegrate back into society. The day before all the buildings, streets, walkways were handmade, people's hard work literally carved into stone. Now we see proper buildings with concrete, neon signs and sooo many cars and motorbikes.

It occurred to me Himalayan time is only measured by the days or minutes it takes to walk. "Nepali time" is different from the average person walking since Sherpa are so much more adept.

Walking is the only way to get from village to village, to mountain, or peak.

Last night we arrived in Kathmandu and I cried when I saw a Western toilet. We as a team went to dinner at Fire and Ice, a pizza place to celebrate. It occurred to me that, surprisingly, I will miss everyone I've met. Never in a million years would I seek out friends here, but we've all experienced this crazy adventure together. Explaining what it means to people who haven't seen it is very confusing. I myself can barely wrap my head around it.

The day before, we left Namche and we walked back down to Lukla. We were back to hiking along the Dudh Kosi River, surrounded by trees and greenery. On those first few days of trekking, it reminded me of home. Now it reminded me how far I had come. It was nice to hear the water trickle in the background, and birds chirping in the forest. Our views were not vast and expansive anymore, but rather, of the charming Nepali countryside.

In three days, we had descended roughly 8,500 vertical feet in elevation. In what took us fourteen days to ascend forty miles, took us three to descend. It was as if the first two weeks of our journey had happened in slow motion and then all of a sudden someone had pressed the rewind button and within three seconds we were back to the beginning.

When we arrived at Lukla we felt the whirlwind of the journey hit. Did we really just trek to Everest Base Camp? Did it really happen? Was it a dream? It felt surreal to me. I could not believe that just three days ago I had been hanging out at 17,500 feet. It started to set in that I had accomplished my goal.

Together, Josh and I made it there and back again.

The tea house we were staying at had high ceilings and was very open. It was unlike most of the others we stayed at that felt as if its tables, chairs and people were bursting at the seams. There were groups of people who like us had just checked off this accomplishment, as well as other groups who were just about to start their own journey.

Our team was elated due to each of our individual achievements. We were high on our newfound oxygen, silly with disbelief and happiness. That night the whole tea house erupted in a dance party, music was playing, and drinks were poured. It was our last night in the Khumbu Valley, the magic of the Himalaya dissipating, our selves slowly dematerializing before the mountain.

In a moment of complete joy, one of our team members turned to me wearing old gray sweatpants with me in my dirt stained yoga pants and asked me if I liked her outfit. We were celebrating in the cleanest items we owned. It was hilarious to us and we both burst out laughing. I realized the rawness of that specific moment translated into the rawness of our entire trip. There were no masks, no makeup, no fancy clothes and nothing to stand behind. It did not matter that I lacked everyday things in common with our group, we had just done this amazing thing together. We laughed, cried, peed behind rocks together, supported each other and offered encouragement in tough moments. All we had to offer was what we carried inside our hearts, exposing our true humanity.

The next day we left Lukla and flew to Ramechhap. I was not as nervous for the plane ride as I was when we landed, which was good. However, there had been a deadly accident two days prior on the runway. A plane had trouble with its landing gear and was unable to stop. It circled and crashed into a helicopter on the landing pad, killing the pilots of both, and crew on the ground. The accident site had not been roped off or moved, but rather a too small tarp was placed over it. That was our viewpoint as we flew down the 1,000-foot runway.

The bus ride from Ramechhap to Kathmandu was nauseating. I do not like roller coasters, I often get car sick on long windy roads and this was no exception. In comparison, travelling on the prop plane felt like the safest place in the world. Being vaulted back into the society of cars, even on rural sandy hills was a shock. We saw many abandoned vehicles tossed along the side of the hills, marking their crash site.

Again, in Nepal there are no speed limits, no stop lights, no barriers and no lanes. Our bus did not have seat belts or air conditioning and we were crammed in there like a clown car. Multiple times both Josh and I glanced at each other reading each other's minds thinking that we were going to crash. Our bus rounded corners as fast as possible only to move over at the last second as another car was doing the same on the opposite side.

Thankfully, we arrived back in Kathmandu at the Yak and Yeti safe and sound. It was disconcerting being back here at this fancy hotel. It was as if no time had passed and yet, in the same moment, all the time in the world had passed. After our long ride, I desperately had to use the bathroom. I remember walking into the lobby facilities, and started to tear up seeing proper doors, the ability to flush, real toilet paper, soap and a sink. My pockets were filled with stolen napkins from tea houses rationed out to use, and here was a real and whole toilet paper roll.

We all got keys to our rooms with beds, comforters, fresh sheets, clean bathrooms and showers. Suddenly, everyday luxuries were thrust upon us. I peeled off the clothes I had been wearing for days, discovering the layers of dirt and sweat that had caked itself upon me. I reintroduced myself to me in the mirror, putting a face back to my own name. I showered in a tiled bathroom with soap and a real drain and walked around barefoot in our hotel room. It was bizarre.

We went to dinner that night, clean and in real street clothes. I remembered what it was like to brush my hair and put on lip gloss. We had been eating as a group for every meal every single day for days. This was different. This was decadent. Parts of our masks edging their way back to us, society offering its own form of makeup.

I wondered if I looked different. I felt different. Could a stranger on the street tell what I had just gone through? We were celebrating as a team in Kathmandu, the Nepalese automatically deducing we had just been to Everest Base Camp and back. Thousands of people complete the trek each year, we were not in the minority. Tourism escalates in huge numbers during Everest season, many Sherpa and Nepalese families earn their yearly income only in those few months each Spring.

Despite what I looked like and my new reimagined mask, I was changed forever.

AFTER

part I

April 21, 2019

Last night we went to our last team dinner at the Rum Doodle Restaurant. Famously, it has boards filled with signatures of all Mt. Everest summiteers and Josh finally signed his part.

We as a team decorated a paper Yeti foot to hang from the rafters representing our team to hang with hundreds of others.

Earlier in the day we walked around Tahmel, looking for souvenirs and just relaxing. It was so very strange to not have a plan for the day, let alone having to walk miles upon miles, or deal with the cold and altitude. Adjusting to "real life" again is a mind bend.

Today we flew from Kathmandu to Pokhara, Nepal. It's a little lakeside town that reminds me of what Old TonSai would be mixed with Costa Rica. It's much cleaner than KTM, prettier with the lake and lots of trees/foliage and much more relaxed. Ideally, you can see the Annapurna range when it is clear out. As much as I did not want to fly or move, I really do like it here. I missed being close to water.

Phewa Lake is in the middle of town. We paddled out to an island in the middle of the lake that has a temple called Tal Barahi, of the goddess Durga, protector of the gods. Many people were offering animal sacrifice which I had never seen before.

Josh had struggled in his attempts to sign the boards at the Rum Doodle Restaurant. In his previous travels to Nepal he had tried multiple different times. He was finally able to submit the correct materials to the restaurant in order to prove his accomplishment on this trip. At long last he was given the reward to sign his signature among legends. The boards date as far back to the early 1980s. Sir Edmund Hillary and Tenzing Norgay who were the first two people to ever reach the summit of Mt. Everest in 1953, signed their respective signatures on the first board created.

The boards themselves are massive, 4 x 4 feet planks of plywood hanging from the walls. Hanging from the rafters are paper Yeti feet of all sizes sharing names, stories, and drawings from Mt. Everest climbers and trekkers through time. There are dedications of the accomplishments of so many, as well as testaments to those who are never to return.

That night was our last night together as a group. Our team decorated our own Yeti foot, with the names of all the trekkers and climbers in our group. We had decided that our team name was "Team Sloth", as our motto had become, "We'll get there when we get there." We talked about the people from our group who were still up on the mountain, excitedly waiting for the opportunity to summit.

We all had gotten "White elephant gifts" that day to exchange with one another. I ended up with Himalayan doggy soap, and Josh ended up with a Christmas tree ornament in the shape of Boudhanath temple, which we hang on our tree every year near the top. It was strange to know that this would be our last gathering together. Mental barriers had already started to build, time distancing ourselves from the great expedition we all had just finished. Dinner was long. I am not sure anyone wanted it to end. We were on the precipice of assimilating back into our homes and routines. Knowing that the unspoken question we were all asking ourselves was how in the world do I go back to a normal life after just having experienced such a life altering event?

Since we had built in contingency days for the trip, our plane flights back to America were scheduled in five days. We had time to utilize. It was strange to think that he and I had just experienced this hugely emotional experience for both of us, yet we were surrounded by near strangers the entire time.

Josh had heard about Pokhara, a small lake town a short flight from Kathmandu. We decided to take a mini vacation there to rest and rejuvenate together. Pokhara was to Annapurna, as Kathmandu was to Mt. Everest. Even though it was an equivalent of a landing point for various trekkers and climbers, unlike Kathmandu, Pokhara was subdued and relaxed.

When we got to Pokhara we puttered around the little shops that surrounded us. We had coffee at a rooftop bar, and it felt strangely normal. There was one very long main street with little shops, hotels and restaurants lining the street. It had everything you might need, but never felt cramped, or too busy. One of the first things I wanted to do was find a pseudo wedding ring. It cost around six U.S. dollars, but I wanted something representative. Our hotel was about two blocks back from the main street, and our view overlooked the city and the water. Parallel to the main street was a dirt road that lined Phewa Lake. You could either walk the length of the central part of the city on the urban street, or along the water.

Pokhara felt like a city that just took a deep breath after a nice long stretch. The people and environment were calming and unhurried. Phewa Lake offered pretty views under an expansive sky with various green mountain peaks in the distance. On our first afternoon, we kayaked to Tal Barahi Temple in the middle of the lake and reflected on our adventure. Tal Barahi was simple, but very colorful in its decor. People prayed, offered sacrifice, and burned incense around us. The water was unlike Thailand, but beautifully different. It felt healing.

*A*pril 22, 2019

We went paragliding today – probably one of the scariest and coolest experiences of my life. Ever since I was a little kid all I can think of is wanting to fly. I think today was the closest experience I will ever get to flying. The wind currents weren't that big, but I was still nervous. All I can think of was the fated Summer that I was seventeen. I honestly wish that it was something I could have done when I was younger. It was scary and exhilarating, but also kind of peaceful.

It is such a different vantage point, viewing the world from above.

Directly after finishing college I started a job at a big company selling books to schools. Sales was never my interest, strength or my degree, but it was a job and I was happy about it. There were many parts about it that I loved, and some that were downright awful. I loved my coworkers and being surrounded by books and providing opportunities for kids to read was my main driving factor. I did not love corporate America. At the end of the day I did not care about the numbers or the sales. Any sales that helped get books in the hands of kids was a win for me, it did not matter to me the monetary worth of what the book cost.

Eventually, I knew that I was on the chopping block as the year came to a close. I had posted a photo I had torn from a magazine of a person paragliding in my cubicle. Many days after not hitting my numbers, being called into meetings about my performance I would look up at the torn magazine clipping. The idea that someday I would not be sitting in an awful, gray, windowless cubicle gave me hope. It gave me solace knowing that someday maybe I really would be able to do something so far out of my comfort zone, jump off the side of the world and just fly.

In actuality, I was apprehensive about paragliding. Being harnessed up with ropes to a parachute far behind you and then literally jumping off the edge of a cliff, waiting for the world to absorb you, or for the parachute to catch you is a little nerve wracking. The guide that I was attached to loved his job. I remember begging him to not make us go upside down, knowing that if that would happen, I was certain I would die. Or in a more possible scenario, all bodily fluids would land on him, which I was guessing he did not want.

On this particular day it was windy, and many paragliders were around us. Pokhara, as it turned out, is one of the best places in the world to paraglide and there was some sort of competition of gliders on the same day we decided to fly. Josh had jumped right after me and as we circled on our own wind currents, many times we would glide past one another. He enjoyed the adventure and unlike me, was not nervous. He flew much higher than me, exploring the wind patterns that were offered to us on that day. Seeing Pokhara from that level was amazing. The middle of the air is quite peaceful. You are moving quickly, but you almost feel suspended. I flew on lower wind currents over jungled parts of the city, flying near the trees, hearing the monkeys cackling, conversing with one another. We flew over Phewa Lake, everything below us so bright and blue.

Paragliding was a bit scary, but still incredible. The wind was not equal in movement, but jarring in nature; my guide continuously adjusting our balance in air, a perfect metaphor for survival.

April 24, 2019

Yesterday we left Pokhara to go back to Kathmandu. We stayed in a different hotel, Kathmandu Guest House, which was like a hidden garden in Tahmel. Our flight was delayed eight hours, so we only had about 18 hours in KTM. During that last leg back, I came to appreciate it all. The Nepalese culture are definitely survivors. So much poverty, hustling their way through life. It made me miss all the Sherpa and Sherpa culture who basically are like warriors. They literally have nothing and carry villages, tourists and climbers on their backs.

Today our flight was delayed an hour and we flew back to Bangkok. I don't hate it as much. But I also don't feel the draw I have toward TonSai, even though this is Thailand, too. A dinner of Thai food was good, but the Indian tikka masala we had last night was AMAZING. We at least have tomorrow to lay by the pool. The 85-degree heat, even now at 10pm makes me happy.

Leaving Pokhara was sad. Time suspended itself there. It gave us a chance to unwind and start to process everything we had just gone through. On our last night, the clouds parted, and we were able to see Annapurna from the city. It was quite brief, the mountain only unshrouding herself for a few moments, showing her beauty. Josh was excited, he had never climbed it.

We were able to have dinner with a former mountain guide and coworker of Josh's who lives in Oregon but was travelling the world trekking with his wife for a year. At home, we could drive about six hours and see him and his wife, but up till then, never have. We all were across the world, both on equally impressive adventures and randomly met up. It speaks to the versatility of mountain guides, the span their friendships hold across countries.

Going back to Kathmandu was strange. By that point all our team members had left to head home, or still remained on the mountain bidding time for their summit. We were the only ones from the big group who were in Kathmandu. I felt as if a part of me was missing. We stayed at the Kathmandu Guest House. I think it was good that we were staying in a different hotel than before. It felt unfamiliar but being back at the Yak and Yeti without everyone would have felt incomplete.

Our hotel was situated in the middle of busy and bustling Tahmel. It had huge pillars at the entrance and a walkway down to where the hotel actually was, away from the city. The walkaway opened into a huge outdoor garden area where there was an outdoor eating area, seating and lounging. All of a sudden, we were transported into greenery and flowers, the air smelled sweet and floral. We were in what felt like a secret garden in the middle of a city.

That night we had our last dinner in Nepal, the best we had the entire trip. Our bed was nearly the size of our room and we settled in. In need of a distraction, we turned on the television. In a paralleling moment reminiscent of me spending so many days unable to get off the couch, *Harry Potter* was playing. Again, the whole world had come full circle.

We strolled through Tahmel for the last time. I absorbed everything around me, memorizing the sights and smells, and how I felt. The transformers held millions of power lines and cords, balancing above us and I still pondered how they did not fall on our heads. I wandered into the bookstore that on every trip to Tahmel I would find myself in. I finally bought a book, unconcerned with the weight, or potential to not fit in my bag.

We flew back to Bangkok and stayed in a hotel for about twenty hours before our next flight. We got some sleep and I happily enjoyed some time laying by the pool. As much energy as I had spent missing Thailand, it was odd being back. No, it wasn't TonSai, but it was fine being back. Fine meaning, we were in a nice, clean hotel; it was warm outside, and everything was suitable.

Nothing was determinedly wrong, but I felt as if I did not fit in.

In TonSai I felt as if I had seen my soul reflected in the Andaman Sea, the jungle and the warm sun. I realized that on the trek to Everest Base Camp I learned other secrets about myself. The mountains call me just a little bit, too. I felt different being back in a country that felt so much like a home I had never felt. I had found a feeling of home but left it and returned. In leaving, I pursued and experienced something I never thought I would do. Upon returning, I was a different person from when I had started.

AFTER

part II

April 26, 2019 — WA time

We got home late last night. Josh estimated that we had been travelling for about 40 hours, which is insane. Getting back home the first thing I noticed was all the good and safe drivers on the roads and how well the roads are maintained. Just seeing Seattle on the way home from the airport makes me realize how excessive so many things are. The fact that we have working, nice cars, roads, sound and structured buildings and electricity and water without fail seems so ridiculous. I missed proper bathrooms very much, but I also see how much America is privileged.

All I can think of is the Sherpa who view travel in terms of days while walking. So far, the entire trip is like a dream. As if I was sucked into a time vortex, like in A Wrinkle in Time *and all the knowledge and experiences I encountered are not even comprehensible in this, my current world.*

Strangely, my constant reminder is the red string the monks tied around us at the blessing in Tengboche. It feels like the past 35 days are wrapped up inside of it. Funny, anytime Josh had previously trekked through the Khumbu I've been a little jealous of his red string. A reminder of what was when he wasn't home.

Today, I cherish mine and finally feel like I understand.

In what felt like a blink of an eye we were home. This journey that I had unknowingly started to prepare for the day Josh and I had met was over. Just under two days ago we were halfway across the world in a culture, poles apart from our average daily life. Now we were thrust back into our daily lives like no time had passed. As unnatural as it was, there was a familiarity of finally being in our home.

While we were gone, we had a arranged a house sitter, a coworker from the rock climbing gym that Josh knew. We did not want to displace our animals, taking them away from their home, on top of us leaving them for five weeks. Ellie and Mushu were overjoyed with us returning, and we were overjoyed to see them. Much of our time spent when we were gone was making up conversations between each other of what the animals might be saying or doing, much to the comedy of our trekking group.

That entire first jetlagged night I stayed up until two in the morning exhaustedly cleaning our house. In my worn-out state I was robotic, scrubbing and wiping down things to look and smell like new. It gave me an opportunity to reacquaint myself with our house, remembering our bathtub, kitchen counters and the inside of our microwave. When I finally laid down in our bed next to Josh, Mushu jumped on my head, and Ellie laid across both of us. In the safety and security of our bed, I felt at ease.

A couple days after coming home we bought a car. We still had never replaced mine after it was totaled. The experience was frustrating, and I lost my patience. Jumping through the hoops to buy a car, listening to a salesperson merely talk for the sake of talking was overwhelming. My endurance to care for meaningless things had ceased even more than it had prior to our trip. I had limited patience for anything that lacked heart or did not get right to the soul of the matter.

I returned to work and Josh returned to climbing Mt. Rainier and hit 100 summits that Summer. Waking up at home, having coffee in our bed, driving to get to destinations and showering whenever I wanted had become the norm again. I still felt as if in most conversations I was internally bursting at the seams. All I could think about was the wonder and enchantment of the Khumbu Valley.

I used the first three weeks as an opportunity to prepare for a half marathon, the same that I had run two years prior corresponding to the day Josh had almost died. I had not run in five weeks and going from zero to 13.1 miles in three weeks was a challenge. It was a challenge that my mind needed. I used my newfound running time to escape my own head, and get away from the small, menial day to day tasks that I was back to doing.

Later that Summer the company that Josh was now working for celebrated their 50-year anniversary of being in business. Jim and Lou Whittaker were in attendance, the former of which was the first American to ever summit Mt. Everest. Josh was nervous, not wanting to meet them, or bother them with a photograph. I, of course, asked them. Josh humbly never talks about climbing or summitting mountains unless someone directly asks him. I told the Whittaker's that Josh had summitted Mt. Everest twice. I am not sure if that really meant anything to either of them, but I was still very proud of Josh, nonetheless.

It seemed as if after Josh initially resigned, along with the others who had stopped guiding full time, that the brotherhood of guiding came to fruition. Now instead of spending time together at work on a mountain, time had to be dedicated. People grew up a bit, got married and started families with their fur babies and real babies. All of a sudden, I finally felt as if I had a little bit of a community with the other guide wives and partners. It was unexpected, especially after many had left the business, but I finally felt as if I had a support network if I needed it.

I learned that support does not just happen on a mountain top, but in everyday life as well. So much of Josh's guiding career I felt alone and isolated. Yet, almost anywhere that we have vacationed to we have spent time with or stayed with someone that Josh has known from his guiding career. I started to wonder if some of the isolation I had always felt was something I had created myself. Many people have stayed at our house, merely for a chance to have a hot shower and clean sheets. We have adopted guides into our family for Thanksgiving and Christmas as they pass through town. It is a very unique career and has brought the most unlikely of people into my life. With that said, having a group of people to rely on and who open their doors no matter what shows how deeply those relationships have been forged.

On a whim Josh decided to see if he could become a firefighter. Over 2,000 people applied and they were hiring sixteen. Josh was one of them. Early on in our relationship I had asked him what he was afraid of. We had just started getting to know each other, asking fun fact type questions about each other, slowly peeling away the layers. Josh responded that he was afraid of water, dying in the mountains, or a fire.

Awhile back I decided to partake in extensive training to become a volunteer for our local hospital Sexual Assault Response Team. Soon after, in a conversation with a friend she asked me my motivation in being a part of this. It's not fun; it's often very frustrating and sad, and generally there is not any closure. I honestly had not really thought about my motivation, it just felt right to me. So, in my response I answered very frankly and said, "To do something outside of my comfort zone." My friend burst out laughing.

She just looked at me and replied, "Most people do things like jump out of airplanes to get out of their comfort zones."

That thought struck me and I thought about it a lot. I am not sure why I chose to do something that can be considered so depressing. To me, I see it as hopeful. A testament to the human spirit. As humans we have the ability to go through a lot in seemingly wretched circumstances. Similarly, when I asked Josh his fears, I smiled. He was a collegiate swimmer, a mountain guide, and now a firefighter. All of the things that he is afraid of he has faced every day of his adult life.

Josh now has a career that is "distinguished." Over the course of our relationship, many people rudely ask when he would "grow up and get a real job." Yet, mountain guiding was the perfect preparation for firefighting. Josh put his life on the line every single day remotely in the mountains, faced death and the toll it took on his life. Fighting fires was a natural transition and seemed easy in comparison. To me, mountain guiding will always be braver and more noble.

In the entire process of Josh becoming a firefighter and thinking about him walking into burning buildings I never felt a sense of fear. Many people have asked me about it being a dangerous job, and if I was worried. I honestly never even thought about it until people started asking. Josh and I had experienced so much. Nothing could cause me more fear or worry than what we already had been through.

I spent countless hours thinking about Mt. Everest. I spent countless hours thinking about what Josh underwent in Nepal and what he went through when he returned home. I spent countless hours thinking about what I went through when he was gone and when he returned home.

None of these thoughts were positive or healthy. They manipulated my mind, playing their awful tricks with me. I could never win the game. I was stuck, frozen in thoughts and feelings of discontent. I was bitter and hostile to anything that even minimally had to do with Mt. Everest.

And then the world presented its opportunity. Leading up to it, there were many moments that I thought that it was just another cruel ploy. Was going to this place, returning with Josh a good idea? I could not even utter the words of Mt. Everest without feeling a hollowness in the pit of my stomach, my tongue poisoned with the words, flashes of death and suffering crossing through my mind.

Undeterred, we went to Mt. Everest together, hand in hand. I realized that everything that had led to this point was not just something that Josh and I suffered, but something that we had endured. We survived. Against all odds he was alive. We made it through.

Still, I continue to spend countless hours thinking about Nepal and Mt. Everest. Now, I think about it for much different reasons. I remember the beautifully astounding mountains and the gentle countryside, reminding us of our true wildness. The Khumbu Valley was filled with magic and awe, healing us.

I remember the unbelievably kind and hardworking Sherpa people who are the backbone of most people's dreams. Their true strength shown by their humble nature. The world is a softer place because of them.

I remember the warm heartedness of all the other mountain guides on our trip. Their decency was unparalleled, and their goodwill was evident. They more than anyone else understood the road that had led us to Nepal.

I remember the clients who I originally felt so far removed from. We all had come on our own separate journey's, but we all trekked the same trail. We experienced high highs and low lows on a level that is incomparable to ordinary daily life. I am grateful for walking side by side with them.

I remember in the moments of fearing my own inabilities to emotionally continue forward, Josh was there to hold my hand and offered encouraging words.

I could not have had any idea of what my future held when I met Josh. I just knew I wanted to be with him. On the surface relationships and marriages are fairly straightforward. There is the natural pathway to follow and check boxes to mark. Nowhere in the instructional manual of life is there a "What to do if your husband almost dies" section. Again, death has many different meanings. I realized that we both had become reborn, rising from our own ashes. Our souls were and are truly entwined together, symbiotically saving each other.

Every day I learn something new.

Some days are a challenge.

Some days we are holding hands and literally so close to being on the top of the world together.

Every day is an adventure.

EPILOGUE

As far back as I can remember I have been afraid of things. My mom would watch crime shows when I was a kid and would let me watch them with her. It took me years of my daily chore of walking across the street to get the mail to realize that I probably was not going to get kidnapped.

Taking chances, or risks was something that I still sometimes must encourage myself to do. To combat that, I surrounded myself with people in my life who were seemingly unafraid. Or rather, less afraid than me. My best friend growing up would always convince me to "do the thing" and her excitement would somehow squash down my fear making me feel brave. That bravery was a contradiction to my daily self-talk that I would tell myself. It takes constant effort to think about the good possibilities that might happen if I in fact, do the thing.

Yet, *doing the thing* never truly caused any great harm. Sometimes things would not go to plan, or we would get in trouble, and of course there were some close calls, but the actual act of doing the thing and sharing it with someone made it all worth it. Looking back, as much as I've preemptively stressed out about doing something, I never actually end up regretting doing it. I have shied away from chances to take part in once in a lifetime opportunities because I am scared or nervous. As I have gotten older, I began to surround myself around people who are quite the opposite of me. It is a constant reminder to myself that taking chances isn't always a bad thing, a contradiction to the little voice in my head.

As an adult I learned that I did not want fear to dictate my decisions. In retrospect, much of my life is an inner monologue filled with questions and anxiety, but I learned that I did not have to let it rule my future experiences. I began to make decisions based on other factors, despite what I might be feeling internally. Most people do not realize what I am feeling inside, as it does not necessarily match what I choose to show the world.

I learned that fear does not have to paralyze me, but it can motivate me.

The Summer I was seventeen was the best "real" Summer that I have ever had. Looking back, it was carefree and innocent. The responsibilities of adulthood blooming, but not yet fully flourished. It was filled with friendship, exploration and love. The experiences and conversations I had during that season set the stage for how I wanted to live the rest of my life and the values I wanted to cherish. Fear had enveloped so much of my life, inhibiting my choices and binding me. That sweet and idyllic Summer made me aspire to the person I am today.

One of the most meaningful conversations of my life happened then. As far back as I can remember, I have always wanted to fly. Not for observation purposes or to eavesdrop on people, but to have the feeling of pure balance on the wind, just floating without a care in the world. Granted, the experience of paragliding was a bit different. Being strapped into safety harnesses felt nerve wracking and unbalanced. I imagine if I had the wings of a bird, instead of being human I would have glided with ease and bliss.

Late one night, in a conversation with one of my best friend's, we started talking about wishes. I had never before said this aloud; it had seemed silly that my wish was to learn to fly, let alone impossible. The response I was given I have held in my heart ever since. It calms me in moments of anxiety, restlessness and fear. I am reminded of who I am, who I aspire to be, and what I am capable of. It gives me hope that those disquieting feelings do not define me and someday I really might just be free.

The irony that I married someone so incredibly different is not lost on me. Josh is extroverted, thrives in social situations, and continues to periodically climb mountains all over the world. He did all those things with apparent ease. Now he literally walks into the fire. Doing the thing does not scare Josh. Unlike me, he is organized and meticulous to a fault, exceptionally tidy and respects the order of things. I am introverted by nature and only really enjoy the company of a few, cherished people. As a social worker I elevate the success of other people, minimizing myself as if I am the crew dressed in black helping set the stage, versus being the star of the show.

I would not describe myself as a person who is adventurous, fearless, or even able-bodied. I have probably run the course of thousands of miles over my lifetime and I still would not consider myself to be an athletic runner. I have summitted Mt. Rainier three times, trekked to Everest Base Camp, hiked trails all over the Pacific Northwest and would not consider myself adventurous. I have written all these words somehow, coming out of my brain, down my body, through my fingers onto the page and yet, I still would hesitate to call myself a writer.

Despite all of my contradictions of my innermost thoughts and feelings to real and true fact, I still cannot deny all of the above things. I have lived through my husband almost dying physically and soulfully, somehow making it through and surviving. I went back to the place that had taken so much away from both of us, only to realize it also had been bountiful.

At some point I realized – I did the thing.

I was undeterred in the humble act of living in the face of my fears.

I finally had learned to fly.

Come to the edge, I said
No, we're afraid
Come to the edge
No, we're afraid we'll fall.
Come to the edge I said again
And they came
And I pushed them
And they flew

ACKNOWLEDGEMENTS

To my mom. For always being there, loving me every morning and night.

To the fur babies. Even though you cannot read or talk, your snuggles and comfort make every day better.

To Dallas. Without you the course of our lives would be drastically tragic. Thank you is not enough. I am forever in your debt.

To Luke. For staying true to your promises.

To Mike and Caroline. You believed in us and gave us the opportunity to heal. Thank you for our happily ever after.

To my Wild Women. Thank you for encouraging me to howl.

To Ben. For believing in the impossible.

To Josh. For always coming home.

TIGER OF THE SNOWS FUND

MISSION STATEMENT

Tiger of the Snows Fund aims to facilitate education for workers involved in outdoor tourism and their families in under-served communities. We believe that access to education should be a fundamental right and that education is the best way to address issues of development, access to opportunity, and social issues. Our goal is also to promote awareness of education issues and the needs of local communities affected by the outdoor tourism industry.

FOR MORE INFORMATION:

www.tigerofthesnows.com
info@tigerofthesnows.com

Tiger of the Snows Fund is a registered 501(c)(3) non-profit organization.

Reprinted with permission from Founder, Mike Hamill

I AM:

THE RED LETTER PSALMS

SHAYNE MASON VINCENT

ACKNOWLEDGMENTS

God: You brought me from the depths and set me among princes. You truly are my Father. These have been incredible decades walking together. The places you have brought me, the valleys of shadow, the glorious mountain tops, all the credit is Yours. For all of my ups and downs, Your Cross has the final word.

Family: You have filled my life with grace, adventure, and meaning. *Gabriela Anca Vincent, Susan V. Vincent, the Heikkila's, the Wenstrom's, the Baciu's, the Beckman's, the Vincent's, & my Pups.* I love you, guys. I miss you. Especially those of you who are now gone. I will always remember the Norman Rockwell moments, and your love and tolerance, as I learned the pathway of the true human being. Thank you, mom, "all things work together for good". And, most of all, to my beloved wife, Gabriela-Anca, for all these years of passion and adventure.

Friends: You have kept me authentic, laughing and seeking truth. *Kyle Gimlin, Steve Lambert, The Watson's, Cali, SoFlo, Cedar-Valley, Floodwood, Hibbing, Duluth, St.Paul, Upper-Lake, Wyoming, Michigan, and my many-many close friends in faith.* Were it not for you, I would not be me. It was journeying together that taught me how to survive, how to thrive, how to make sense out of living. I owe you my humor, my apologies, my chosen paths, my being, and those golden nostalgic memories.

Mentors: You have made me powerful, mended, and a healer. *Michael Tscheu, Drs. David & Beverly Sedlacek, David Watson, Pastor Dan Holmes, and my Churches.* What can I say, but that my views are actually yours. I would not have known what to know were it not for you pouring yourself into my heart and mind. I just put the lego blocks together. I owe you my wisdom. It's my hope that my insights honor you.

CONTENTS

INTRODUCTION

At the age of five, I would go with my grandmother, Ina, to an old country church, hidden away in a sleepy hollow called, Cedar Valley. On cold winter days, while Jack Frost was doing his Michelangelo's, I would sit in the back with the old timers, my numb toes burning under the whoosh of the wood stove. Those jolly old men made church just as warm as that stove. Inevitably, my attention would drift and my gaze would fall on this immense painting of the ascension of Christ keeping sentinel above the pulpit. Whenever my gaze fell upon it, it was like I could sense the Spirit in my bones. I can still smell the musty wood and brewing coffee of that happy memory.

Throughout the years, God continued speaking to my heart. In my early twenties, I was a very disillusioned young man. A high school drop out, homeless, fatherless, drug addicted. A broken soul. And right there is where God came looking for me; I wasn't even looking for Him, yet, He came and *"lifted me up from the dunghill and set me among princes"*, Psalm 113:7-8 *NKJV*.

The dunghill and the prince is actually quite a literal experience. I was living in a city park when God came and found me. Through individuals of various faiths, God cleaned me up, gave me a family, and an education. But, what truly blew me away, is when my brother-in-law, a composer and conductor, invited my wife and I to a VIP event, where we were seated with a prince and princess of Romania. While *Psalm 113:7-8* was a life verse for me, I never expected God to fulfill the text to the very letter! Indeed, as David said, *"O' Lord, our Lord, how magnificent is your reputation throughout the earth!" Psalm 8:9 NET*.

God stepped in as a surrogate father for me, as it says in *Psalm 27:10 "Though your father and mother may abandon you, I, the Lord, will take care of you."* And that is exactly what He did. Through all my adventures over the years, God has taken care of me, and taught me His wisdom. I am telling you this, because, in reinterpreting the Psalms, I want you to know that I am deeply invested in representing my Father in Heaven accurately. I am also keenly aware that there are many billions on this planet who equally love Him, or, at the very least, respect the Bible as sacred. Therefore, I thought it expedient to include some insight into how I approached reorienting the Psalms.

While contemplating the Psalms, the idea came to me like a whisper in my ear, "Flip the Psalm". It was an intriguing concept, born, perhaps, of a longing to hear God's voice. So, I tried it: "The Lord is my Shepherd, I shall not want", became, "I, the Lord, am your Shepherd, you shall want for nothing". I was struck with the beauty of the shift in perspective. But, needing to leave for work, I promptly forgot about it altogether. Yet, as providence would have it, later that week, while attending worship, the speaker's topic was the Psalms. Again, the whisper came back to me, "Flip the Psalm". I tried it again, and, sure enough, it worked flawlessly.

And, so, began a five-year-long project of flipping the perspective of the entire book of Psalms. It became a devotional journey for me. The more I researched, the more it became obvious that the whisper I heard was indeed the Spirit. The reversed point of view worked for the entire 150 chapters without any real complexity. Certainly, there were a few sticky passages; David was, after all, a man of war as much as of poetry. But, what truly convinced me, was the beauty of God's love exploding from Psalm after Psalm, revealing just how intimately God cares for humanity. And so, here I sit, five-years later, writing the introduction, ready to send my editors the final draft.

Inevitably, there will be critics of my attempting to, "speak for God", as it were. But you can't accomplish anything new in this world without the arm-chair quarterback league opining. Whatever your opinion, just know, I did everything in my power to faithfully translate the original text, and to avoid paraphrasing and bias as much as possible. Moreover, I have prayerfully labored to translate in view of the larger theological framework of who God has revealed Himself to be, throughout the entirety of Scripture.

My source material for translating comprised: the original Hebrew, lexicons, Strongs, Bible Dictionaries, sixteen-English translations, and twelve-reference/commentaries, all for clarity of translation in passages. In addition, the reader must recognize that the term, "Psalm", means, "song". The Psalms are actually poetry, music, and art, not simply narrative; therefore, it requires some thought translation to bring the musicality and implied meanings of Hebrew language into another tongue. Hence, why it has taken me five-years of research to complete this book.

In varied passages, the reader will notice key, historical turns of phrase, were, at times, preserved, and, in others, altered. I recognize how delicate of a subject this can be. But, as this is likely the first time this form of reinterpretation has ever been attempted, it was essential that some scholarly liberty be applied. Translating

Hebrew is not a simple straight forward process. For example, the Literal-Translation method can come across as wooden, failing to convey the full intent of the Hebrew poetry. While going too far with Paraphrase methodology can unintentionally introduce bias. Therefore, my modality could be considered a mixture of Literal-Translation, Thought-Translation, and as little Paraphrase as is plausible for readability.

In regard to difficult passages, such as in imprecatory Psalms, I chose to translate in harmony with God's character in the larger view of Scripture, as opposed to corrupt human motives found in the Psalms (such as: lust, violence, anger, revenge, pettiness, hatred, etc). Take Psalm 137:9[NIV] for example "Happy is the one who seizes your infants and dashes them against the rocks". While those complex texts are a small minority compared with the breadth of the Psalms, they do exist, and I do not believe God behaves toward His enemies in the same manner as human beings. Therefore, there was a necessity of some paraphrasing when attempting to "speak for God" in first-person.

Let the reader be aware, there was only one area of translation I did, at times, intentionally, and with scholarly bias, paraphrase and alter the wording: that is in the case of cherished historical terms such as righteousness, which I changed to love and justice; and sin, which I changed to selfishness or corruption. I am aware of the risk of changing these revered wordings, especially when it comes to literalists. But I translated the terms with the intent of conveying the actual spiritual biblical meaning, rather than making an idol of the phrasing alone.

I am of the deep conviction that my chosen translation of these core-religious-teachings are supported by both the original Hebrew, and by the intent and redemption theology of the entire Bible. Why? Because it relates directly to the main theme of the entire Bible: the personality and character of a God who is love, and who is in conflict with Lucifer, the fallen-angel, who introduced the untenable lie that selfishness can make us happier than God's selfless love.

In addition, God has historically been given the reputation of being an arbitrary tyrant, who threatens humanity with torture and suffering, if they do not obey His will. This could not be farther from the truth, than night is from day, than east is from west. God is love, and He has done everything possible to show us that His teachings, and actions, are the pathway to sustainable joy.

- *Detailed theological methodology and apologetics can be found in the Exegetical Appendix.*

There is one last important insight I feel compelled to share. It was probably the primary revelation I discovered while translating the book. David was a brutally honest believer, and God actually loved that about him! Why? Because, while David may complain, or cry out in anxiety or depression, he always ended with, "Yet, I will trust You". Essentially, every single Psalm out of the original 150, except for just a handful, like Psalm 88, ends with faith.

David knew He could trust God. Because God never required blind faith. Rather, He always proved Himself worthy of David's trust, by following through on what He promised him. And trust is probably the hardest lesson for any of us to learn in this broken world. Especially when God's answers often come to us in disguise.

And, so, it is my sincerest hope, that in reading, "I AM: The Red Letter Psalms", you will find that God loves you, just as He loved David; and that you may also come to see that God is worthy of *your* trust. In reinterpreting the perspective of the Psalms, it is my sole intent that the beauty of God would become clearer to all peoples of faith, and perhaps even for the esoteric and secular reader, that we might all come to know, God is indeed, "Love".

Psalms 36:7 (NKJV Strong's) "How precious is Your lovingkindness, O, God! Therefore the children of men put their trust under the shadow of Your wings."

"I raise the poor from the dust; I lift the needy from the garbage heap; to make them sit among princes."

— PSALMS 113:7-8 (IAV)

BOOK 1

Chapters 1-41
Psalms of Praise

-GENESIS-

Davidic Grouping I

I AM: YOUR GUIDE

*B*lessed are those who reject the advice of the godless, who do not follow the example of sinners, nor join in with skeptics and mockers. ² Instead, their joy is in My teachings, they contemplate My laws day and night. ³ They will be like a tree planted by a riverbank, that grows fruit in and out of season, whose leaves never dry up; whatever they do will prosper.

⁴ Wicked people are not like this at all; they are like husks that the wind blows away. ⁵ They will not survive the time of judgement, for there will be no sin in the community of the righteous. ⁶ For I, the Lord, watch over the journey of the loving, but those who follow the path of selfishness will end in death.

I AM: BRINGING JUSTICE

*W*hy do the nations rebel, and their people make futile plans? ² Their leaders revolt, the rulers plot together against Me and against My Chosen One, saying, ³ "Let us break His chains and free ourselves from slavery to God". ⁴ From My throne in heaven I roll my eyes and scoff at them. ⁵ I rebuke them in My outrage, and frustrate their plans in My fury.

⁶ I will install My King in Zion, My holy mountain. ⁷ My Begotten Son will proclaim My decree, for I am His Father. ⁸ I will give Him all the nations for an inheritance; the whole earth will be His possession. ⁹ He will break the corrupt nations with an iron rod; He will shatter them in pieces like clay pots.

¹⁰ Now be wise, you leaders; be warned, you rulers of the earth. ¹¹ Serve Me with reverence and tremble. ¹² Submit to My Son, for if He rejects you, you will die in your ways when the Judgement comes. But I will bless all who take refuge in Him.

3

I AM: YOUR SAFETY

I, the Lord, see how your enemies have increased. So many have turned against you! ² There are many who say, "God will never rescue you." ³ But I am a shield around you, I am your glory, I am the One who holds your head up high. ⁴ You cried out to Me for help, and I heard you from My holy mountain.

⁵ When you lay down to sleep, you will wake up in safety, because I watch over you. ⁶ So don't be afraid, even if ten-thousand people surround you on every side. ⁷ For I will arise and will save you, for I am your God! I will slap your enemies in the face and will shatter the teeth of the wicked. ⁸ For salvation comes from Me, and My blessing is upon My people.

I AM: YOUR FRIEND

I hear you when you call, for I am a loving God. I will give you relief from your troubles. I will have mercy on you and will hear your prayer. [2] I will not allow these people to perpetually insult your honor. Their love of vanity and falsehood will come to an end.

[3] You can be sure of this, I, the Lord, have set apart My faithful ones as My own; I hear them when they call to Me. [4] So when you are angry, don't let it make you sin. Be calm and silent, and take time to think about it. [5] Offer the sacrifices of love instead, and put your trust in Me.

[6] For there are too many who pray: "Please bless me with prosperity God. Let the light of Your face shine on me." [7] But I will fill your heart with joy, more than success ever will. [8] So when you lie down to sleep, sleep in peace, because, I alone, will keep you safe.

I AM: YOUR SHIELD

I hear your words, I pay attention to your pain. ² I, your God and King, listen to your cries for help when you pray to Me. ³ I listen to your voice at sunrise, when you look up and lay your requests before Me.

⁴ I am not a God that takes pleasure in corruption; evil cannot even dwell in My presence. ⁵ Therefore the arrogant may not stand before Me, for I despise corruption. ⁶ Indeed, I will destroy all those who are liars. For I, the Lord, abhor murderers and deceivers.

⁷ But because of My unfailing love, you will enter My house in awe, and worship in My holy temple. ⁸ For I will lead you in My righteousness; I will make your path plain to follow and will protect you from your enemies.

⁹ Do not trust a single word from the enemy's mouth, for their heart is filled with malice. Their words may be flattering and smooth, but they are full of deadly lies. ¹⁰ They are guilty, and their plots will become their own downfall. For I will banish them because of the multitude of their sins, for they have rebelled against My love.

[11] But let all those who put their trust in Me rejoice; they can always shout for joy, because I defend them. Let those who love My name be joyful in Me. [12] For I, the Lord, bless the innocent; My love will surround them like a shield.

I AM: ANSWERING YOU

I, the Lord, will not be angry and rebuke you. I will not discipline you in wrath. ² I will have compassion on you, for I see you are weak. I will heal you. I can see you are completely exhausted. ³ I see your soul drowning in darkness, and I know you are wondering how long I will wait before I come to help you. ⁴ I will return and rescue you. In mercy, I will save you. ⁵ For in death you cannot remember Me, in the grave you cannot give Me thanks.

⁶ You are worn out with your sighing; every night you flood your bed with tears; your pillow is soaked with your weeping. ⁷ Your eyes waste away because of grief; they grow weak as you constantly watch for your enemies. ⁸ Keep away from My child you workers of evil! For I, the Lord, have heard the voice of their weeping. ⁹ I have heard their cry for help and will answer their prayers! ¹⁰ All your enemies will be disgraced and terrified; they will be turned back and put to shame.

I AM: YOUR DELIVERER

*T*ake refuge in Me, the Lord your God. For I will rescue you from those who persecute you. ² I will deliver you, before they tear you apart like a lion; I will never allow them to carry you off where no one can rescue you. ³ But if you have wronged anyone, if there is guilt on your hands, ⁴ if you have betrayed your friends, ⁵ or robbed your enemies, then they will capture you, they will trample you into the ground, and drag your honor in the dust.

⁶ Yet, I will arise in jealous anger. I will stand up against the fury of the enemy; I will rise up and bring justice. ⁷ For the nations will assemble before Me; I will sit enthroned over them upon high, ⁸ and will judge all the nations. Then I will vindicate you and declare you righteous because of your integrity. ⁹ For I will bring an end to the violence of those who are evil, and will protect those who are innocent. For I am a righteous God, who examines deep within the mind and heart. ¹⁰ I am a shield, saving all those whose hearts are right and true.

¹¹ I am an honest judge, and the endless wickedness angers Me. ¹² If they do not change their ways, I will sharpen My sword, I will draw My bow and make it ready; ¹³ I will prepare My deadly

weapons, and aim My flaming arrows. [14] For whoever is pregnant with evil conceives plots and gives birth to fraud. [15] They prepare a trap, digging a deep pit, but they will fall into the snare they made. [16] The trouble they make for others will backfire on them, and their violence will land on their own heads.

[17] So give praise, for I am just, and you will sing songs of thanksgiving to Me, the Lord Most High.

I AM: YOUR FATHER

I am the Eternal Lord, My name is known throughout all the earth. My glory reaches beyond the stars. [2] Yet the lips of children and nursing babes call forth My praise, silencing My adversaries. [3] As you ponder the heavens, the work of My hands, the moon and the stars, which I personally appointed, [4] you wonder why I am mindful of humanity? It is because I care about them.

[5] I made you almost like the angels, crowning you with glory and honor. [6] I gave you dominion over the work of My hands, putting all things under your feet: [7] sheep and cattle, and wild animals too, [8] even the birds and the fish that pass through the paths of the seas. [9] I, the Eternal God, did this, and My name is known throughout all the earth.

I AM: DEFENDING THE NEEDY

*G*ive thanks with all your heart; tell others of all the wonderful things I will do. ² Be glad and rejoice, honor Me with songs of praise. ³ When your enemies finally run away, they will stumble and perish in My presence. ⁴ For I will maintain the justice of your cause, I will sit upon My throne and judge what is right. ⁵ I will rebuke the nations and will destroy the wicked; I will blot out their names forever and ever. ⁶ The enemy will be finished, in everlasting ruin. I will uproot their cities, and even the memory of them will disappear.

⁷ But I, the Lord, will reign forever, executing judgement from My throne. ⁸ I will judge the world in righteousness and will administer the verdict for the nations with equity. ⁹ For I am a refuge for the oppressed, a place of safety in times of trouble. ¹⁰ Those who know Me put their trust in Me, for I do not abandon those who seek Me.

¹¹ So sing and celebrate, for I am the Lord who dwells in Zion; go and declare what I will do among the nations! ¹² For I remember the victims of violence and will avenge their blood; I do not forget the cry of the afflicted. ¹³ I will have mercy on you. I see how those that hate you torment you. But I will lift you up from the gates of

death, [14] that you may declare your joy in the gates of Zion, and rejoice in My salvation!

[15] The nations will sink down into the pit they have dug for others; their own feet will be caught in the net they have hidden. [16] For I am known for bringing justice, and the wicked are already condemned by the works of their own hands. [17] They will all go down into the grave. That is the fate of all the nations who chose to forget Me, their God. [18] But I will never forget the needy, the hopes of the poor will never perish. [19] For I will arise; mere mortals will not always defy Me, for all the nations will be judged in My presence. [20] Then they will rightly be afraid; at that time, the nations will know for themselves that they are only mortal beings.

I AM: YOUR PROTECTOR

J, the Lord, am not far off. I do not hide Myself in times of trouble. ² The corrupt, in their arrogance, oppress the poor; but they will be caught in the schemes they devise. ³ They boast of their crimes and bless the greedy while they revile Me, their God. ⁴ In their pride, the wicked do not seek Me; there is no room for Me in any of their thoughts. ⁵ Because they are always succeeding, and My judgements are far above, out of their sight, they view all their rebukes with contempt. ⁶ They think in their heart, "I will never fail; I will never be in trouble." ⁷ So they fill their mouth full of cursing, manipulation, and oppression; their tongues become perverse and evil.

⁸ They lurk in the cities, seeking to harm the innocent. Their eyes watch in secret for their helpless victims. ⁹ Like a lion in cover, they lie in wait for the poor; catching them in their traps, dragging them away. ¹⁰ Their victims are crushed, they collapse, they fall under their power. ¹¹ These criminals say to their own heart, "God will never notice; He has closed his eyes and will never see." ¹² But I, the Lord, will rise up! I will lift up My hand against them! I will not forget the helpless! ¹³ Why do the wicked renounce Me, their God? Do they think in their heart that I won't hold them accountable?

[14] For I have seen the trouble and grief they cause; I have taken note of it and will repay them by My own hand. That is why helpless victims commit themselves to Me, because I am the helper of the fatherless. [15] I will break the power of these evil people! I will call these criminals to account for their sins; secret crimes that would not otherwise be known. [16] For I, the Lord, am King forever and ever. All these nations will be swept off My land. [17] I listen to the longings of the helpless; I hear their cries and comfort them. [18] I will bring justice for the fatherless and the oppressed, so that corrupt mortals may never again cause them fear.

I AM: ALWAYS HERE

*Y*ou have put your trust in Me, your Lord. That's why you don't listen when people tell you, "Escape like a bird to the mountains for safety!" ² You can see the wicked stringing their bows, and fitting their arrows against the string; all so they can shoot from the shadows at those whose hearts are right. ³ When law and order collapse, what can the righteous do?

⁴ I have not moved. I am still in My holy temple, ruling from my throne in heaven! My eyes observe everyone on earth, and examine them. ⁵ I am examining both the upright and the corrupt, and I despise those who are lovers of violence. ⁶ Coals of fire will rain down upon the wicked; a scorching wind of fire and sulfur will be their fate. ⁷ For I am a loving God, and I love what is right, therefore, only the virtuous will see My face.

I AM: YOUR SECURITY

I, the Lord, will help you. It may seem like there are no faithful people left, like loyal people have vanished from the human race. ² Yet, people have always been lying to one another, manipulating one another with flattery. ³ But, one day, I will silence the flattering tongues and the bragging mouths of ⁴ those who say, "Lies are the pathway to success. We can do whatever we want. Who is Lord over us?"

⁵ I, the Lord, have seen the violence done to the helpless. I have heard the groans of the needy. I will arise and rescue them as they have longed for Me to do. ⁶ My promises are sure, they are as pure as silver refined seven times in a smelting pot. ⁷ I will protect you. I will keep you safe from those around you forever; ⁸ even when the wicked parade around, when what is vile is applauded by the human race.

I AM: NOT IGNORING YOU

*T*hough it may feel like forever, I, the Lord, have not forgotten you. I am not hiding from you. [2] The things that trouble your soul will come to an end. The sorrow that fills your heart day after day will cease.

Your oppressors will not be over you forever. [3] I, the Lord your God, am watching over you, and I will give you light to see; you will not sleep the sleep of death. [4] The enemy will not be able to say, "I have overcome them". Those who trouble you will not be able to gloat over your downfall.

[5] Because you have trusted in My unfailing love, your heart will rejoice in My salvation! [6] Therefore, sing for Me, for I will always be good to you.

14

I AM: THE RESTORER

*O*nly fools believe in their heart that I do not exist. It is because they are selfish; they have done vile things, none of them do what is right. ² I, the Lord, look down from heaven upon these children of men to see if there are any who are wise, any who seek Me. ³ They have all turned their backs; they have become altogether corrupt. Where are those that do what is right? I can't find even one!

⁴ Do all these selfish people know nothing? They devour My people as though eating bread; and they never call upon Me. ⁵ There is a time coming that they will be terrified, for, I, God, take the side of those who obey Me. ⁶ The wicked may frustrate the plans of the poor, but I am their refuge. ⁷ The salvation of My people will come out of Zion; they will rejoice and be glad when I restore My captive people.

I AM: SEEKING HONESTY

Who will I, the Lord, allow into My sanctuary? Who will live on My sacred Mountain? ² A person who has integrity and does what is right, speaking the truth from a sincere heart. ³ Those who do not slander others, nor harm their neighbors, or spread rumors about their friends. ⁴ The one that despises those who are vile, and honors those who revere Me. They stand by what they promise, no matter how much it may cost them. ⁵ The one who helps others financially without self-interest. Who cannot be bribed to testify against the innocent. Those who do these things, will never be cast out of My presence.

I AM: ALL YOU NEED

I, your God, will protect you, for you have put your trust in Me. ² Your soul cries out to Me because your goodness is nothing apart from Me. ³ Seek those who are loving on the earth, they are noble and you will find encouragement in them. ⁴ But those who run after idols will only find sorrow; do not offer anything to them, nor take their names upon your lips.

⁵ For I am your inheritance and your cup of blessing. I am the One that holds your future. ⁶ The land that I will give you is in pleasant places, it is a beautiful inheritance. ⁷ So be thankful, for I will give you counsel and will instruct your heart, even at night. ⁸ Always set Me before your eyes. When I am at your right hand, you cannot be moved.

⁹ Therefore let your heart be glad, let your soul rejoice, and your body rest. ¹⁰ For I will not leave you in the grave, I will not abandon My faithful one to the pit. ¹¹ I will show you the path that leads to life; for in My presence there is fullness of joy; at My right hand, you will find never ending fulfillment!

I AM: THE WAY

I, the Lord, hear your plea for justice; I listen to your cry. I hear your prayer, because it is honest. ² I will vindicate you, because I see who does what is right. ³ I know your heart for I have visited you in the night; I have examined you completely and found no evil, not even in in the words you say. ⁴ Though people have tried to lead you astray, you have followed My word and kept away from the paths of the violent. ⁵ Your feet have not slipped because you always held to My paths.

⁶ You call to Me, your God, because you know I will answer you, for I bend My ear to you and listen as you pray. ⁷ Indeed, I will show you the wonders of My great love; by My right hand I save all those who trust in Me from their enemies. ⁸ I will keep you as the apple of My eye; I will hide you in the shadow of My wings. ⁹ I will protect you from the wicked who oppress you, those murderous enemies that surround you. ¹⁰ For they have closed up their calloused hearts, and their mouths speak only of pride. ¹¹ They are around you even now, wherever you turn, watching for a chance to pull you down. ¹² They are like lions, hungry to tear at their prey, like young lions hiding in ambush.

[13] But I, the Lord, will arise! I will confront them, and overthrow them! I will deliver you from the clutches of the godless by My sword. [14] By My powerful hand, I will save you from these debased people whose only reward is in this life. They will suffer the wrath I have stored up for them; even their children and grandchildren will live with the consequences of their wickedness. [15] But as for you, you will behold Me face to face; and you will be fully satisfied when you rise in My likeness.

18

I AM: YOUR STRENGTH

*Y*ou love Me, for I am your strength. ² I am your rock, your fortress, and your Savior. I, God, am the rock in whom you trust; your shield, the power of your salvation, and your safety. ³ You called upon Me, for I am worthy of praise, and I saved you from your enemies. ⁴ When the noose of death entangled you, and the waves of destruction terrified you, ⁵ when the cords of the grave coiled around you, and you were confronted by the danger of death, ⁶ in your distress, you called out to Me, the Lord, and cried out to Me, your God. I heard your voice from My sanctuary and your cry reached My ears.

⁷ Then the earth trembled and shook; the foundations of the mountains rocked and quaked because of My jealous love. ⁸ Smoke poured out of My nostrils; a consuming flame flew from My mouth, burning coals blazed out from it. ⁹ I tore the sky open and came down with a dark cloud under My feet. ¹⁰ I flew swiftly with My most powerful angels; traveling upon the wings of the wind. ¹¹ I hid Myself with darkness; I made a canopy from thick clouds, full of water. ¹² From the brightness of My presence, dark clouds advanced, with hailstones and flashes of lightening. ¹³ When I, the Most High, uttered My voice, it thundered from heaven. ¹⁴ I shot My arrows and scattered the foe, vanquishing

them with flashes of lightning. ^{15} Then, at My rebuke, at the blast of breath from My nostrils, the floor of the ocean was laid bare, the bones of the earth were uncovered.

^{16} I reached down from on high and took hold of you; I drew you out of the deep waters. ^{17} I delivered you from your powerful enemy, from those who hated you; for they were too strong for you. ^{18} They confronted you in your day of trouble, but I, the Lord, supported you. ^{19} I brought you out into a safe place; I rescued you because I delight in you. ^{20} I, the Lord, have blessed you because you have done what is loving; because of your innocence, I have blessed you. ^{21} For you have kept My ways; you have not turned away from Me, your God. ^{22} For all My laws were there before you, and you did not push My teachings away. ^{23} You were also sincere with Me, and you have kept yourself from sin. ^{24} And so I blessed you, because you have done what is right, I saw that your hands were innocent.

^{25} For I will show mercy to those that are merciful; with those that are innocent, I will show Myself to be innocent; ^{26} to the pure, I will show Myself to be pure. And with with the devious, I will show Myself clever. ^{27} For I save those who are humble, but I humble those who are arrogant. ^{28} For I, the Lord, will light a lamp for you and will turn your darkness into light. ^{29} With My help, you can conquer your enemies and overcome their defenses. ^{30} For My path is perfect; all of My promises prove true. I am a shield for all who trust in Me for protection.

^{31} Who is God, but Me? And who is your rock except Me? ^{32} It is I, the Almighty, who equips you with strength, who makes your way secure. ^{33} I make you as sure footed as a deer, and set you in high places. ^{34} I train you for battle, so that you can use the strongest weapons. ^{35} I have given you the shield of My victory, and My right hand holds you up. It was My support that made you great. ^{36} It was I that widened the path under you, so that you did not slip.

37 And so you pursued your enemies and overtook them; you did not turn back until they were consumed. 38 You wounded them, and they could not rise; they lay defeated before you. 39 All because I fortified you with strength for the battle, subduing those who rose up against you, 40 making your enemies turn their backs and run; and so you destroyed those who hated you. 41 They cried out for help, but no one rescued them. They even called to Me, the Lord, but I did not answer them. 42 They were ground down to dust in the wind and were flung out like filth in the gutter.

43 I delivered you from a rebellious people and made you head over the nations; a people you didn't even know became your subjects; 44 foreigners bow before you. As soon as they hear you, they obey, 45 losing all their courage, they come out trembling from their strongholds.

46 For I, the Lord, am a living God! Therefore give thanks to Me, your rock. Exalt in me, for I am the God of your salvation. 47 For it is I that avenge you and subdue people under you. 48 I rescue you from your enemies and hold you safe beyond their reach. I deliver you from their violence. 49 So share My praise among the nations; sing your songs of thanksgiving in My name. 50 For I give great deliverance to My royal people; I show mercy to My anointed, to all of My chosen people, forevermore.

19

I AM: FAIR

*T*he heavens declare My glory; and the skies show My artistry. ² Day after day attests to it; night after night reveals this knowledge. ³ They use no speech, nor language, there is no sound to be heard; ⁴ yet their voice has gone throughout the earth, and the whole world can hear what they say. In these very heavens I made a dwelling for the sun; ⁵ it comes out in the morning like a groom from the honeymoon, and rejoices like an athlete eager to run a race. ⁶ It rises from one end of the earth and goes across to the other. Nothing can hide from its warmth.

⁷ I am the Lord, and My law is truth; it converts your soul. My word is trustworthy, giving wisdom to the simple. ⁸ My teachings are upright, giving joy to the heart. My commands are right, giving wisdom to see. ⁹ Respect for Me is pure, and it lasts forever. My laws are just and true. ¹⁰ They are more desirable than the finest gold; they are sweeter than the purest honey and the honeycomb. ¹¹ By them, My people are given counsel; and in keeping them, there is great reward.

¹² Who can now know all the sins lurking in their heart? Therefore I will cleanse you from your hidden faults. ¹³ I will also keep you

from presumptuous sins; I will not let them have dominion over you. Then you will be blameless and innocent of rebellion. [14] Then the words you speak and the deep thoughts in your heart will be pleasing to Me, for I, the Lord, am your strength and your Redeemer.

2 0

I AM: YOUR DEFENDER

*I*n times of trouble, I will answer your cry. I, the God of Jacob, will defend you. ² I will send you help from My sanctuary and will strengthen you from Zion. ³ I will remember your offerings and accept your sacrifices. ⁴ I will give you the desires of your heart and will help all your plans succeed. ⁵ Then you will rejoice in My salvation, and will plant your banner of triumph in My name. For I will answer all your prayers.

⁶ Then you will know that I save My anointed, when I answer you from My heavenly sanctuary, and rescue you by My right hand. ⁷ Some trust in chariots, and some in horses, but you trust in My name, for I am the Lord your God. ⁸ The nations will be brought to their knees and will collapse, but you will rise up and stand firm. ⁹ For I will give you victory; I will answer your cry for help.

I AM: YOUR POWER

*A*s royalty, you will rejoice in My strength; how great will be your joy in the victories I give! ² I will grant you your heart's desires and will not withhold your requests. ³ For I will come to greet you with rich blessings, and will set a crown of pure gold on your head.

⁴ You asked for life from Me, and I will give it to you, length of days, forever and ever. ⁵ Your honor will be great because of My salvation, for I will place splendor and majesty on you. ⁶ I will bless you eternally, and will make you rejoice in the joy of My presence. ⁷ My royal one, you trust in Me, the Lord Most High; through My unfailing mercy, you will not be shaken.

⁸ I will lay hold of all My foes; My right hand will seize those who despise Me. ⁹ When I appear, it will be like a blazing furnace; they will be swallowed up, for the fire of My glory will consume them. ¹⁰ Even their descendants will be wiped from the earth; I will bring an end to all of them.

¹¹ For they plot evil, and devise corrupt schemes, but they will not succeed. ¹² They will turn their backs and flee, on the day I aim My bow toward their face; ¹³ When My strength is on full display, I,

the Lord, will be exalted! Then you will sing and praise My mighty power.

I AM: NOT FAR FROM YOU

ou cry to Me, "God, O' God, why have You forsaken me? Why are You so far from saving me? So far from my cries of anguish?" ² I can hear you call out to Me throughout the day, I hear you lift up your voice to Me when you can't sleep at night. ³ I am enthroned in lovingkindness, and for this, My people praise Me. ⁴ When your ancestors put their trust in Me, they were delivered. ⁵ They cried out to Me and were saved; they trusted Me and were not put to shame.

⁶ You feel like a worm, not even human, reproached by everyone, and despised by the people. ⁷ All who see you mock you; they hurl insults and shake their heads saying, ⁸ "You trusted in the Lord; let Him deliver You; let Him rescue the One in whom He delights!" ⁹ But I am the One who took you out of the womb, I taught you to trust as you nursed at your mother's breast. ¹⁰ From birth, you were placed in My care; since you left your mother's belly, I have been your God. ¹¹ I am not far from you, I see that trouble is near, that there is no-one to help.

¹² Enemies have indeed surrounded you like bulls; they encircle you, like the mighty bulls of Syria. ¹³ They open their mouths against you like a lion, roaring and tearing. ¹⁴ Your strength pours

out of you like water, and all your bones feel out of joint; your heart is like wax, melting within you. [15] Your mouth, dried up like a clay pot, with your tongue sticking to the roof of your mouth, laid out for burial in the dust of death. [16] For a pack of dogs have surrounded you, like a gang of villains they close you in. They pierce your hands and feet. [17] All your bones are on display. They stare and gloat over you. [18] They divide your garments among themselves, and for your robe, they cast dice.

[19] But I, the Lord, am not far from you! I am your strength and will come quickly to help ! [20] I will deliver your soul from the sword; I will save your precious life from the power of these dogs. [21] I will rescue you from the lion's mouth and from the horns of the wild bull. I will answer you. [22] And you will declare My name to the people; in the midst of their assembly, you will give praise to Me. [23] Then all who revere Me, will shout for joy! All the descendants of Jacob, will glorify Me! All the children of Israel, will love Me. [24] For I do not disdain nor loathe the afflicted, nor do I turn away from them; when you cry to Me, I hear!

[25] You will praise Me when you are in the great multitude. Then your vows will be fulfilled in the presence of all who fear Me. [26] Then the poor will eat and be satisfied; and those who seek Me will thank Me; when their hearts rejoice forever! [27] For all the ends of the world will remember this and turn to Me, the Lord. And all the families of all races will worship before Me.

[28] For dominion belongs to Me, and I rule over all the nations. [29] All will be prosperous in the earth, and they shall feast and worship. Even all who have gone down into the dust will kneel before Me, those who could not keep themselves alive. [30] Your children will also know Me; future generation will be told about Me. [31] You will declare My love to a people yet to be born, telling them of what I have done!

23

I AM: YOUR SHEPHERD

I, the Lord, am your shepherd; you shall want for nothing. ² I give you rest in green pastures and lead you beside still waters; ³ I restore your soul. I lead you in paths of lovingkindness; for I keep My word. ⁴ Even though you walk through the valley of the shadow of death, you have nothing to fear, for I am with you. My shepherd's rod and staff are there to comfort you. ⁵ I will prepare a banquet for you in the presence of your adversaries. I will anoint your head with oil, until your cup overflows. ⁶ Surely My goodness and mercy will follow you all the days of your life; and you will live in My house, forever.

I AM: KING OF THE EARTH

*T*he Earth and everything in it belongs to Me, the entire world and all its inhabitants. ² For I founded it among the seas and established its rivers.

³ Who can ascend into My mountain? And who can stand before Me in My sacred place? ⁴ Only those who have clean hands and a pure heart, who have not given their soul to idols, nor are they liars. ⁵ They will receive blessings and righteousness from Me, for I am the God of their salvation. ⁶ Such are the people who seek Me, who seek the face of the God of Jacob.

⁷ So lift up O' you gates, swing wide you everlasting doors, and let the King of Glory enter. ⁸ Who is the King of Glory? It is I, the Lord strong and mighty, the Lord, victorious in battle. ⁹ Lift up O' gates, fling wide O' everlasting doors, that the King of Glory may come in. ¹⁰ Who is this King of Glory? I, the Lord of Hosts, am the King of Glory.

I AM: FAITHFUL

*G*ive your life to Me. ² You trust in Me, your God; I will not let you be put to shame; I will not let your enemies triumph over you. ³ Indeed, none who wait upon Me will ever be put to shame. But disgrace will come to those who are treacherous. ⁴ I will show you My ways; I will teach you My paths. ⁵ I will lead you in My truth and teach you, for I am the God of your salvation. You can always trust in Me.

⁶ I, the Lord, remember My tender mercies and lovingkindness, for they have existed from eternity. ⁷ Therefore I will not call to mind the mistakes of your youthful rebellion. I will only remember you according to My love, for I am merciful.

⁸ I am good and honorable and I teach the correct way to those who go astray. ⁹ I guide the humble in what is right, and teach the meek My ways. ¹⁰ For all My paths are love and truth toward those who keep My covenant and decrees. ¹¹ I keep My word, and will forgive your sins, though they are many.

¹² I will show those who revere Me the path they should choose. ¹³ They will live in prosperity, and their children will inherit the earth. ¹⁴ For I confide in those who respect Me, and I teach My covenant to them. ¹⁵ Because your eyes are always on Me, I will

rescue you from the traps of your enemies. ¹⁶ I will turn to you and will have mercy on you, because you are lonely and fearful. ¹⁷ Your problems have grown worse, so I will deliver you from your anguish. ¹⁸ I see all your troubles and pain, and will forgive all your sins.

¹⁹ I have also seen your many enemies, and how they hate you with such vicious hate. ²⁰ I will protect you and keep your soul alive. I will not allow you to be disgraced, for you have put your trust in Me. ²¹ Take heart, for your integrity and honesty will protect you. ²² For I, God, will ransom My people from all their troubles.

I AM: REFINING YOU

I, the Lord, will vindicate you, for you have walked with integrity. You have trusted in Me, and have not wavered. ² I have examined you, and tried you, I refined your heart, and your mind. ³ You have kept My unfailing love before your eyes, and have walked in My truth. ⁴ You have also not kept company with deceitful people, and have had nothing to do with hypocrites. ⁵ For you abhor the company of those who do evil, and refuse to dwell with those who hate Me.

⁶ Therefore, wash your hands in the laver of innocence, that you may come to My altar ⁷ and sing songs of thanksgiving, proclaiming all My wonderful works. ⁸ For you have loved My sanctuary, the place where My glory dwells. ⁹ And so I will not sweep your soul away with the sinners; I will spare your life from the fate of murderers, ¹⁰ in whose hands are sinister schemes, and whose right hands are full of bribes. ¹¹ But as for you, because you walk in honesty, I will be merciful to you and redeem you. ¹² Your feet stand on secure ground; and in the great congregation, you will praise Me, the Lord.

I AM: HERE FOR YOU

I, the Lord, am your light and your salvation; there is no need to fear. I am the strength of your life; there is no reason to be afraid. ² When evil people come against you, to devour you, it is your enemies and foes who will stumble and fall. ³ Though a whole army lay siege against you, your heart need not fear; even if they go to war against you, you can still be confident.

⁴ For you have desired one thing from Me, the one thing that you seek most: that you may dwell in My house all the days of your life, to behold My glory, and meditate upon truth in My temple. ⁵ Therefore in times of trouble, I will hide you in My shelter, under the cover of My sanctuary I will keep you safe, and I will set you upon the Rock on high. ⁶ I will hold you head and shoulders above the enemies who surround you; and you will offer the sacrifices of joy in My temple, singing of your gratitude to Me.

⁷ I hear your voice when you pray; I will have mercy on you and answer you. ⁸ When I whispered, "Come to My presence", your heart said to Me, "Lord, I will seek your face". ⁹ Therefore I will not hide Myself from you. I will not turn away in anger from you. I have always been your help; I will never leave you nor forsake you, for I am the God of your salvation.

[10] Though your father and mother may abandon you, I, the Lord, will take care of you. [11] I will teach you My ways, and will lead you along a safe path, to protect you from your enemies. [12] I will not abandon you to the fall into their hands, for false witnesses accuse you of things you've never done, threatening you with violence. [13] Do not lose heart, believe that you will see My goodness in the land of the living. [14] Wait for Me; be of good courage, and I will strengthen your heart; wait patiently for Me.

I AM: HEARING YOU

*C*ry out to me, the Lord, your Rock, I will not turn a deaf ear to you. If I remained silent, you would be like those who go down into the grave. ² I hear your prayer for mercy as you cry out to Me, as you lift your hands toward My sanctuary.

³ I will not take you away with the wicked, with those who are trouble makers; who speak peaceably with their neighbors, but deceit is in their hearts. ⁴ I will give them according to what they gave, according to the wickedness of their actions. I will turn back on them the evil their own hands have done; rendering to them what they deserve. ⁵ They do not care what I have done, nor for the things My hands have made, therefore I will tear them down, to never be built again.

⁶ Give thanks, for I have heard the sound of your pleading. ⁷ I, the Lord, am your strength and shield; you trust in Me with your entire heart, so I will help you. Then your heart will leap for joy, and burst into songs of thanksgiving. ⁸ For I am the strength of My people; I am a fortress of salvation for My chosen. ⁹ I will save My people and bless My chosen ones. I will be their Shepherd and take care of them forever.

I AM: POWERFUL

*H*eavenly beings ascribe unto Me glory and power. ² They give Me the glory due My powerful name; revering Me in sacred beauty.

³ My voice echoes over the waters; for when I, the God of glory, roar, My voice thunders over mighty oceans. ⁴ My voice is powerful and full of majesty. ⁵ It can splinter and shatter the cedars of Lebanon ⁶ making them jump like a calf, making the Mountains of Lebanon and Syria leap like a young wild bull. ⁷ My voice makes lightning like flames of fire, ⁸ and can shake the wilderness, just like I shook the desert where Israel wandered. ⁹ My voice can twist mighty oaks, stripping forests bare. In My temple, everyone cries, "Glory!"

¹⁰ For I, the Lord, was enthroned at the time of the flood, and I will continue to sit as King forever. ¹¹ My voice gives My people strength, for I am the One who blesses them with peace.

I AM: TURNING YOUR SORROW INTO JOY

*E*xult in Me, the Lord, for I have rescued you out of the depths, and have not let your enemies triumph over you. ² You cried out to Me for help, and I, your God, healed you. ³ I brought your soul up from the grave and kept you alive, sparing you from going down into the pit.

⁴ So sing praise, all My faithful people, remember and give thanks for My loving name. ⁵ For My displeasure lasts only a moment, but My favor lasts for a lifetime. Weeping may endure for the night, but joy comes with the morning.

⁶ In your prosperity, you said, "I will never be moved". ⁷ When I favored you, you were as strong as a mountain. But when I hid My face, you were troubled. ⁸ You cried out to me, "O' Lord", and implored Me for compassion, saying: ⁹ "What good is there in my death, if I go down into the grave? Will the dust praise You? Can it proclaim Your truth? ¹⁰ Hear me, O' Lord, and have mercy on me. Lord, be my helper!"

¹¹ And so I turned your mourning into dancing; I removed your sackcloth and clothed you with joy; ¹² so sing praise, and do not be silent. For I am the Lord your God, and you will be grateful, forever.

I AM: DEPENDABLE

*Y*ou have come to Me, the Lord, for protection; I will never let you be disgraced. I will save you in My righteousness. ² I will turn My ear to you and will come quickly to your rescue. I will be your rock of refuge, a fortress of defense to save you. ³ I am your rock and fortress, therefore I will lead you and guide you, for I honor My word. ⁴ I will pull you out of the traps your enemies have laid for you; for I am your protector.

⁵ Commit your Spirit into My hands. For I, the God of truth, have redeemed you. ⁶ Because you have trusted only in Me and have despised serving lifeless idols, ⁷ you will be glad and rejoice in My love. For I have seen your troubles and know your soul's anguish, ⁸ I will not hand you over to the enemy, rather, I will set your feet in a spacious place.

⁹ I, the Lord, will have mercy on you, for you are in trouble; your eyes waste away from sorrow, your soul and body with grief. ¹⁰ For your life is consumed by heartache, and your years with sighing; your strength fails because of your guilt; even your bones are wasting away. ¹¹ You are ridiculed among your enemies, especially among your neighbors. Even your friends dread being

around you. When people see you in the street, they run the other way. ¹² You are forgotten as though you were dead; you are like a broken pot thrown away. ¹³ You hear people slandering you; fear is all around you, because they conspire against you, scheming how to harm you.

¹⁴ But you trust in Me, saying, "You are my God. ¹⁵ My life is in Your hand". Therefore, I will deliver you from the hand of your enemies, from those who persecute you. ¹⁶ I will make My favor shine upon you, My child; I will save you, because of My unfailing love. ¹⁷ I, the Lord, will not let you be disgraced, for you have called upon Me. But the corrupt will be disgraced; they will be silenced by the grave. ¹⁸ All the lying lips who speak arrogantly and contemptuously against the godly will be silenced.

¹⁹ How abundant are the good things I have stored up for those who honor Me! Before a watching world, I will lavish them upon those who trust in Me. ²⁰ I will hide them in from those who plot against them in the secret place of My presence; I will keep them safe from accusing tongues under My shelter. ²¹ So, give praise when you are under siege, for I will show you the wonders of My unfailing love. ²² In your panic you cried out, "I am cut off from God". But I heard your prayers, when you called out to Me for help. ²³ For I only want love from My loyal people. Indeed, I preserve those who are true to Me; but I will repay the proud and arrogant as they deserve. ²⁴ So, be strong, and let your heart take courage, all you that hope in Me, the Lord.

3 2

I AM: YOUR HIDING PLACE

*O*h, the joy of those whose guilt is forgiven, whose sins are covered. ² Blessed are those who I, the Lord, do not count as guilty, and in whose spirit is no deceit. ³ For when you kept silent about your iniquity, even your bones wasted away, and you complained all day long. ⁴ Day and night My hand of conviction was heavy upon you; and your vitality became like drought in summer. ⁵ But you acknowledged your guilt to Me, and you did not hide your wrongdoings. You decided to confess your sin to Me, and I forgave all your sins.

⁶ Likewise, let everyone who is faithful pray to Me while I still may be found. Surely when the great flood comes rushing in, it will not come near you. ⁷ For I am your hiding place; I will protect you from trouble. I will surround you with songs of deliverance. ⁸ I will instruct you and teach you in the way you should go, and I will counsel you with My loving eye on you.

⁹ So don't be like a horse or like the mule, which have no understanding, and must be harnessed with a bit and bridle or else they won't listen. ¹⁰ For the wicked will only find many sorrows. But the one who trusts in Me, the Lord, will be surrounded by

lovingkindness. [11] So, be glad and rejoice in Me all you who are loving; and shout for joy all you who are upright in heart.

I AM: UNFAILING

*R*ejoice in Me, the Lord, all you that are loving! For gratitude from the upright is beautiful. ² Give thanks with the harp, play music for Me with stringed instruments. ³ Sing Me a new song, find a skillful player, and shout for joy! ⁴ For My word is straightforward, and everything I do is truth. ⁵ For I love what is right and just, and the earth is filled with My goodness.

⁶ By My word the heavens were made, all the starry seas of them by the breath of My mouth. ⁷ I gathered the waters of the sea together like a dam and laid up the oceans in storehouses. ⁸ So, let all the earth revere Me, let all the inhabitants of the world stand in awe. ⁹ For I spoke, and it was done; I commanded and it stood firm.

¹⁰ I bring the counsel of nations to end in nothing; I make their plans have no effect. ¹¹ But My counsel stands forever and the plans of My heart last through all generations. ¹² Blessed is the nation over whom I am their God, the people I chose as My own. ¹³ I, the Eternal Lord, look down from heaven and see all of humanity. ¹⁴ From where I am enthroned, I look upon all the inhabitants of earth. ¹⁵ For I fashioned your hearts individually and I understand everything you do.

^{16} No king is saved because of the size of an army; a warrior does not triumph because of their great strength. ^{17} A horse is a vain hope for deliverance; despite all of its great strength, it cannot save you. ^{18} But My eye watches over those who revere Me, those who hope in My unfailing love. ^{19} I will deliver their soul from death and keep them alive in famine. ^{20} So, let your soul wait on Me, the Lord; for I am your help and your shield. ^{21} Let your heart rejoice in Me, because you have trusted in My loving name. ^{22} My stedfast love will be with you because you put your hope in Me.

I AM: GOOD

*Y*ou will praise Me, the Lord, for all time; gratitude will continually be in your mouth. [2] Your soul will boast in Me and the humble will hear it and be glad. [3] So, boast in Me and exalt in My loving name together. [4] For you sought Me and I heard you and delivered you from all your fears. [5] You looked to Me and were beaming with joy, your face unclouded by shame. [6] Your poor soul cried out and I heard you; I saved you from all your troubles. [7] For My angel encamps around those who honor Me and delivers them.

[8] Taste and see that I, the Lord, am good, for those who trust in Me are blessed. [9] Honor Me all My people, for those who honor Me lack nothing. [10] Even young lions lack and suffer hunger, but those who seek Me will not lack any good thing. [11] Come, My children, listen to Me and I will teach you respect. [12] Whoever among you loves life and desires to see many good days, [13] keep your tongue from mischief and your lips from speaking lies. [14] Turn away from trouble and do good, seek peace and pursue it. [15] For My eyes are on the loving and My ears are open to their cries. [16] But I am against those who are corrupt, I will cut off the remembrance of them from the earth.

¹⁷ The loving cry out, and I hear them, and deliver them from all their troubles. ¹⁸ I, the Lord, am near to those who have a broken heart, and I save those who are crushed in spirit. ¹⁹ The loving may have many troubles, but I will deliver them out of them all. ²⁰ I guard all their bones and not one of them are broken. ²¹ But calamity will destroy the wicked, and those who hate the righteous will be condemned. ²² But I will redeem the souls of My people; and none of those who trust in Me will be condemned.

I AM: YOUR SALVATION

I, the Lord, will rebuke those who strive against you, and will fight against those who fight against you. [2] I will take hold of My shield and armor and will rise up to help you. [3] I will draw out My spear and stop those who pursue you. Let Me reassure your soul, "I am your Salvation". [4] Those who seek after your life will be put to shame and disgrace. Those who plot against you will be turned back and humiliated. [5] They will be like dust blown by the wind when My angel drives them away. [6] Their path will become dark and slippery when My angel pursues them.

[7] Without cause they laid a trap for you and dug a pit to catch you, though you had done nothing wrong. [8] But destruction will come upon them unexpectedly; they will be caught in their own net and I will cause them to fall into their own pit. [9] Then your soul will be joyful because of Me; you will rejoice in My salvation. [10] Your whole being will exclaim, "Lord, who is like You, You deliver the weak from those that are too strong for them, yes, the poor and needy from those who plunder them?!"

[11] Malicious witnesses testify against you and accuse you of things you know nothing about. [12] They reward your kindness with evil, making you sick with despair. [13] When they were sick, you dressed

in mourning, and when your prayers returned unanswered, you humbled yourself with fasting . ¹⁴ You paced around as though they were your friend or brother, you were bent over in sorrow like one who grieves for their mother.

¹⁵ But now when you are in trouble, they join together and rejoice, gathering attackers against you who you didn't even know to slander you. ¹⁶ Like godless mockers at a feast, they gnash at you with their teeth. ¹⁷ So you cry, "How much longer, Lord, will You just look on? Rescue me from their fierce attacks; save my precious life from these lions! ¹⁸ Then I can give You thanks in the great assembly, and share my gratitude before them all."

¹⁹ I will not let those treacherous enemies gloat over your defeat; I will not let those who hate you without cause squint their eyes. ²⁰ For they do not speak like a friend; instead they plot against innocent people who live peacefully in the land. ²¹ They open their mouths wide, shouting, "Aha, Aha, we have seen it with our own eyes." ²² But I have also seen, and I will not keep silent, for I am not far from you. ²³ I, the Lord your God, will awake and rise up in your defense. ²⁴ I will vindicate you in My righteousness; they will not be allowed to gloat over you. ²⁵ They will never have their heart's desire; they will never swallow you up. ²⁶ Those who rejoice at your suffering, and exalt themselves above you, will be brought to shame and confusion.

²⁷ But those who delight in your vindication will shout for joy and gladness and will continually say, "How great is the Lord! He takes pleasure in the well-being of His followers." ²⁸ Then your tongue will proclaim My lovingkindness, and you will sing praise all day long.

I AM: SATISFYING

*S*in whispers to the wicked deep within their hearts: they have no fear of Me before their eyes. ² In their blind arrogance, they cannot see how perverse they really are. ³ Everything they say is crooked and deceitful; they refuse to be wise and to do good. ⁴ Even on their beds they lie awake plotting corruption; they commit themselves to their sinful course, and make no attempt to turn from their depravity.

⁵ But My mercy reaches to the heavens; My faithfulness reaches to the skies. ⁶ My love is like the highest mountains; My justice is like the great ocean. I, the Lord, preserve both people and animals. ⁷ How priceless is My unfailing love. All humanity finds shelter under the shadow of My wings. ⁸ I feed them from the abundance of My house; letting them drink from the river of My goodness. ⁹ For I am the fountain of life, the light by which you see.

¹⁰ I will pour out My lovingkindness on those who know Me, giving justice to those with honest hearts. ¹¹ I will not let the foot of the proud come against you, nor the hand of the depraved drive you away. ¹² For the workers of evil will fall, they will be cast down, and will not be able to rise.

I AM: GIVING YOU THE EARTH

*D*on't worry because of the wicked, or be envious of those who do wrong. ² For like grass, they will soon wither, like green plants, they will soon die away. ³ Trust in Me, the Lord, and do good; then you will dwell securely in the land and will feed on My faithfulness. ⁴ Find your delight in Me and I will give you your heart's desire. ⁵ Commit your way to Me, trust in Me, and I will bring it to pass.

⁶ I will bring forth your innocence like the dawn, and justice like the noonday sun. ⁷ Rest in Me and wait patiently for Me. Do not worry about evil people who prosper or fret about their selfish schemes. ⁸ Stop being angry, and let go of resentment. Do not lose your temper, because it only causes trouble. ⁹ For the corrupt will be cut off; but those who wait on Me, the Lord, will inherit the Earth. ¹⁰ In only a little while, wicked people will be no more; indeed, you will look diligently for them, but they will be no more. ¹¹ But the humble will inherit the earth and they will delight themselves in the abundance of peace.

¹² The wicked may plot against the innocent and gnash at them with their teeth. ¹³ But I laugh at this, for I see that their day is coming. ¹⁴ The selfish have drawn their swords and have bent

their bows to bring down the poor and needy, to harm those who do what is right. ¹⁵ But their swords will enter their own heart and their bows will be broken.

¹⁶ The little that a godly person owns is worth more than all the wealth of those who are evil. ¹⁷ For the power of the wicked will be broken, but I take care of the loving. ¹⁸ The innocent are daily under My care, and they will receive an inheritance that lasts forever. ¹⁹ In times of disaster they will not wither, and in times of famine they will have plenty. ²⁰ But the corrupt will perish, and all My enemies will vanish like the flowers of the meadow, like smoke they will vanish away.

²¹ Thieves borrow and do not repay, but loving people are generous givers. ²² Therefore, those who I bless will inherit the Earth, but those who I curse will be cut off. ²³ For I guide the steps of the upright because I delight in their way. ²⁴ If they fall, they will not stay down, for I hold them up with My hand. ²⁵ You were once young and now you are old, and have you ever seen the righteous abandoned? Or their children begging for food? ²⁶ They are always generous, lending freely, and their children are a blessing.

²⁷ If you depart from evil and do what is good, you will live forever. ²⁸ For I, the Lord, love justice, and do not abandon My faithful people; I will preserve them eternally. But the descendants of the wicked will be cut off. ²⁹ The loving will inherit the earth and live in it forever, ³⁰ for their mouths speak wisdom, and they always talk of what is just. ³¹ Because My law is in their hearts, their feet do not slip from My path. ³² The corrupt stalk the godly, seeking to harm them. ³³ But I will not leave them in their hands, nor let them be condemned when brought to trial.

³⁴ Wait on Me, the Lord, and keep My ways, and I will honor you by giving you the Earth; for when the wicked are destroyed, you will see it. ³⁵ You have all seen the ruthless in power, spreading themselves out like massive native trees. ³⁶ Yet they pass away,

and they are no more. Though you look for them, there is nothing left to be found. [37] But mark those with integrity, observe the upright, for their future is peace. [38] For all the selfish will end up destroyed; there will be no future for the guilty.

[39] The salvation of the loving is from Me; I am their strength in times of trouble. [40] I will help them and deliver them; I will deliver them from the wicked, and save them, because they trust in Me.

3 8

———————

I AM: ALWAYS FOR YOU

I, the Lord, am reprimanding you, but not in wrath, I am only disciplining you. ² For My arrows pierce deep when My hand presses down on you. ³ You feel sick because of My displeasure; you feel it deep within your bones because of your sin. ⁴ Your guilt has overwhelmed you, it is a burden too heavy to bear. ⁵ Your wounds grow foul and fester because of your foolishness. ⁶ You are troubled, completely bowed over, going around sad all the time. ⁷ Your insides are on fire, and your health is broken. ⁸ You are worn out and utterly crushed, groaning because of the anguish in your heart.

⁹ All your longings lie open before Me; your sighing it is not hidden from Me. ¹⁰ I see that your heart is throbbing, that your strength is failing, and that even the light has gone from your eyes. ¹¹ Your loved ones and friends don't want to deal with your affliction; even your relatives avoid you. ¹² Those who want to harm you lay traps for you, and those who want to hurt you plan your destruction, plotting all day long. ¹³ But you, like the deaf, refuse to hear them, like the mute, you do not open your mouth. ¹⁴ You don't hear a word they say, nor do you speak a word in response. ¹⁵ For your hope is in Me; and I, the Lord your God, hear

you. [16] I will not let them gloat over you, or rejoice when your feet slip.

[17] Because your grief is always with you, you feel ready to fall, [18] but in anguish over your sins, you have confessed your guilt to Me; [19] and though your enemies are powerful and those who hate you for no reason are numerous, [20] remember, those who repay hate for kindness are your enemies only because you seek to do what is right. [21] I will never abandon you; I, your God, will never leave you. [22] I will rush to your aid, for I am your Lord and Savior.

I AM: NOT AN ENABLER

*Y*ou said: "I will watch my ways, so that I won't sin in what I say. I will hold my tongue when the ungodly are around me." [2] You remained mute with silence and held your peace, not even saying something good; yet your sorrow grew worse. [3] Your heart became hot within you, while you ruminated, the fire burned until you said your thoughts out loud:

[4] "Lord, show me how my life will end, and how long I will live, so that I will know how fleeting My life is. [5] You have made my life a mere handbreadth in length, the span of my life is as nothing before You; everyone, even at their best state is but a breath." [6] Truly, everyone walks around in an illusion. They busy themselves for nothing, piling up assets they can never keep, without knowing whose they will finally become.

[7] What then, can you hope in Me? You have put your hope in Me. [8] Therefore I will deliver you from all your transgression. I won't make you the reproach of fools. [9] For you were mute and didn't open your mouth because I was the one who wounded you. [10] But I will remove My scourge from you, for you have been overcome by the blow of My hand. [11] For when I rebuke and correct mortals

for their sin, I consume like a moth what is dear to them, only because their life is like a mere breath.

[12] I, the Lord, hear your prayers, and listen to your cries for help; I am not deaf to your weeping. For you are only a foreigner and a wanderer in this world, as were all those who went before you. [13] Therefore I will remove My glare from you, that you may regain your strength, before you lay this life down and are no more.

40

I AM: GRACIOUS

*Y*ou waited patiently for Me, the Lord, and I listened to you. ² I brought you up out of a horrible pit, out of the mud and mire, and set your feet upon a rock, establishing your path. ³ I put a new song in your mouth, a hymn of gratitude for Me. Many will see this, and come to revere and trust in Me.

⁴ O' the joy of those who put their trust in Me, who put no confidence in the proud who turn away to idols. ⁵ Were you to proclaim all the many wonders I have done and still have planned for you, they could never be counted, for they are two numerous to list. ⁶ For I have no desire for sacrifice or offering, nor for burned offerings or sin offerings. I only wish that your ears would be open.

⁷ As I have said, the Messiah will come, in the scroll of the book it is written about Him. ⁸ He delights to do My will; for My law is within His heart. ⁹ He will proclaim the good news of deliverance in the great assembly; and will not be afraid to speak out. I, the Lord, know this to be true. ¹⁰ He will not hide My righteousness in his heart. He will declare My faithfulness and My salvation. He will not conceal My lovingkindness and My truth from the people.

[11] Therefore I will not withhold My tender mercies from you. My love and faithfulness will continually preserve you. [12] For innumerable troubles surround you, and your sins have overtaken you, so that you are unable to look up; they are more than the hairs of your head, and your heart fails within you. [13] But I, the Lord, delight in delivering you. I will come quickly to help you! [14] Those who seek to destroy your life will be brought to shame and confusion. All those who wish you harm will be driven back and brought to disgrace. [15] Those who point fingers at you will be astonished because of their own shame.

[16] All those who seek Me will rejoice and be glad in Me. All those who love My salvation will continually say, "How great is our Lord!" [17] Yes, you are poor and needy, yet I am thinking about you. I am your help and your deliverer. I am your God, and I will not delay.

I AM: HOLDING YOU UP

*B*lessed are those who are concerned for the poor; I, the Lord, will deliver them in times of trouble. ² I will protect them and preserve them; they will be counted among the blessed on the earth; I will not abandon them to the will of their enemies. ³ I will strengthen them when they are sick and will restore them to health.

⁴ I will be merciful to you, I will heal your soul, though you have disobeyed Me. ⁵ For enemies speak maliciously about you, wishing you would die and be forgotten. ⁶ And when they come to see you, they only speak lies while their hearts gather gossip; when they go out, they spread it abroad. ⁷ All who hate you whisper together against you imagining the worst. ⁸ They say, "A fatal disease has afflicted you; you are on your deathbed." ⁹ Even your best friend, the one you trusted and shared your food with has turned against you.

¹⁰ But I, the Lord, will be merciful to you and raise you up, that you may shut all their mouths. ¹¹ By this you will know that I am pleased with you, when your enemy fails to triumph over you. ¹² For I uphold you in your integrity, and will set you before My

presence forever. [13] For I, the God of Israel am blessed, from everlasting to everlasting.

BOOK 2

Chapters 42-72
Psalms of Need

-EXODUS-

Davidic Grouping II
Sons of Korah Grouping I

I AM: WHAT YOU THIRST FOR

*a*s a deer pants for streams of water, so your soul longs for Me, your God. ² Your soul thirsts for Me, the living God. You long to come and meet with Me. ³ For tears have been your food day and night, while people continually mock you, saying, "Where is your God?"

⁴ You pour out your soul remembering how you used to go with the crowds to My house, shouting for joy and singing praise among the festive throngs of pilgrims. ⁵ But don't let your soul be discouraged. Don't let your heart be sad. Put your hope in Me, for you will praise Me once again, for I am your Savior and your God.

⁶ I see that your soul is deeply discouraged. Reflect upon Me from the land of the Jordon that flows from the heights of Mount Hermon and small Mount Mizar, ⁷ where the deep sea calls to the river in the roar of My waterfalls; let their waves and billows sweep over you, ⁸ for in the same way, I, the Lord, will pour My lovingkindness over you by day, and by night My songs will be upon your lips like a prayer, for I am the God of your life.

⁹ I, your God, and your Rock, have not forgotten you. I see your sorrow because of oppressive enemies. ¹⁰ Like a sword shattering

your bones, your enemies reproach you, saying all day long, "Where is your God?" [11] But don't let your soul be discouraged. Don't be troubled within. Put your hope in Me, for you will once again praise Me, for I am your Savior.

I AM: YOUR GOD

I, your God, will declare you innocent and defend your cause against ungodly people; I will rescue you from these unjust liars. ² For I am your safe haven, I have not rejected you. I see you wandering around in grief because of the oppression of the enemy.

³ I will send you My light and My truth; let them guide you, let them lead you to the sacred mountain where I dwell. ⁴ Come to My altar, for I am the source of all your joy; so sing praise on stringed instruments, for I, the Almighty God, am your God.

⁵ Why is your soul discouraged? Why are you troubled within? Hope in Me, for you will yet thank Me, for I am your Savior and your God.

I AM: NEAR

*Y*ou have heard with your own ears, your ancestors have told you what, I, your God, did in their days, in the days of old. ² How I drove out the corrupt nations with a powerful hand, and planted My own people. I broke apart their nations, and made your ancestors flourish. ³ They did not conquer the land with their own weapons, nor did their own power save them: it was by My right hand, by My power, and the light of My presence that helped them, because I loved them.

⁴ For I, your God and King, give victory to My people. ⁵ It is through My power you are able to push down the enemy, only by My name can you overcome the foe. ⁶ So, don't put your trust in your bow or sword, for they cannot save you. ⁷ I am the One who saves you from the enemy, I put those who hate you to shame. ⁸ You can boast in Me all day long and give praise forever.

⁹ It may seem like I have cast you off and humbled you; as though I no longer go with you into the battle. ¹⁰ For you have been forced to retreat from the enemy, while those who hate you plunder what is yours. ¹¹ Like sheep sent to the slaughterhouse, you have been scattered among the nations, ¹² sold for next to nothing, without even making a profit. ¹³ You have become a joke among your

neighbors, receiving scorn and contempt from those around you. [14] You have become a proverb among the nations, and they shake their heads at you. [15] You are unable to escape the constant humiliation, so you cover your face in your shame. [16] The taunts of those who revile you is continually in your ears, for your enemy is bent on revenge.

[17] All this came upon you, but you did not forget Me, nor did you break the covenant I made with you. [18] Your heart did not turn back, nor did your steps depart from My way. [19] I sorely broke you among a place of dragons; I shrouded you in the shadow of death. [20] If you had forgotten Me, your God, and stretched out your hand to another god, [21] I would have discovered it because I know all your secret thoughts. [22] It is for My sake that you have faced death all day long and are regarded as sheep for the slaughter.

[23] I, the Lord, am wide awake, for I do not sleep. I will rouse Myself, for I have not rejected you. [24] I am not hiding My face, nor have I forgotten your suffering and oppression. [25] I see your soul, bowed down to the dust, lying defeated on the ground. [26] I will rise up and help you. I will redeem you because of My unfailing love.

I AM: OVERFLOWING

*B*eautiful words stir in My heart. With My tongue flowing like the pen of a skillful poet, I will recite a lovely a poem about the coming King: ² For He is the most excellent of men, and grace has been poured upon His lips. Therefore, I, your God, will bless Him eternally. ³ So, buckle Your sword upon Your thigh, O Mighty One; clothe Yourself in glory and majesty. ⁴ In splendor, ride forth victoriously in the cause of truth, of humility, and justice. With Your right hand, You will perform awe-inspiring deeds. ⁵ For Your arrows are sharp, piercing the enemies heart, let the nations fall at Your feet.

⁶ Your throne, O God, is forever and ever; a scepter of justice is the scepter of Your kingdom. ⁷ For You love what is right and hate evil. Therefore God, I, Your God, have anointed You with the oil of joy, more than all others. ⁸ Your robes will be fragrant with myrrh, aloes, and cinnamon. Out of palaces adorned in ivory the music of stringed instruments will make You glad. ⁹ Daughters of kings will be among your court, and at Your right hand will stand the Bride in finest gold.

¹⁰ Listen O Bride, and consider this carefully - leave your people behind, your own families house, ¹¹ for the King desires your

beauty. Adore Him, for He is your Lord. [12] Then the port of Tyre will pour out gifts to you, and the rich among them will seek your favor. [13] The royal Bride, so glorious within the palace, her gown woven in gold. [14] She will be brought before the King in an embroidered robe of many colors, her virgin bridesmaids in her train. [15] With joy and gladness they will come and enter the palace of the King!

[16] Your children will become royalty like their Father, they will become rulers over all the earth . [17] And I will cause Your name to be celebrated by all generations; and Your people will give praise to You, for ever and ever.

I AM: YOUR SANCTUARY

I, your God, am your refuge and strength, I am an ever-present help in trouble. ² So, don't be afraid, even though the earth is shaking and mountains fall into the depths of the sea; ³ though its waves roar and boil and mountains shake with its surging. ⁴ There is a river whose streams bring joy, it is in My city, in the sacred place of the sanctuary, where I, the Most High, dwell. ⁵ I am in the midst of her and she will never be destroyed, for from the very break of day, I, God, will help her.

⁶ Nations will be in turmoil, and their kingdoms will totter. When My voice thunders the earth will melt. ⁷ But I, the Lord of hosts, will be with you; for I am your refuge. ⁸ Come and see what I will do: I will make the earth desolate. ⁹ I will make wars cease all over the world. I will break the bow and cut the spear in two, and will burn their chariots with fire. ¹⁰ So, be still, and know that I am God. For I will be exalted throughout the nations, supreme over all the world. ¹¹ I, the Lord of heaven's armies, am with you. For I am your refuge.

I AM: RULER OF THE EARTH

*C*lap your hands, all My people! Shout to Me, your God, with the voice of triumph! [2] For I, the Lord Most High, am awesome in power and majesty. I am the great King over all the earth. [3] I subdue the nations before you, putting them under your feet. [4] I even chose your inheritance for you, the Promised Land of Jacob's descendants, whom I love.

[5] I have ascended amidst shouts and the blast of trumpets. [6] So, sing your thanksgiving, sing praises; sing of gratitude for your King; sing praises. [7] For I am King over all the earth. Sing for Me psalms of thanksgiving! [8] For I am seated upon My sacred throne, reigning above all nations. [9] The rulers of the world will all gather together with the people of the God of Abraham, [10] for all the kings of the earth belong to Me, your God, and I am greatly exalted.

I AM: YOUR DEFENSE

I, the Lord, am powerful and worthy of Praise. ² My city sits on My sacred mountain, beautiful in its lofty heights, Mount Zion in the far north, the city of your great King. From there I bring joy to the whole earth; ³ for I am in her palaces, revealing Myself as her protector.

⁴ When kings assembled their forces and advanced together, ⁵ they saw it and were stunned and fled in terror. ⁶ Fear took hold of them and they writhed in pain like a woman about to bear a child. ⁷ I broke them like the ships of Lebanon when they are shattered by an east wind. ⁸ As you have heard, so now you have seen, this is the city of the Lord of hosts, the city of your God, and I will preserve it forever.

⁹ Within My temple you can contemplate My unfailing love, ¹⁰ for My goodness is praised to the ends of the earth, because My right hand is filled with love. ¹¹ So, let Mount Zion rejoice. Let the peoples of Judah be glad, for My judgements are just.

¹² Walk around Zion, go all around her and count the watchtowers, ¹³ reflect upon her defenses and walk among her strongholds, so that you can tell the coming generations, ¹⁴ "this is

just what God is like, He is your God, forever and ever, and He will guide and protect you even to the end of your life."

I AM: YOUR RANSOM

*H*ear this, all peoples! Listen, all you inhabitants of the world, ² both low and high, rich and poor together. ³ My mouth speaks wisdom, and the thoughts of My heart give you understanding. ⁴ Listen carefully to this proverb and solve a riddle.

⁵ Why should you fear when trouble comes, when you are surrounded by enemies? ⁶ They trust in their wealth and boast of their great riches. ⁷ Yet not one them can ransom the life of another; there is no price they can pay Me for it; ⁸ for the redemption of a soul is too costly, you can never pay enough ⁹ to live forever and never see the grave.

¹⁰ You can see that even the wise die as well as the arrogant and the fool. They all leave their wealth to others.¹¹ Their inner hope is that their houses will last forever, here to stay for all generations; they even name the land after themselves. ¹² But, humans, despite their wealth, do not endure; just like the animals, they all die.

¹³ This is the fate of those who are foolish, and the fate of their followers who approve of their sayings.¹⁴ Like sheep, they are laid in the grave and death will be their shepherd. While their bodies rot in the grave far from their mansions, the upright will rule over

them in that morning. [15] For I, your God, will redeem your souls from the power of the grave and will surely bring you to Myself.

[16] So don't be afraid of the rich and powerful, when the prestige of their name increases; [17] for when they die, they will take nothing with them, and their splendor will not follow them into the grave. [18] Though, while they live, they count themselves blessed, for people always praise you when you do well for yourself, [19] yet they will join all those who have gone before them into death, to never see the light of life. [20] Those who boast of wealth, lack wisdom, for they die just like the animals.

I AM: SEEKING GRATITUDE

I, the Almighty God, will speak and summon the whole earth; from the rising of the sun in the east, to its going down in the west. [2] Out of Zion, perfect in its beauty, I will blaze forth. [3] I, your God, will come, and I won't be silent, for a devouring fire will be before Me and a tempest all around Me.

[4] I will summon the heavens above, and earth, to witness the judgement of My people. [5] I will gather My faithful people to Myself, those who made a covenant with Me by sacrifice. [6] Then all the heavens will declare that I am loving, for I, God, am a just judge.

[7] O My people, listen as I speak, for I have charges against you. [8] Now I have no complaint against your sacrifices or your offerings which you always offer Me. [9] Yet, I have no need of bulls from your farms nor goats from your flocks, [10] for every animal of the forest is mine, as well as the cattle on thousands of hills; [11] I even know every bird in the mountains and all that moves in the field is Mine.

[12] If I were hungry, I wouldn't even tell you, for the world and everything in it is Mine. [13] Do you really think I eat the sacrifice of the bulls, or drink the blood of the goats you offer? [14] Make

gratitude your offering to Me, your God, and follow through on your commitments to Me! ¹⁵ Then you will call out to Me in the day of trouble, and I will deliver you, and you will thank Me.

¹⁶ But to those who are hostile toward Me, I say: What right do you have to proclaim My teachings, or to take My covenant in your mouth, ¹⁷ seeing as you hate My guidance and cast My Words behind you? ¹⁸ When you see a thief you join in with them and partake with adulterers. ¹⁹ You give your mouth to corruption, and use your tongue for deceit. ²⁰ You'll even sit and testify against your sibling, slandering your own mother's child!

²¹ You have done all these things, and I have kept silent, so you thought that I was exactly like you. But I will rebuke you and lay the charges clearly before your eyes. ²² So, consider this: you, who chose to forget Me, will be destroyed, and there will be no one to deliver you. ²³ Those who offer gratitude are the ones that truly honor Me. And if you keep to My path, I will reveal My salvation to you.

I AM: FORGIVING

I, your God, will have mercy upon you, because of My unfailing love. According to the multitude of My tender mercies, I will blot out your sin. ² I will wash you completely from your guilt and cleanse you from your selfishness. ³ For you have acknowledged your transgression, indeed, your sin is always before you. ⁴ Before Me and Me only is your guilt known, doing what is evil in My sight. So, you know I am right in My verdict, because My judgement is justified.

⁵ Indeed, you were born sinful; you were corrupt from the time your mother conceived you. ⁶ Yet, I desire truth deep in your heart; therefore, since the womb, I have been teaching you wisdom. ⁷ Therefore, I will cleanse your wounds and apply medicine, and you will be clean; I will wash you, and you will be whiter than snow. ⁸ I will return your joy and happiness, that your broken bones may dance once again.

⁹ Therefore I will hide My face from your sins, and blot out all your guilt. ¹⁰ I, your God, will create a clean heart within you, and I will renew your faithful spirit within. ¹¹ I will not cast you away from My presence, I will not take My Holy Spirit away from you. ¹² I will, instead, restore the deep joy of My salvation to you, and I

will hold you up by My generous Spirit. [13] Then you can teach others, so they too will turn back to Me. [14] I, the God of your salvation, will also deliver you from the guilt of bloodshed, and your tongue will sing aloud of My forgiveness. [15] For I will open your lips with joy filled praise.

[16] I don't want sacrifice, and I know you would give it; nor do I take pleasure in offerings. [17] The sacrifice I want is a humble spirit. I, your God, will never reject a broken or crushed heart. [18] For it brings Me pleasure to prosper Zion and rebuild the walls of Jerusalem. [19] I am only delighted by sacrifices done in love, with any and all of these type of offerings you place on My altar.

I AM: ENDING CORRUPTION

*W*hy do you who are powerful boast about your corruption? All day long you boast, yet you are a disgrace in My eyes. ² Your tongue is like a sharp razor, scheming destruction through deceit. ³ You love corruption more than kindness and lies rather than speaking justice. ⁴ You love malicious gossip because you're a fraudulent liar.

⁵ But I, God, will bring you down to everlasting ruin; death will take you away, snatching you right out of your home, removing you from the land of the living. ⁶ Those who are upright will see it and be shocked; they will laugh in relief, saying, ⁷ "Look at what happens to the one who did not make God their strength, but trusted instead in the abundance of their riches, strengthening themselves with corruption."

⁸ But My children will be like an olive tree flourishing in the house of their God; for they trust in My unfailing love forever and ever. ⁹ They will thank Me eternally because of what I have done. In the presence of all the other faithful, they will put their hope in My name because it is trustworthy.

I AM: SEEKING JUSTICE

*F*ools have said in their heart, "There is no God." But they are corrupt and their actions are evil; not one of them does what is loving. ² I, God, look down from heaven on all of humanity, to see if there are any who are wise, any who seek the True God. ³ But every one of them has turned away; they have together become corrupt; not one of them does what is right, not even one.

⁴ Will those who are evil never learn? They devour My people like bread and would never think to pray to Me, their God. ⁵ But terror will grip them as they have never known before when I scatter their bones. They will be put to shame when I reject them. ⁶ On the day that Salvation comes out of Zion, I will deliver My people from their captivity, Jacob will shout for joy and Israel will rejoice!

I AM: LISTENING

I will rescue you because of My great love! I will defend you by My power. [2] I hear your prayer and I am paying attention to your pleas. [3] For strangers are attacking you and violent people seek after your life; people who care nothing about Me, your God. [4] But I am your helper; I, the Lord, am the one who sustains you.

[5] The evil plans of those who slander you will recoil back upon themselves. They will be destroyed. [6] Then you will freely worship Me and give praise to My name, for I am loving. [7] For I will deliver you out of all your troubles and help you triumph over your enemies.

55

I AM: AWARE

I, your God, hear your prayers; I will not hide Myself from your pleas; [2] I am paying attention to you, and will answer you. [3] You're restless and anxious, feeling overwhelmed because of the voice of the enemy, because of the oppression of the wicked. For they bring trouble down upon you, and assail you in their hate.

[4] Your heart pounds within your chest; the terror of dying has fallen upon you. [5] Fear and trembling have gripped you, the horror has overwhelmed you. [6] So you said, "If only I had wings like a dove so I could fly away and be at peace. [7] I would run far away and live in the country. [8] If only I could quickly escape far from this raging storm and hatred."

[9] But I, the Lord, will confuse them, and confound their plans; for I have seen the violence and strife in the city; [10] day and night they prowl around its walls, filling it with crime and abuse. [11] It is collapsing at its core because oppression and fraud never leave the streets.

[12] If it were an enemy reproaching you, you could endure it; if it were someone who hated you rising against you, you could have hidden from them. [13] But it was your equal, your companion and

close friend, ¹⁴ with whom you once enjoyed sweet fellowship at My sanctuary among the worshippers. ¹⁵ Yet, death will stalk your enemies; the grave will swallow them alive, because evil has made its home within them.

¹⁶ As for you, call upon Me, your God, and I will save you. ¹⁷ Morning, noon, or night, when you pray and cry out to Me, I can hear your voice. ¹⁸ I will redeem your soul with peace from the battles you fight against so many enemies.

¹⁹ For I have ruled since eternity and I hear you; I will defeat them. For they refuse to change their ways and do not respect Me, their God. ²⁰ They have betrayed those who were at peace with them and have broken their promises. ²¹ The words of their mouth were smoother than butter, but there was war in their hearts; their words were as soothing as oil, but they cut like drawn swords.

²² So cast your burdens on Me, the Lord, and I will sustain you; for I will not allow the people in whom My righteousness dwells to slip and fall. ²³ For I will bring the wicked down to the pit of destruction; the treacherous and bloodthirsty will not live out half their life. But as for you, put your trust in Me.

I AM: RECORDING YOUR TEARS

I, your God, will be merciful to you, for your enemies are in hot pursuit, attacking you all day long . ² They hound you endlessly and many are boldly fighting against you. ³ But whenever you are afraid, trust in Me. ⁴ Boast in My Word and put your trust in My promises! Why should you be afraid? What can mere mortals do to you?

⁵ They are always twisting your words and spend their time scheming against you, plotting ways to harm you. ⁶ They conspire together, lurking, marking everything you do, lying in wait to ruin your life. ⁷ Do they think they will get away with their crimes? For I, your God, will cast them down to the ground!

⁸ I am keeping a record of your struggles; I have put your tears in My bottle, they are all in My book. ⁹ When you cry out to Me for help, I will turn your enemies back. You know that I am for you! ¹⁰ You boast in My Word, raving about it, ¹¹ and have put your trust in Me, so don't be afraid. What can mere mortals do to you?

¹² You will fulfill your vows to Me and will praise Me for My help, ¹³ for I will deliver your soul from death. I will keep your feet from falling, so that you may walk before Me in My life-giving light.

I AM: LOVING

I, your God, will be merciful to you, for your soul trusts in Me. Take refuge under the shadow of My wings until the danger has passed. ² Cry out to Me, the Most High, who accomplishes all things for you. ³ I will reach from heaven and save you, defeating those who would swallow you up. I will send forth My love and faithfulness. ⁴ For your soul is surrounded by lions and you live among people who breathe fire. Their teeth are like spears and arrows, and their tongues are like sharp swords.

⁵ But I am exalted across the heavens, and My glory covers all the earth. ⁶ Though enemies have prepared a net for your steps and your soul is weary with stress, though they dig a deep pit in your path, they will fall into it themselves.

⁷ So, let your heart be confident in Me, your God, let your heart be stedfast. Sing and make psalms! ⁸ Awaken your soul! Wake up your guitar and harp! Awaken the dawn with your songs! ⁹ For you will praise Me among the nations and you will sing of Me among them all.

¹⁰ For My great love ascends as far as the heavens and My faithfulness is as high as the skies. ¹¹ For I am exalted among the heavens and My glory is over all the earth.

I AM: BRINGING JUSTICE

*D*o you rulers ever speak justly? Do you judge fairly? ² No! In your heart you plot injustice, and your hands spread violence on the earth. ³ The wicked go astray from the womb; they spread lies from the day they are born. ⁴ Their venom is like the poison of a snake, like a deaf cobra that plugs its ears ⁵ ignoring the voice of the charmer, no matter how clever the enchanter.

⁶ I, God, declare, their teeth will break in their mouths, the fangs of these young lions will be torn out. ⁷ They will vanish like water that drains away; like grass they will be trodden down and wither. ⁸ They will be like snails that dissolve as they move along, or like a stillborn child who never sees the sun.

⁹ Faster than your pot can heat over the flame, the selfish will be swept away like a tornado, whether young or old. ¹⁰ The loving will be grateful when they see injustice avenged; the blood of the corrupt will wash up at their feet. ¹¹ Then people will say, "Surely there is a reward for those who live for God; truly there is a God who judges the earth."

I AM: RELIABLE

I, your God, will deliver you from your enemies; I will protect you from those who rise up against you! ² I will rescue you from these criminals; I will save you from those who are after blood. ³ I see how they lie in wait for you, how those in power conspire against you, though you have not sinned or offended them. ⁴ You have done nothing wrong, yet they are ready to attack. I see what is happening and will rise up and help you.

⁵ I, the Lord God of Heaven's host, the God of Israel, will rise up and judge the nations; grace will not cover those who are wicked and treacherous. ⁶ For they come out in the dark, growling like dogs as they prowl about the city. ⁷ I see the filth they spew from their mouths. Their tongues are as sharp as swords, and they think that no one hears them. ⁸ But I scoff at them; all these nations are a mockery.

⁹ So wait for Me, for I am your strength and your fortress. ¹⁰ In My unfailing love I will go before you and you will look down in triumph over your enemies. ¹¹ Yet, I will not utterly destroy them, for My people soon forget such lessons; instead, I, your Lord and shield, will stagger them with My power and bring them to their knees. ¹² Then they will be caught in the snare of their own sins

and cruelty; by their pride, corruption, and lies. ^{13} They will be destroyed and completely wiped out. Then it will be know that I, the God of Jacob, rule to the very ends of the earth.

^{14} So when they come out at night, growling like dogs, prowling about the city, ^{15} wandering around for food, howling when they are not satisfied, ^{16} sing of My power; yes, sing aloud of My mercies which will come in the morning. For I have been a fortress for you, a refuge in times of trouble. ^{17} I am your strength, so sing praise! I am a reliable defense.

60

I AM: STILL WITH YOU

I, your God, have not cast you off; I have broken you down, because I was displeased. But I will restore you again. ² I made the earth tremble, and tore it open; but I will heal its wounds, for it is crumbling. ³ I have shown my people hard times; I have given them wine that made them reel. ⁴ But for those who revere Me, I have raised a banner, a rallying point in the face of attack. ⁵ I will rescue you, My beloved, and will save you and help you with My right hand.

⁶ I, your God, make you a sacred promise: In triumph I will make a present of Shechem and hand out the Succoth Valley as a gift. ⁷ Gilead will be yours, and Manasseh. Ephraim will be a helmet, and Judah will be a scepter. ⁸ Moab will be your servant; you will hurl your shoe at Edom, and shout in triumph over Philistia. ⁹ You wondered who would lead you against these strongholds? Who would lead you to Edom? ¹⁰ You thought, I, your God, had cast you off, and no longer went out with you in your battles? ¹¹ But I will give you help when you are in trouble, for human help is worthless. ¹² Through Me, your God, you will do mighty things, for I am the one who tramples down your foes.

I AM: YOUR SHELTER

I, your God, hear your cry; I listen to your prayer. ² From the ends of the earth, you call to Me when your heart is overwhelmed, so I lead you to the Rock that is high above you. ³ For I have been your shelter, a strong fortress against the enemy, ⁴ and will dwell in My sanctuary forever, trusting in the shelter of My wings.

⁵ I, your God, have heard your vows, and I will give you the inheritance reserved for those who revere My name. ⁶ I will increase the days of your royal life; your years will span the generations. ⁷ You will abide in My presence forever, for My love and truth with protect you. ⁸ Then you will sing praise to My name forever; and you will fulfill your goals day after day.

I AM: TRUSTWORTHY

*L*et your soul find rest in Me, your God, for salvation comes from Me. [2] I alone am your Rock and your salvation; I am your defender, and you shall never be defeated.

[3] How long will they attack you? How long will they try and destroy someone no stronger than a broken-down fence? [4] They scheme to cast you down from your place of honor, taking pleasure in telling lies; with their mouth they say blessings, but in their heart they curse.

[5] Let your soul find rest in Me, your God, for your hope comes from Me. [6] For I am your Rock and your salvation; I am your defender, and you will never be shaken. [7] I, your God, am your salvation and honor. I am the Rock of your strength, and your refuge is in Me. [8] So trust in Me at all times, My people. Pour out your heart to Me, for I am your refuge.

[9] Surely ordinary peoples lives are like a breath, yet even the powerful are only a facade. If you weighed them on a scale, they are all lighter than a breath of air. [10] So, do not make your living through oppression, or hope to gain anything by robbery. Even if your riches increase, you shouldn't set their heart on them.

¹¹ For I, God, have spoken plainly, and you have heard it many times: true power belongs only to Me, the Lord. ¹² My love is indeed unfailing, yet I will still render to each one according to what they have done.

I AM: WHAT YOU LONG FOR

I am your God and you have earnestly sought Me. Your soul thirsts for Me, your flesh longs for Me like a dry and weary land thirsts for water; ² You have beheld My power and glory in My sanctuary, ³ and have see that My unfailing love is better than life itself, and so you praise Me. ⁴ You have thanked Me and prayed in My name all your life, ⁵ for I satisfy your soul like the richest of foods, therefore your mouth sings to Me for joy!

⁶ Often at night, you lie in bed and remember Me, meditating about Me, ⁷ for I have always been there to help you; under the shadow of My wings you sing for joy, ⁸ your soul clinging to Me, while My strong right hand upholds you.

⁹ All those who seek to destroy your soul will go down into the grave; ¹⁰ they will die by the sword and will be prey for wolves. ¹¹ But you find your joy in Me, your God; indeed, all those who commit their lives to Me will celebrate; but the mouths of hypocrites will be silenced.

I AM: LISTENING TO YOUR PRAYER

I, your God, hear your prayer. I will protect your life from the threats of the enemy. ² I will hide you from the secret plots of the selfish, the schemes of the wicked, ³ who sharpen their tongues like swords and aim bitter words like arrows. ⁴ They ambush the innocent, attacking suddenly without any fear of repercussion. ⁵ They encourage themselves in these evil plots, scheming how to set their traps in secret, saying, "No one will know." ⁶ As they plot their crimes they say, "we have devised the perfect plan!"

Certainly, the human mind and heart are cunning. ⁷ But I, your God, will shoot them with My arrows and they will be struck down suddenly. ⁸ I will turn their own tongues against them and all who see them will shake their heads in scorn. ⁹ Then all will respect Me; they will declare My mighty deeds and reflect about what I have done. ¹⁰ My loving people will rejoice and trust in Me, the Lord. And all those with an honest heart will thank Me.

I AM: GOOD TO YOU

A mighty chorus of praise awaits Me in Zion, where all vows will be fulfilled, ² where all of humanity will come before Me, the God who answers prayer. ³ Though you are overwhelmed by your sins, I will forgive them all!

⁴ How joyful will those I have chosen be when I bring them near to live in My courts; they will be satisfied with the goodness of My house, the blessings of My loving temple. ⁵ By wondrous deeds of righteousness I will answer you, for I am the God of your salvation; I am the hope of everyone on the earth, and across the farthest seas.

⁶ I will form mountains by My strength, for I am clothed with power. ⁷ I will still the noise of the seas and the roar of their waves, and I will calm the tumult of the nations. ⁸ The whole world will stand in awe of My signs and wonders, from where morning dawns, to where evening fades, it will call forth songs of joy.

⁹ I will care for the earth and water it; I will make it rich and fertile. My rivers will be full of water, and I will provide the earth with grain, for I ordain them all. ¹⁰ I will drench its fields, melting the furrows and leveling the ridges, softening the soil with showers, and blessing the plants to grow.

¹¹ I will crown the year with bounty, and your wagons will overflow with abundance. ¹² The grasslands of the wilderness will become a lush pasture, and the hillsides will blossom with joy. ¹³ The meadows will be clothed with flocks, and the valleys will be mantled with grain, all shouting songs of joy.

I AM: GUIDING YOU

*L*et the whole earth shout joyfully to Me, their God. ² Sing about the glory of My name; make it glorious! ³ For My works are awe-inspiring. Even My enemies cringe before My power. ⁴ Let the whole earth worship and sing praise, shouting out My name in glorious song.

⁵ Come and see what I, your God, have done, My wonderful miracles for humanity. ⁶ I turned the sea into dry land so My people could cross on foot, and they rejoiced in Me. ⁷ By My power, I rule forever and keep My eye on the nations; rebels cannot raise a finger against Me! ⁸ So, let all the races of the nations bless Me, your God, let the sound of thanksgiving be heard!

⁹ For I have preserved your lives, and have not allowed your feet to slip. ¹⁰ I, your God, have tried you, like silver purified by fire, I have refined you. ¹¹ You were lured into a net and experienced the heavy burdens of slavery laid upon your backs. ¹² So, I put a leader over you who brought you through fire and flood. I led you through all this to bring you to a place of rich fulfillment.

¹³ So, come and enter My sanctuary through the offering of gratitude; fulfill your vows, ¹⁴ those promises you made to Me

when you were in trouble. ¹⁵ Offer Me the very best sacrifice, the sweet fragrance of roasted lamb.

¹⁶ Come and listen, all you who revere Me and I will declare what I have done for your soul. ¹⁷ You cried out to Me for help, praising Me as you spoke; ¹⁸ and if you had cherished sin in your heart, I, the Lord, would not have listened to you. ¹⁹ But I have certainly heard you and have listened to the words of your prayer. ²⁰ And so you will praise Me, for I have not rejected your prayer, nor will I withdraw My love from you!

I AM: FOR EVERYONE

I, your God, will be gracious to you and bless you. I will make My face shine upon you, ² that My ways will become known throughout the earth, then all nations will know of My salvation.

³ Let all nations worship Me, the True God. Let all races come with thanksgiving! ⁴ 'Let the nations be glad and sing for joy! For I will rule them justly and will guide the people of the whole world.

⁵ Let the nations praise Me, let every race give praise! ⁶ Then the earth will yield its harvest and I, the True God, your God, will richly bless you all. ⁷ Yes, I will bless you, and all the ends of the earth will revere Me.

I AM: YOUR SAVIOR

*W*hen I rise up, My foes will scatter; those who despise Me will flee; [2] as smoke disappears on the wind, so they will be driven away; as wax melts in front of a fire, so too the selfish will perish at My presence. [3] But the loving will be glad and rejoice in My presence; yes, they will be happy and joyful. [4] They will sing to Me, their God, they will sing in exultation to My name when I ride upon the clouds. For My name is, "I AM", and they will rejoice at My presence.

[5] For I am a Father to the fatherless, a defender of widows. From My sacred dwelling [6] I give the lonely a family. I free prisoners and lead them to prosperity. But those who rebel live in a dry and empty land.

[7] When I led My people out from Egypt, when we marched through the desert, [8] the earth shook and the heavens poured down rain at My presence; Mount Sinai itself trembled at the My presence, the God of Israel. [9] I sent plentiful rain to restore the dry and weary land My people would inherit; [10] My flock found a home there, because I provided from My goodness for the poor and needy.

^{11} When I, the Lord, gave the command, the great multitude proclaimed the good news, stating, ^{12} "The kings and their armies have fled, they are on the run!" The women of Israel divided up the Canaanite spoil I gave them. ^{13} When they bed down among the sheepfolds, they opened their bags and found figures of doves covered with silver, their wings glittering with fine gold. ^{14} On that day, I, the Almighty God, scattered the kings, like the snow that fell on windy Mount Zalmon.

^{15} O' majestic Mountains of Bashan, you are high and rugged, with many peaks, ^{16} so why do you gaze in envy when you look at the mountain I have chosen as My dwelling place? I will reside on Mount Zion forever; ^{17} with tens of thousands of chariots, even unnumbered thousands of angels, I, the Lord, will be among them in My sanctuary, just as I was at Mount Sinai.

^{18} When I ascended on high, I lead a crowd of captives free, I received gifts from them, even from those who rebelled against Me. I will live among you there. ^{19} So give praise, for I will load you with benefits every day; for I am the God of your salvation, ^{20} I am the God who saves, and I will rescue you from death!

^{21} I will surely put an end to all of My enemies; those who persist in going on in their corruption. ^{22} I will bring your enemies back, I will even bring them up from the depths of the sea, ^{23} and you will plant your feet over them in conquest; even your dogs will have their share.

^{24} Then they will see My procession, the procession of your God and King, into the sanctuary. ^{25} The singers will go before Me and the musicians will follow after; among them will be young women playing tambourines, singing, ^{26} "Bless God in the great choir; praise the Lord, who is Israel's fountain of life!" ^{27} First will come Benjamin, the smallest tribe in the lead, then the princes of Judah as a group, followed by the princes of Zebulun, and the princes of Naphtali.

²⁸ Then I will summon My power and will show My strength as I have done in the past. ²⁹ And all the kings of the earth will bring gifts to My temple in Jerusalem. ³⁰ I will rebuke these enemy nations, those wild animals lurking among the reeds. I will rebuke that herd of bulls among the weaker calves; I will humble their arrogance and they will bring bars of silver as tribute, all these nations who love to make war. ³¹ Princes will come to Me out of Egypt, and the Ethiopians will bring gifts to Me, the one True God. ³² Then all the kingdoms of the earth will sing to Me and will revere Me, the Lord.

³³ For I am He who rides among the stars of the ancient heavens. Indeed, I send out My voice and it is a mighty roar. ³⁴ So ascribe power to Me, for My majesty shines down on Israel and My power is mighty in the heavens. ³⁵ For I, your God, am terrifyingly powerful in My sanctuary, yet I am the God of Israel, who gives strength and power to My people. So, give praise!

I AM: BUILDING YOU UP

I, your God, will save you. I see that the waters have come up to your neck, ² that you are sinking in miry depths without a foothold. You have come into deep waters and the flood is engulfing you. ³ I see you weary with crying, your throat scratchy and dry, your eyes failing as you look for Me, your God. ⁴ Those who hate you without cause are now more numerous than the hairs of your head. There are many who seek to destroy you, being your enemies for no reason; though you stole nothing, they demand restitution.

⁵ But I, know how foolish you have been; your sins are not hidden from Me. ⁶ Yet I, the Lord God of Heavens Host, will not let those who hope in Me be ashamed because of you. I will not let those who seek Me be embarrassed by your actions. ⁷ It is for My sake that you have chosen to endure insults; their scorn is written all over your face. ⁸ You have even become a stranger to your own family, you are like a foreigner to your own siblings.

⁹ It is zeal for My house that consumed you; and the insults, which were hurled at you, fall on Me. ¹⁰ Even when you wept and humbled your soul by fasting, they still insulted you; ¹¹ when you dressed yourself in mourning clothes, they mocked you. ¹² You

have become the subject of gossip in the streets, and drunkards make up songs about you.

[13] But you kept praying to Me, the Lord, hoping for a time of favor. And in the abundance of My stedfast love, I will answer you with the assurance of My salvation. [14] I will deliver you out of the mire; I won't let you sink. I will rescue you from those who hate you, I will pull you from the deep waters. [15] I won't allow the floodwaters to sweep over you. I won't let you drown in the depths, nor will the grave close its mouth over you.

[16] I, the Lord, hear your prayers, for My unfailing love is good and My mercy is plentiful. [17] I will not hide My face from you, for you are in trouble and I will answer you quickly. [18] I will draw near your soul and redeem you, delivering you from the enemy.

[19] I know you are scorned, shamed, and dishonored; your adversaries are all known to Me. [20] Their insults have broken your heart and filled you with despair. You looked for someone to take pity, but there were none; you looked for comforters, but you found none. [21] They gave you bitter herbs to eat, and for your thirst, they offered you vinegar.

[22] But their table will become a snare before them; a retribution and a trap. [23] Their eyes will go blind, so that they cannot see, and their knees will knock together in terror, [24] for I will pour out My indignation upon them; when fiery judgement takes hold of them [25] their homes will be left deserted, because not one will be left.

[26] For they persecute the ones I have smitten, and add pain to those I disciplined; [27] they heap guilt upon guilt, therefore they will not have any part in My salvation. [28] Their names will be erased out of the book of life; they will not be written among My loving people.

[29] Indeed you are afflicted and sorrowful, but I will protect you with My salvation. [30] Then you will praise My name in song, and will glorify Me with thanksgiving. [31] That will please Me more

than sacrificial offerings. [32] And when the poor see this, they will be glad. Indeed, all you who seek Me, let your hearts come alive! [33] For I, the Lord, listen to those in need and do not forget My captive people.

[34] So, let heaven and the earth sing praise, even the seas and all that move in them; [35] for I will save Zion and will rebuild the cities of Judah. Then My people will settle there and possess it; [36] the descendants of those who obey Me will inherit the land, indeed, all those who love My name will live there in safety!

I AM: YOUR HELPER

I, your God, will rush to rescue you! I, the Lord, will come quickly to help you! ² Those who seek to harm you will be put to shame and confusion. Those who desire to hurt you will be turned back in disgrace. ³ Those who say "Aha, we've got you", will fall back, exposed in their shame. ⁴ So, let all who seek Me rejoice and be glad in Me. Let those who love My salvation repeatedly shout, "God is powerful!" ⁵ For you are poor and needy, therefore I will rush to your side. For I am your help and your deliverer and I will not delay.

I AM: WITH YOU ALWAYS

*I*n Me, your Lord, you have put your trust; I will never let you be put to shame. [2] I will deliver you because I do what is right and will rescue you. I am always listening to you and will save you. [3] I am your rock of safety where you can always hide. I have given the command to save you, for I am your rock and your defensive castle. [4] I, your God, will deliver you from the power of the wicked, from the grasp of those who are selfish and cruel. [5] For I am your hope. The one you have trusted in since you were young.

[6] I have been with you since the day you were born; I am the one who brought you out safely from your mother's womb. You will always have a reason to thank Me. [7] That's why your life has been an example to so many, because I have been your strong refuge. [8] That is why you praise Me and proclaim My glory, [9] because I will never cast you away, not even in your old age; I would never abandon you when your strength is gone!

[10] Your enemies may slander you, conspiring together to harm you. [11] They believe I have abandoned you, so they are out to get you, believing there is no one to rescue you. [12] But I, your God, am not far from you; I will always rush to help you. [13] And your

accusers will be startled and consumed with humiliation; those who try to harm you will be bathed in scorn and disgrace.

[14] You will always have hope, and a reason to praise Me more and more, [15] for even if you told of My love and salvation all day long, you would not be able to tell it all. [16] So go forward in My strength, letting them know that it is found in My righteousness, and Mine alone.

[17] For I, your God, have taught you ever since you were young, and you constantly proclaimed My wondrous works. [18] And now that you are old and your hair is gray, I will not abandon you. I will be with you as you proclaim My power to the next generation, My victorious power to all who are to come. [19] For My love reaches to the highest heavens; I have done so many wonderful things, who can you compare Me to?

[20] Though I have allowed you to see some bitter troubles and calamities, yet, I will revive your life again; I will raise you from your grave and will bring you up again. [21] I will restore you to even greater honor, and will comfort you once again. [22] Then you will praise My faithfulness with stringed instruments. You will sing praises for the Holy One of Israel. [23] And you will shout for joy as you sing to Me, for I have ransomed your soul. [24] Your tongue will proclaim My love all day long, because those who intended to harm you, will be defeated and disgraced.

I AM: GIVING YOU MY SON

I, God, will give My love of justice to the King; My royal Son will be endowed with My love, ² that He may judge My people with righteousness, that the poor will be treated fairly. ³ Then the land will give peace to the people; it will experience the fruits of love. ⁴ He will defend the poor among the people and will save the children of the needy, breaking their oppressors in pieces. ⁵ And they will revere Him as long as the sun and moon endure, throughout all ages to come.

⁶ He will be like rain that falls on the fields, like showers that water the earth. ⁷ Love will flourish in His days, and the abundance of peace, until the moon is no more. ⁸ He will have dominion from sea to sea, from the Euphrates to the ends of the earth. ⁹ The people from the wilderness will bow down before Him; even His enemies will throw themselves to the ground. ¹⁰ The western kings of Tarshish and of the islands will bring gifts; the southern kings of Sheba and Seba will also bring him gifts. ¹¹ Yes, all kings will bow down before Him; all nations will serve Him.

¹² For He will deliver the poor and needy when they cry, all those who have no helper. ¹³ For He feels pity for the poor and needy

and will save their souls. ¹⁴ He will redeem their life from oppression and violence, for their blood is precious in His sight.

¹⁵ My king will live forever. The gold of Sheba will be given to Him and the people will continually pray to Him, praising Him always. ¹⁶ Grain will abound throughout the earth, swaying on the hill tops; fruit trees will flourish like the trees of Lebanon and the people in the cities will blossom like the grass of the field. ¹⁷ His name will endure forever; it will continue as long as the sun. And all nations will be blessed through Him and will call Him blessed.

¹⁸ So give thanks to Me, the Lord God, the God of Israel. For I alone do these wonderful things. ¹⁹ You will bless My glorious name forever! For the whole earth will be filled with My splendor. Amen and Amen. ²⁰ I will fulfill all the prayers of David, the son of Jesse.

BOOK 3

Chapters 73-89
Psalms of Hope

-LEVITICUS-

Asaph
Sons of Korah Grouping II

I AM: ALL YOU NEED

I, God, am indeed good to My people, to the pure in heart. ² You had nearly lost your footing and your steps were on slippery ground ,³ for you were envious of the arrogant when you saw them prosper in spite of their wickedness. ⁴ They seem to have no struggles and are strong and healthy. ⁵ As though they are free from the troubles of common people, like they're not plagued with problems like everyone else.

⁶ They wear pride like a necklace and violence like a robe, ⁷ having more than they could wish, bulging with abundance, ⁸ they scoff with indifference and arrogance about their oppression. ⁹ They openly speak against Me, the God of heaven, and their arrogant tongues boast throughout the earth, ¹⁰ therefore people turn to them and eagerly drink in all their words. ¹¹ They say, "What does God Know? How can the Most High even know what is happening?"

¹² You see these corrupt people enjoying a life of ease while their riches multiply ¹³ and it makes you wonder if it is in vain that you have kept yourself pure, and have lived in innocence? ¹⁴ You feel as though I have made you suffer all day long; that every morning I have disciplined you afresh. ¹⁵ And if you had spoken these

thoughts to others, you would have felt like a traitor. ¹⁶ When you tried to think this problem through, it troubles you deeply.

¹⁷ But then you went into My sanctuary, and you understood the final destiny of the wicked. ¹⁸ Surely they have put themselves in slippery places, for they will be cast down to destruction. ¹⁹ They will be brought to desolation in a moment and will be utterly consumed with destruction. ²⁰ They are like a dream that goes away when you awake, for when I rise up, they will disappear like an illusion.

²¹ When your heart was grieved and your spirit was embittered, ²² you became senseless and stubborn, like a brute beast before Me. ²³ Yet I was always with you and held you by your right hand, ²⁴ for I am guiding you by My counsel, and in the end, I will take you into glory. ²⁵ Who else do you have in heaven but Me? You know there is nothing on this earth you desire besides Me!

²⁶ Your body and heart may fail, but I, God, am the strength of your heart; I am your portion, forever. ²⁷ Those who are far from Me will certainly perish; I will put an end to those who play the harlot. ²⁸ But as for you, it is good for you to draw near Me, your God. For you have put your trust in Me as your refuge, and you will tell everyone the wonderful things I have done for you.

I AM: KEEPING A RECORD

$\mathcal{T}$hough My frustration smolders against the sheep of My pasture, I, your God, have not rejected you. ² I remember that you are the people I chose long ago, the tribe I redeemed as My own special possession; for Mount Zion is where I chose to dwell. ³ I have walked through the awful ruins of the city and I see how the enemy has destroyed everything in My sanctuary.

⁴ The enemy is roaring in the heart of My meeting places; setting up their own standards as signs. ⁵ They behave like woodsmen wielding axes cutting through thick trees. ⁶ With axes and hammers, they break down all its intricate work. ⁷ They have set fire to the sanctuary and defiled the dwelling place of My name, burning it to the ground. ⁸ They said to themselves, "Let's destroy it completely"; so they burned up every place where I, your God, am worshipped.

⁹ Because you do not see any signs from Me and there are no longer any prophets, nor do any of you know how long this will last, ¹⁰ you ask Me, "How long will the adversary reproach us, O God? Will the enemy dishonor Your name forever? ¹¹ Why do you

withhold Your hand, Your right hand? Unleash Your power and finish them!"

[12] But I am King from of old, working out salvation on the earth. [13] It was I that split open the sea by My power; I broke the heads of the dragons in the waters; [14] I am the one that crushed the heads of the leviathans and gave them as food for the animals of the wilderness. [15] It was I that broke open the fountains in the flood, and who dried up its never ending stream. [16] The day is Mine, the night also is Mine. I created the moon and the sun. [17] It was I that set all the boundaries of the earth, and made both summer and winter.

[18] I, the Lord, remember how the enemy has mocked Me, I see the foolish people that have reviled My name. [19] I would never deliver the soul of My dove to these wild beasts; I never forget the lives of My afflicted people. [20] I will honor My covenant; indeed, the dark places of the earth are haunts full of cruelty, [21] but I will never let the oppressed be disgraced again.

So, let the poor and needy give thanks to My name. [22] For I, God, will rise up and defend it. I will remember how fools scoffed at Me daily. [23] I will not forget the voice of My enemies; for the chaos of those who rise up against Me is becoming an uproar.

I AM: GOD

Give thanks to Me, your God, give thanks, for I am near. People everywhere testify of My wonderful deeds. ² For I have set an appointed time for judgment and I will judge with fairness. ³ When the earth totters and all its inhabitants melt with fear, I will keep its foundations steady.

⁴ I have warned the proud to not be arrogant; and I have warned the wicked to not lift up their fists; ⁵ do not raise your power against heaven, or speak so stubbornly. ⁶ For no one from the east or from the west, or from the south should exalt themselves. ⁷ For I, God, am the judge: only I can decide who will rise or fall.

⁸ In My hand, I hold a cup, and the wine is red and foaming, it is full of mixture, and when I pour it out in judgment, all the wicked of the earth will drink it down to the last drop. ⁹ But My people will rejoice forever, they will sing of gratitude to Me, the God of Jacob. ¹⁰ For I will cut off the power of the wicked; but the power of the loving will forever be lifted up.

I AM: WORTHY OF RESPECT

I am honored in Judah; My name is great in Israel. ² For I made Jerusalem My dwelling and Mount Zion My home. ³ From there I will break the fiery arrows, the shields and swords, yes, all the weapons of war. ⁴ Indeed, I, your God, am glorious and more majestic than the everlasting mountains.

⁵ The mightiest will lie plundered, they will sink into the sleep of death and not one of their warriors will lift their hand against Me. ⁶ At My rebuke both horses and chariots will fall still. ⁷ Is there any wonder that people fear Me, for who can stand before Me once My indignation rises? ⁸ When I pronounce judgment from heaven the earth will tremble and stand silent before Me; ⁹ for I will stand up in judgement and will save all the oppressed of the earth.

¹⁰ Surely My judgement against humanity will end in praise; and whatever wrath is left, I will restrain. ¹¹ So, when you make your vows to Me, the Lord your God, follow through with them. Let all the nations who are around Me bring tribute, because I am worthy of reverence; ¹² for I humble arrogant rulers and terrify even great kings.

I AM: LEADING YOU

*Y*ou cried out to Me, your God, for help, you shouted for Me to hear you! ² In your time of trouble you sought Me. Stretching out your hand at night in prayer, you waited, but your soul could not be comforted. ³ When you thought about Me you were troubled, and you felt overwhelmed; ⁴ you were so worried you couldn't even speak; it kept you awake all night!

⁵ So you thought about the good old days, as well as the ancient times. ⁶ You recalled it in songs throughout the night and searched your heart. And in your spirit you wondered, ⁷ had I, your Lord, rejected you? Would I ever again show you favor? ⁸ Has My unfailing love vanished forever? Were My promises at an end for all time? ⁹ Have I ceased to give you grace? Have I, in anger, withdrawn My compassion?

¹⁰ You appealed to the years when I, the Most High, gave you the favor of My right hand. ¹¹ You called to mind the many miracles I've done, including the great deeds of long ago. ¹² You contemplated My miracles and spoke of all My powerful deeds. ¹³ For you know that My ways are loving, and that there are no other gods as mighty as I am!

[14] Indeed, I am the God who works miracles, showing My power among the nations. [15] By My power I redeemed My people, the descendants of Jacob and Joseph. [16] When the Red Sea saw Me its waters were afraid, the sea trembled to its very depths. [17] The clouds poured down rain and thunder crashed from the sky while arrows of lightning flashed. [1]

[8] My thunder roared in the whirlwind, the lightning lit up the earth as it trembled and quaked. [19] For My way led through the sea and through the mighty waters. A pathway no one even knew was there. [20] So too, will I lead you, just as I did the flock of My people by the hand of Moses and Aaron.

I AM: GOOD TO MY PEOPLE

*L*isten to My teachings My people, pay attention to what I am saying, ² for I have used parables to explain hidden lessons since ancient times, ³ stories you have heard and known, told to you by your ancestors. ⁴ Don't hide these truths from your children. Tell the next generation about My glorious deeds, about My power and the miracles I have done.

⁵ For I gave the witness in Jacob and My laws to Israel. I instructed your ancestors to teach them to their children. ⁶ So that generations to come might know them, and they in turn, would teach their children. ⁷ Thus each generation would learn to trust in Me, their God, never forgetting the miracles I did, and keeping My commandments. ⁸ Then they will avoid becoming like their predecessors, a stubborn and bitter generation who refused to give their hearts to Me, whose spirit was unfaithful to Me.

⁹ The descendants of Joseph, though armed and carrying bows, turned their backs and fled on the day of battle. ¹⁰ They did not keep My covenant and refused to live by My law. ¹¹ They forgot what I had done, the great wonders I had shown them; ¹² the miracles I did for their ancestors in the land of Egypt at the Nile Delta. ¹³ I divided the sea and took them through it. I made the

waters stand up like a heap! [14] I led them with a cloud by day and throughout the night with a pillar of fire. [15] I split the rocks open in the wilderness and gave them water as abundant as the sea. [16] I made streams pour out of a rock and made waters flow down like a river.

[17] But they murmured against Me even more, rebelling in the wilderness against the Most High. [18] They deliberately put Me to the test by demanding the food they craved. [19] They spoke against Me saying, "God should spread out a buffet for us in this wilderness! [20] If He can strike a rock and water gushes out, can't He also give His people some fresh bread and some meat?"

[21] When I, the Lord, heard these words, I was indignant, fiery wrath burned against Jacob as My anger with Israel grew. [22] For they did not believe Me, nor did they trust that I could save them. [23] I had already commanded the clouds above and opened the doors of the heaven, [24] raining down manna for the people to eat. I had given them bread from the sky! [25] They were eating the food of angels and had already been given all the food they could eat!

[26] Therefore, I caused an east wind to blow, and by My power I stirred up the south wind, [27] I rained meat down on them like dust! I sent down birds, as many as the grains of sand on the seashore; [28] I even had them fall in the middle of the camp all around their tents. [29] And the people ate until they were gorged, for I, God, gave them what they lusted after. [30] But before they had satisfied their craving, while the meat was still in their mouths, [31] fed up, My anger erupted, and I struck down the strongest men and best young men of Israel with a plague.

[32] In spite of all this, the people kept on with their rebellion; regardless of My miracles, they did not believe. [33] So I ended their days in futility, all their years were filled with troubles. [34] For, it was only when I disciplined them that they would finally seek Me; only then would repent and sincerely seek Me. [35] They would remember that I was their Rock, and that I, the Most High, was

their Redeemer. ³⁶ But their words were all flattery. Nothing they said was sincere. ³⁷ Their hearts were not loyal to Me, nor were they faithful to My covenant.

³⁸ But I, God, being full of compassion, forgave their guilt, and did not destroy them. Yes, many times I turned My anger away and restrained My fury. ³⁹ I remembered that they were only mortal beings, like a breath of wind that blows by and is gone. ⁴⁰ Oh, how often they rebelled against Me in the wilderness, grieving My heart in that wasteland. ⁴¹ Again and again they put Me to the test, provoking Me, the Holy One of Israel. ⁴² They forgot My power and how I had redeemed them from the enemy. ⁴³ Nor did they acknowledge how I had performed mighty miracles in Egypt, all of the wonders I did on the plain of Zoan.

⁴⁴ For I turned Egypt's rivers and streams into blood, so that the Egyptians had no water to drink. ⁴⁵ I sent swarms of flies that tormented them, and frogs that ruined their land. ⁴⁶ I gave their crops to the caterpillar and their produce to the locust. ⁴⁷ I destroyed their grapevines with hail and their fig trees with frost. ⁴⁸ I struck their cattle with hail and their livestock with bolts of lightning. ⁴⁹ I unleashed on Egypt the fierceness of My anger, all of My fury, indignation, and hostility, by sending angels of destruction among them. ⁵⁰ I did not restrain Myself, nor did I spare a soul from death; I gave their lives over to the plagues, ⁵¹ destroying all the first-born in Egypt, the first-fruits of the descendants of Ham.

⁵² I then led My people out like a shepherd, guiding them through the wilderness like a flock. ⁵³ I led them safely, they had nothing to fear, for the sea engulfed their enemies. ⁵⁴ I then brought them to the border of My holy land, to the hill country which My right hand had acquired. ⁵⁵ I drove out the nations before them and gave their lands to them as an inheritance, settling all the tribes of Israel in their homes.

⁵⁶ Even after all this, they rebelled against Me, the Most High God, and put Me to the test. They did not live by My teachings, ⁵⁷ but turned away and were faithless like their parents, unreliable as a crooked arrow. ⁵⁸ They provoked Me to anger with their shrines of worship to other gods, provoking Me to jealously with their idols.

⁵⁹ I was furious when I saw it; I abhorred Israel. ⁶⁰ So I abandoned My dwelling in Shiloh, the home where I had lived among mortals. ⁶¹ I allowed their enemies to capture the Ark of our Covenant, the symbol of My glory. ⁶² I was indignant with My own people and let them be destroyed by their enemies. ⁶³ Young men were killed in war and young women had no wedding songs. ⁶⁴ Priests fell by the sword and their widows could not mourn their deaths.

⁶⁵ Then I, the Lord, woke as though from sleep. I was like a warrior shouting because of wine. ⁶⁶ I drove Israel's enemies back, I put them in perpetual shameful defeat. ⁶⁷ But I rejected the descendants of Joseph; I did not choose the tribe of Ephraim. ⁶⁸ Instead, I chose the tribe of Judah, and Mount Zion which I loved. ⁶⁹ I built My Sanctuary there, towering like the heavens and as solid and enduring as the earth. ⁷⁰ I then chose My servant David, calling him from tending sheep and lambs in the pasture. ⁷¹ I brought him to be the shepherd of My people, Israel, My inheritance. ⁷² David cared for them with a true heart, leading them with wise and skillful hands.

I AM: SALVATION

I, God, see that unbelievers have invaded My land, that they have defiled My sanctuary, leaving Jerusalem in ruins. ² They left the dead bodies of My followers for the vultures, the flesh of My godly people were left for wild beasts to feast upon. ³ Their blood was shed like water all through Jerusalem, and there was no one left to bury the dead. ⁴ You are mocked by your neighbors, an object of scorn and ridicule to all those around.

⁵ So you asked Me, "Lord, how long this will go on? Will You be angry with us forever? Will Your jealousy burn like a wildfire? ⁶ When will You pour out Your indignation on the people that refuse to acknowledge You, on the nations that do not call on Your name?" ⁷ Indeed, I see that they have devoured My people, making the land a desolate wilderness. ⁸ I will not hold the guilt of past generations against you. My tender mercies will come quickly to meet you, for you are in desperate need.

⁹ I, the God of your salvation, will help you, I will deliver you and provide atonement for your guilt, for I am honorable. ¹⁰ For why should the nations say, "Where is your God?" I will make known among the nations that I avenge the outpoured blood of those who

follow Me. [11] For the cry of the prisoners have come before Me, and with My powerful arm I will save those condemned to die. [12] I, the Lord, will pay back the enemy seven times the contempt they have hurled at Me. [13] Then you, My people, the sheep of My pasture, will thank Me forever and praise Me for all time to come.

I AM: RESTORING YOU

J, the Shepherd of Israel, am listening, for I lead My people like a flock. I, who am enthroned between angelic cherubim, radiant in glory, will come and save you. ² I will show My strength for the tribes of Ephraim, Benjamin, and Manasseh and will come and save you. ³ I will restore you; I will make My face shine upon you, so that you may be saved.

⁴ I, the Lord God of Heavens' Armies, will not be grieved by the prayers of My people forever. ⁵ For I have fed you with the bread of sorrow, I have given you tears to drink by the bucketful. ⁶ I made you an object of scorn to your neighbors and your enemies laugh among themselves. ⁷ But I, the Almighty, will restore you; I will make My face shine upon you, that you may be saved.

⁸ I transplanted a vine from Egypt, I drove out the nations and planted it. ⁹ I prepared the ground for it, and it took deep root and filled the land. ¹⁰ It blanketed the hills with its shadow, even the mighty cedars were overshadowed by its boughs. ¹¹ It extended its branches to the Mediterranean Sea, even as far as the Euphrates River. ¹² But I was forced to break down its walls so that anyone passing by could pluck its fruit; ¹³ then wild boars from the forest

began to uproot it and wild animals from the fields began devouring it.

^{14} But I, the God of hosts, will return; for I look down from heaven and see your plight; I will again take care of the vine, ^{15} the vineyard which My right hand planted, the branch that I, Myself, made strong. ^{16} For the enemies that have cut the vine down and set it on fire will perish at the rebuke of My appearing.

^{17} My hand will protect the one who is at My right hand, the Son of Man whom I, Myself, made strong. ^{18} Then you will never turn away from Me, for I will revive you and you will call on My name. ^{19} I, the Lord God of Heavens' Armies, will restore you, I will make My face shine upon you , that you may be saved.

I AM: LONGING FOR YOU

*S*ing aloud to Me, the God of your strength; make a joyful shout for Me, the God of Jacob! ² Start the music, strike the tambourines, play some beautiful music on the harps and the lute. ³ Sound the shofar horn at the time of the New Moon, at the full moon, on the day of the festival. ⁴ This is an appointed time in Israel, a decree from Me, the God of Jacob.

⁵ I gave it to the people of Joseph as a testimony of when I subdued the land of Egypt. When they heard a voice, they did not know say, ⁶ "I removed the burdens off your shoulders; I freed your hands from the heavy tasks. ⁷ You cried to Me in your trouble, and I delivered you." I answered them from the thundercloud on the mountain and tested them at the waters of strife. ⁸ Saying, "Hear Me, My people, when I warn you. O' Israel, if only you would listen to Me! ⁹ There must be no foreign gods among you; never worship another god. ¹⁰ For I, the Lord your God, am the One who brought you out of Egypt. When you open your mouth wide, I will fill it!"

¹¹ But My people would not listen to My voice; Israel wanted nothing to do with Me. ¹² So, I eventually let them go after their own stubborn hearts, to follow their own ideas. ¹³ O' how I wish

My people would listen to Me, that Israel would walk in My ways. [14] How quickly I would subdue their enemies and turn My hand against their foes! [15] For those who hate Me, may pretend to submit to Me, but their fate will last forever; [16] I could have fed them with the finest wheat, I would have satisfied them with wild honey from the rock!

I AM: JUDGE

I, God, preside over heaven's court; I render judgment among the rulers who act as gods. [2] How long will they judge unjustly and show partiality to the corrupt? [3] Defend the weak and the orphans; uphold the cause of the oppressed and the destitute! [4] Rescue the poor and needy, free them from the hands of criminals.

[5] You know nothing, you understand nothing! You walk around in darkness, and now the foundations of the world are unstable. [6] I said, "You are gods; all of you are children of the Most High." [7] But you will die like mere mortals; you will fall like every other ruler. [8] For I, God, will arise and judge the earth, because all nations are My inheritance.

I AM: SUPREME

I, God, will not remain silent; I will not hold my peace; I will not stand aloof! ² I see how My enemies are in revolt, how those who hate Me have reared their heads. ³ They devise crafty schemes against My people and conspire against those I cherish.

⁴ "Come," they say, "Let us destroy their nation, so the name of Israel will be forgotten forever." ⁵ With one mind they plot together, forming an alliance against Me; ⁶ the people of Esau and Ishmael, Moab and the Hagrites; ⁷ Gebal, Ammon, and Amalek, Philistia and the residents of Tyre. ⁸ Even Assyria has joined them to reinforce Lot's descendants.

⁹ I will deal with them as I did Midian and Sisera and Jabin at the river of Kishon; ¹⁰ they were destroyed at Endor and became like dung on the ground. ¹¹ Their leaders will die like Oreb and Zeeb; indeed, all their rulers will die like Zebah and Zalmunna ¹² who said, "Let us seize for our own use these pasturelands of God!"

¹³ I will scatter them like dust-devils, like tumbleweeds blown away by the wind. ¹⁴ As wildfire consumes the forest, or as a flame sprints up the mountainside, ¹⁵ I will pursue them with My raging

tempest and terrify them with My storms. [16] I, the Lord, will cover their faces in shame and they will acknowledge My power. [17] They will be ashamed and dismayed forever and will perish in complete disgrace. [18] Then they will know that I alone can be called "Lord", for I am the Ruler over all the earth.

84

I AM: OVERFLOWING

How lovely is the sanctuary where I, the Lord of heaven's armies, dwell. ² Your soul longs, even faints, for My courts. Your body and soul cry out for Me, the living God. ³ Even the sparrow has a home, and the swallow builds her nest, raising her young near My altars, where I, the almighty, am your King.

⁴ Those who live in My house are filled with joy, they are always singing of gratitude. ⁵ Blessed are those whose strength is in Me, whose hearts are set on pilgrimage. ⁶ As they pass through the dry valley of weeping, it will become a place of springs, the autumn rains will cover it with pools. ⁷ They will grow stronger and stronger, as they go until each appears before Me in Zion.

⁸ I, the Lord God of heaven's armies, hear your prayers. I am listening. ⁹ I will bless the King, who protects you, I will show favor to My anointed. ¹⁰ One day in My court is better than a thousand anywhere else. You would rather serve as a doorkeeper in My house, than live in the mansions of the corrupt.

¹¹ For I am your sun and your shield, and I will give grace and honor to you; I will withhold no good thing from those who walk

sincerely. [12] Blessed is the one who trusts in Me, the Lord Almighty.

I AM: FULL OF MERCY

I, the Lord, will pour out blessings on My land; I will bring back the captives of Israel. ² I will forgive My people's sin and pardon all their guilt. ³ I will set aside all My fury and hold back My fierce anger. ⁴ I, the God of your salvation, will restore you and will put away My displeasure with you. ⁵ I will not be angry with you forever, nor will I prolong My indignation to all generations.

⁶ I will revive you, so that My people may rejoice in Me. ⁷ I will show you mercy and grant you My salvation. ⁸ Listen carefully to what I am saying, for I will speak peace to My faithful people, but they must not go back to their foolish ways. ⁹ Surely My salvation is near those who revere Me, for that is how My glory dwells in your land.

¹⁰ Then mercy and truth will meet together; righteousness and peace will kiss one another; ¹¹ truth will spring forth from the earth, and love will look down from heaven. ¹² I, the Lord, will indeed give what is good and your land will yield its harvest. ¹³ For justice will go before Me and I will make My footsteps, your pathway.

I AM: COMFORTING YOU

I will bend down and hear your prayer, for you are poor and needy. ² I will guard your life because you are devoted to Me. I am your God and I will save you, for you trust in Me. ³ I will have mercy on you, for you cry out to Me all day long.

⁴ I will bring joy to your soul, because you put your trust in Me. ⁵ For I, the Lord, am good, and ready to forgive. I am abundant in mercy to all those who call upon Me. ⁶ I, the Eternal, hear your prayer and will listen closely to your cries for help. ⁷ Whenever you are in trouble, call upon Me, for I will answer you.

⁸ Among the gods, there is none like Me. Not one has done what I have done! ⁹ All the nations that I have created will come and bow before Me, they will glorify My name, ¹⁰ for I am majestic and My works are wondrous; indeed, I alone am God.

¹¹ I will teach you My ways, so you can walk in My truth; I will grant you a pure heart that you may honor My name. ¹² With all your heart you will praise Me, the Lord your God, and you will glorify My name forevermore. ¹³ My love for you is great, therefore I will deliver your soul from the depths of the grave.

[14] I see the proud have risen against you; ruthless mobs seeking to harm you— people that have no regard for Me. [15] But I am a compassionate and gracious God, slow to anger, abounding in love and faithfulness. [16] I will turn to you and have mercy on you. I will give My strength to you and save you, because you follow Me just as your mother did. [17] I, the Lord, will show you proof of My goodness, that those who hate you may see it and be put to shame, for I, the Eternal, will help you and comfort you.

I AM: SAVING ALL WHO ARE MINE

I, the Lord, founded My city on the sacred mountain; ² I love the gates of Zion, more than all the cities of Israel. ³ Glorious things are spoken of you, O' My city.

⁴ I will also acknowledge from Egypt and Babylon all those who know Me; the people of Philistia too, and Tyre, along with Ethiopia, and I will say, "this one was born of Zion".

⁵ And of Zion it will be said that, "everyone enjoys the rights of citizenship there". And I, the Most High, will personally establish it. ⁶ I will record in the register all the peoples that are born of Zion. ⁷ As they make music they will sing, "All the springs of life are from You."

I AM: STILL HERE

*B*efore Me, the God of your salvation, you have cried out day and night. ² Your prayer has come before Me and I have turned My ear to your cry. ³ Your soul is so overwhelmed with troubles that your life draws near to death; ⁴ you are counted among the dying who go down into the grave, for all your strength is gone. ⁵ You feel adrift among the dead, like a corpse lying in the grave, remembered no more, and cut off from My care.

⁶ You believe I have thrown you into the lowest pit, into the darkest depth. ⁷ Because My displeasure lies heavy upon you, you are engulfed by all its waves. ⁸ Even your friends have been driven away because you are repulsive to them. You feel trapped, unable to escape. ⁹ Your eyes are blinded by tears because of your grief. Every day you beg Me for mercy, stretching out your hands, pleading: ¹⁰ "Are Your wonderful deeds of any use to the dead? Shall the dead rise up and praise You? ¹¹ Can Your lovingkindness be declared from the grave? Or Your faithfulness in the place of decay? ¹² Can Your wonders be known in its darkness? Or Your righteous deeds in the land of the forgotten?"¹³ And so you cry out to Me, the Lord; every morning your prayers come before Me.

¹⁴ But I, the Lord, have not rejected your soul. I have not hid My face from you. ¹⁵ You have suffered and been close to death since the days of your youth and you are worn out with the terror and hopelessness. ¹⁶ Wrath has swept over you and you are terrified you have been cut off. ¹⁷ It surrounds you like a flood and has completely engulfed you. ¹⁸ Because your loved ones and friends have been taken from you, it feels like darkness is your only friend.

89

I AM: ALWAYS FAITHFUL

*Y*ou will sing of My great love forever, you will make My faithfulness known to young and old. ² You will tell them how My unfailing love will stand firm forever, for I have established My faithfulness in heaven itself. ³ I made a covenant with My chosen servant David, ⁴ I promised him I would establish his seed forever and make his throne firm from now until eternity.

⁵ All the heavens extol My wonders, myriads of angels praise Me for My faithfulness. ⁶ For who in the heavens can be compared to Me, who among the heavenly beings is anything like Me? ⁷ In the council of the holy ones, I, your God, am greatly feared; I am revered by all those around Me. ⁸ For I am the Lord God of heaven's armies, majestic in power, and clothed with integrity!

⁹ I rule over the oceans, subduing their storm tossed waves. ¹⁰ I crushed Egypt and scattered My enemies by My mighty arm. ¹¹ The heavens are Mine, the earth also is Mine; the world and everything in it are Mine, for I created it all. ¹² I created the north and the south; Mount Tabor and Mount Hermon rejoice in My name. ¹³ My arm is endowed with power, My right hand is mighty and exalted!

¹⁴ For righteousness and justice are the foundation of My throne; mercy and truth go before Me. ¹⁵ Those who hear the call to worship are filled with joy, for they walk in the light of My presence ¹⁶ They rejoice all day long in my wonderful name, exulting in My love. ¹⁷ For I am their glory and strength and in My favor they are made strong; ¹⁸ I, the Lord your King, the Holy One of Israel, am their protector.

¹⁹ I spoke in a vision to My prophets and said: "I have found a mighty hero for My people; I have exalted one chosen from the people. ²⁰ I found My servant David and anointed him My sacred oil. ²¹ My hand will sustain him; surely My arm will strengthen him. ²² The enemy shall not outwit him, nor will the corrupt subdue him. ²³ I will crush his foes before him and strike down those who hate him. ²⁴ My faithfulness and mercy will be with him, and by My authority, he will grow in power. ²⁵ I will set his hand over the sea, his right hand over the rivers. ²⁶ He will call out to Me, 'You are my Father, my God, and the rock of my salvation.' ²⁷ I will make him My first-born, higher than the kings of the earth. ²⁸ I will love and be kind to him forever, and my covenant with him will never fail; ²⁹ his seed will endure forever, and his throne, as the days of heaven."

³⁰ But if his children forsake My law and do not live according to My commands, ³¹ if they disregard My instructions and do not keep My commandments, ³² then I will discipline them for their rebellion with the rod, and their disobedience with stripes. ³³ Nevertheless, I will not take My lovingkindness away from him, nor allow My faithfulness to fail. ³⁴ I will not break My covenant, nor alter the words that have gone out of My lips. ³⁵ Once for all, I have sworn by My sanctity, I will not lie to David: ³⁶ His seed shall endure forever and his throne will endure before Me like the sun. ³⁷ It shall be established forever like the moon, that faithful witness in the sky.

³⁸ Yes, I rejected and I spurned because I was dismayed with My chosen one. ³⁹ I renounced the covenant with My servant, I defiled

his crown, casting it to the dust. ⁴⁰ I broke through all his walls and brought his strongholds to ruin. ⁴¹ All who pass by plundered him and he became a reproach to his neighbors. ⁴² I exalted the right hand of his adversaries and made all his enemies rejoice. ⁴³ Indeed, I turned back the edge of his sword and did not sustain him in battle. ⁴⁴ I made his glory cease and cast his throne down to the ground. ⁴⁵ I shortened the days of his youth and covered him with a mantle of shame.

⁴⁶ But I, the Lord, will not hide Myself forever. My displeasure will not always burn like a fire. ⁴⁷ I remember how short your time is, the futility of humanity. ⁴⁸ No one can live and never see death, for who can escape the power of the grave? ⁴⁹ But I, the Lord, will remember My unfailing love which in My faithfulness I swore to David. ⁵⁰ For I remember how My servant was mocked; how you bore in your heart the insults of all the nations; ⁵¹ how your enemies taunted you, how they mocked every step of My anointed one. ⁵² You will thank Me, your Lord, forever, surely you will.

BOOK 4

Chapters 90-106
Psalms of Deliverance

-DEUTERONOMY-

Congregational Praise Grouping I

90

I AM: HUMBLING YOU

I, the Lord, have always been your home, throughout all generations. ² Before the mountains were born, before I gave birth to the earth, from eternity to eternity, I am God. ³ I turn people back to dust, saying, "Return to dust, O mortal children". ⁴ For a thousand years to Me are like one day; they are like yesterday, already gone, like a short watch in the night. ⁵ People are swept away by death, they last no longer than a dream. They are like grass that sprouts in the morning, ⁶ they grow and burst into bloom, then dry up and die by evening.

⁷ You wither with fear beneath My wrath and are terrified by My fury; ⁸ for your guilt is set out before Me, and your secrets are revealed in the light of My presence. ⁹ Therefore all the days of your life pass by under fear of My displeasure, finishing your years with a sigh. ¹⁰ Seventy years is all you have, eighty years if you are strong; yet the best of them are but labor and sorrow; for they quickly pass, and you fly away.

¹¹ Who can comprehend the full power of My fury? My wrath is as great as the fear that it is due. ¹² So I will teach you to realize how short your life is, that you may gain a heart of wisdom. ¹³ For at the right time, I, the Lord, will return and have pity on My

servants. ^{14} I will satisfy you each morning with unfailing love, that you may sing for joy and be glad all your days. ^{15} I will make you glad for as many days as you were afflicted, for all the years you saw trouble.

^{16} Then I will show My mighty deeds to My servants, and My splendor to their children. ^{17} I, the Lord your God, will let My favor rest upon you and I will establish the work of your hands for you; yes, I will bring success to all you do!

I AM: YOUR REFUGE

$\mathcal{T}$hose who take refuge in the shelter of the Most high, will be safe under My Almighty shadow. [2] They will say of Me, "Lord, You are my shelter and my mighty protector. You are my God; I place all my trust in You." [3] Surely I will deliver you from the snares of the enemy, and from deadly diseases. [4] I will cover you with My feathers, and under My wings you will find shelter; My faithfulness will be your shield and armor of protection.

[5] So don't be afraid of the terrors of the night, nor the sudden attacks that fly by day. [6] Do not dread the disease that stalks in darkness, nor the disaster that strikes at high noon. [7] A thousand may fall at your side, and ten-thousand at your right hand, but it will not come near you [8] For with your own eyes you will see the punishment of the corrupt.

[9] Because you have made Me, the Lord, your refuge, even the Most High, your dwelling, [10] no harm will come near you, nor will plague come near your home. [11] For I will command My angels to protect you wherever you go. [12] They will lift you up in their hands, lest you strike your foot against a stone. [13] Then you will

trample upon lions and snakes, you will crush fierce lions and poisonous snakes under your feet.

[14] I will rescue those who love Me, I will protect those who trust in My name. [15] When you call on Me, I will answer you; I will be with you in trouble, and I will deliver you and honor you; [16] I will reward you with long life and show you My salvation.

I AM: YOUR ROCK

*I*t is beautiful when you give thanks to Me, singing praises in My name; [2] when you proclaim My love in the morning and My faithfulness at night [3] on stringed instruments like the lute and harp. [4] You sing for joy because of what My hand has accomplished, so you rejoice in all I have done for you. [5] Indeed, the works I do are vast, for My thoughts are very deep.

[6] Ignorance refuses to see it, and fools do not understand, [7] that even though the wicked sprout like weeds, and those who do evil succeed, they are doomed to eternal destruction. [8] But I, the Lord, will be exalted forever. [9] Look at My enemies, surely all of them will perish, everyone who lives selfishly will be scattered to the winds.

[10] But I have made you as strong as a wild ox. I have poured fresh oil over you. [11] Your eyes will see the downfall of your enemies, and your ears will hear the retreat of the wicked that rise up against you. [12] For the loving will flourish like palm trees; they will grow like the cedars of Lebanon. [13] Those who are planted in My house will flourish in My courts. [14] They will still bear fruit in old

age and will always remain vital and flourishing. [15] They will proclaim that I, the Lord, am just. For I am their Rock, and there is no evil in Me.

I AM: MIGHTY

I, the Lord, reign, clothed in majesty, robed and armed with strength. Just as the world is set firmly in place and cannot be moved, ² so too My throne has stood from time immemorial, for I am eternal. ³ So when the ocean floods the shore, when the sea is roaring, and the waves are pounding, ⁴ know that I am mightier than the noise of the raging ocean, mightier than the crashing waves of the sea. ⁵ For My promises stand firm, and I will reign in love forever.

I AM: THE AVENGER

I am the Lord God, to whom vengeance belongs. I will avenge and justice will shine forth. ² I, the Judge of the earth, will rise up and will render judgement upon the proud. ³ You ask Me, "Lord, how long will the corrupt triumph?" ⁴ I see how they pour out their arrogant words; these selfish people only boast about themselves. ⁵ They crush My people and oppress those who belong to Me. ⁶ They kill widows and foreigners and murder the fatherless. ⁷ They say, "The Lord does not see us; the God of Israel does not care."

⁸ Think again you dimwits, when will you fools be wise? ⁹ I who made the ear, do I not hear? I who made the eye, do I not see? ¹⁰ If I discipline nations and correct them, do you think that I, who teach humanity knowledge, would lack knowledge? ¹¹ I, the Lord, know your very thoughts, and they are futile.

¹² Those who I convict and teach out of My law are happy. ¹³ I give them relief in troubled times, until the pit is dug for the corrupt. ¹⁴ For I will not reject My people. I will never forsake those who belong to Me! ¹⁵ Justice will be restored in the judgment, and all those with good hearts will support it!

16 I will stand up for you against the wicked. I will protect you from the wicked! 17 For unless I, the Lord, give you help, you would have disappeared into the silence of death. 18 When you say, "My foot is slipping", My unfailing mercy will hold you up! 19 When doubts fill your mind, My comfort will give hope to your soul.

20 I will not align with corrupt governments who bring misery through their laws, 21 who gather together against the loving and condemn the innocent. 22 For I, the Lord, am a defense. I am the Rock in whom you can take refuge. 23 And I will repay evil people for their sins, and destroy them for their corruption. I, the Lord your God, will wipe them out.

I AM: CALLING YOU

_C_ome, sing for Me, the Lord. Shout joyfully, for I am the Rock of your salvation. ² Come before Me with thanksgiving and sing joyful songs of praise. ³ For I am the great God, the great King above all gods.

⁴ In My hand are the deep places of the earth, even the heights of the mountains belong to Me. ⁵ The sea is Mine for I made it, My hands also formed the dry land. ⁶ Come, bow down in worship, kneel before Me, your Maker. ⁷ For I am your God, and you are the people of My pasture, the flock under My care.

Today, if you hear My voice, ⁸ do not harden your hearts with defiance as Israel did at the waters of Meribah, like the day they complained in the wilderness of Massah. ⁹ Your ancestors tested Me, wanting Me to prove Myself, though they had already seen what I had done for them.

¹⁰ For forty years I was grieved by that generation. Which is why I said, "they are a people whose hearts go astray from Me, and do not follow My ways". ¹¹ Therefore in My anger I declared an oath, they will never enter My rest.

I AM: A JUST GOD

*S*ing to Me a new song; let all the earth sing to Me. [2] Sing to Me, the Lord, giving thanks to My good name; proclaim the good news of My salvation day after day. [3] Declare My glory among the nations, My marvelous deeds to all peoples. [4] For I am majestic and am worthy of praise.

I am revered above all so called gods, [5] for all the gods of the nations are only idols; but I created the heavens! [6] Splendor and majesty surround Me; strength and beauty fill My sanctuary. [7] Attribute to Me, the Eternal, all you families of nations, attribute to Me glory and might. [8] Give to Me the glory due My name. Bring your offerings and come into My courts [9] worshipping in the beauty of love.

[10] Say among the nations, "The Lord reigns!" For just as the world is set firmly in place and cannot be moved, so too will My judgement of the nations be fair. [11] So let the heavens rejoice and let the earth be glad; let the seas roar and every creature in them; [12] let the fields be joyful and all that is in them; let all the trees in the forest sing for joy! [13] Let all creation rejoice before Me, the Lord, for I am coming to judge the earth. I will judge the world faithfully, according to what is loving and just, for all the races of the nations.

I AM: GUARDING YOU

I, the Lord, reign, let the earth rejoice, let even distant shores be glad. ² I ride upon the thick storm clouds that surround Me, for the foundation of My throne is justice and righteousness. ³ Fire goes before Me and consumes My foes on every side. ⁴ My lightning lights up the world; the earth sees it and trembles. ⁵ The mountains melt like wax before Me, the Lord of all the earth.

⁶ The heavens proclaim My love and every nation can see My glory in it. ⁷ Those who serve human images, who boast in their idols, will be put to shame, for all gods bow down before Me, the Lord. ⁸ Zion hears this and rejoices, all the cities of Judah are glad, because of My judgements. ⁹ For I am the Most High, ruler of all the earth; I am exalted far above all gods.

¹⁰ Let those who love Me hate evil, for I guard the souls of My faithful ones; I deliver them out of the power of the wicked. ¹¹ For light shines on the loving, as does joy for those whose hearts are right. ¹² So, rejoice in Me, your Lord, you who are vindicated, and give thanks when you remember My sacred name.

I AM: KEEPING MY PROMISES

*S*ing a new song to Me, the Lord! Indeed I have done a marvelous thing! My right hand and My sanctifying arm have won a mighty victory! ² I have made My Salvation known and have revealed My justice to the nations. ³ I kept My promise to love and be faithful to Israel, even the very ends of the earth have seen My salvation!

⁴ So, let all the earth shout for joy to Me, the Lord your God; break forth into jubilant song and praise! ⁵ Sing to Me with the harp and with melodious songs. ⁶ Blow trumpets and rams horns, and shout joyfully before Me, your King!

⁷ Let the sea roar and everything in it shout praise! Let the world and all living things join in! ⁸ Let the rivers clap their hands and the mountains sing joyfully together before Me, the Lord. ⁹ For I am coming to judge the earth and I will judge the people of the world with justice and fairness.

I AM: EXALTED

I, the Lord, reign, and the nations tremble in awe. For I sit enthroned between the angelic cherubim; even the earth quakes before Me. ² For I am majestic in Zion and I am exalted over all nations. ³ Let everyone give thanks to My great and good name, for I am Love itself. ⁴ For I, the Mighty King, love what is just and have established fairness and I have done what is just and true in Israel. ⁵ So, exalt in Me as you bow before Me, for I am the Lord your God, and I am Love!

⁶ Moses and Aaron were among My priests, and Samuel was among those who called upon My name; they cried out to Me, the Lord, and I answered them. ⁷ I spoke to them from the pillar of cloud and they heeded the laws and commands I gave them. ⁸ I answered them and was to them, "the God who forgives"; though I disciplined them when they went wrong. ⁹ So, rejoice in Me, the Lord your God, as you worship at My sacred mountain, for I am Love.

I AM: HAPPINESS

*L*et all the earth shout with joy before Me, the Lord. ² Serve Me with gladness! Come into My presence with singing! ³ Know this: I, the Lord, am the True God. I am the One who made you and you are Mine; you are My people, the flock of My pasture. ⁴ So, enter My gates with thanksgiving and come into My courts with praise. Share your gratitude with Me and bless My good name; ⁵ for I, the Lord, am good, My mercy is everlasting, and My truth endures to all generations.

I AM: PROUD OF YOU

*Y*ou are always singing of My love and justice, praising Me in song. ² I will indeed come and help you; for you have been careful to live a life of integrity, and have conducted your affairs with a honest heart, even in your home! ³ You refuse to set anything that is vile before your eyes, hating the way faithless people live; you will have no part in it! ⁴ You keep away from perverse people, staying away from evil. ⁵ Nor do you tolerate those who slander their neighbor behind their back, or put up with anyone who is proud and arrogant. ⁶ Your eyes have sought out the faithful in the land to be your friends, and you only allow those who walk with integrity to work with you. ⁷ Those who make a practice of deceit are not allowed to stay in your home as you don't make alliances with those who are liars; ⁸ for you have made a point of removing the wicked in the land, cutting off every evildoer from holding positions of power in My city.

102

I AM: ALWAYS WITH YOU

I, the Lord, hear your prayer; your cry for help has come to Me. ² I won't turn away from you in your time of trouble. I will bend down and listen to you, I will answer you quickly in the day that you call. ³ For your life is vanishing like smoke; your bones burn like glowing embers. ⁴ Your heart is beaten down and withered like grass and you have lost your appetite.

⁵ In your distress, you groan aloud; you are reduced to nothing but skin and bones. ⁶ You are like a wild bird in the wilderness, like an owl among abandoned ruins; ⁷ you lie awake, lonely as a solitary bird on a rooftop. ⁸ All day long your enemies insult you; those who rail against you use your name as a curse. ⁹ For you have eaten ashes like bread and your tears run down into your drink. ¹⁰ Because of My wrath, you feel like I have picked you up and thrown you out. ¹¹ Your life passes as swiftly as a shadow and you wither away like a flower.

¹² But I, the Lord, sit enthroned forever; My fame endures throughout every generation. ¹³ So I will arise and have mercy on Zion, for the time has come to show grace to her; the appointed time has come. ¹⁴ For My people hold its very stones dear and

cherish even the dust in her streets. ¹⁵ Then the nations will tremble at the name of the Lord and all the kings of the earth will tremble before My glory. ¹⁶ For I, the Lord, will rebuild Zion when I appear in My glory.

¹⁷ I will respond to the prayer of the destitute; I will not reject their pleas. ¹⁸ Let this be recorded for future generations, that the people not yet born may praise Me, the Lord. ¹⁹ For I look down to earth from My heavenly sanctuary, ²⁰ I hear the groans of her prisoners and I will release those condemned to die.

²¹ Then My name will be celebrated in Zion and they will praise Me in Jerusalem ²² when the nations and kingdoms assemble to worship before Me. ²³ For I broke your strength in midlife, cutting your days short. ²⁴ And so you cry out to Me, "O' God, don't take me away while I am so young! For You are eternal and Your years continually unfold throughout all generations!"

²⁵ Indeed, I laid the foundations of the earth long ago, even the heavens are the work of My hands. ²⁶ Yet even they will perish and still I will endure. They will all wear out like old clothing; I change them like a garment and discard them. ²⁷ Yet I remain the same, for My years have no end. ²⁸ So too, the children of My people will live in safety and their children will thrive in My presence.

I AM: SLOW TO ANGER

*B*less Me, the Lord, with all your soul, let all that is within you give praise for My loving name. ² Give thanks with all your heart, and do not forgot all of My benefits. ³ For I forgive all your sins and heal all your diseases. ⁴ I will redeem your life from the grave and crown you with love and mercy. ⁵ I will satisfy your desires with good things, so that your youth is renewed like the eagle's. ⁶ For I will give righteousness and justice to all the oppressed.

⁷ I even revealed My plans to Moses and my miracles to the children of Israel; ⁸ for I, the Lord, am compassionate and gracious, slow to anger, and abounding in love. ⁹ Therefore, I will not always chide you, nor will I keep My anger forever. ¹⁰ For I have not dealt with you according to what your sin deserves, nor punished you according to your faults. ¹¹ For as high as the heavens are above the earth, so great is My love for those who revere Me. ¹² As far as the east is from the west— that is how far I have removed your transgressions from you.

¹³ As a father has compassion on his children, so I, the Lord, am tender and compassionate with those who revere Me. ¹⁴ For I know how weak you are, I remember that you are only dust. ¹⁵

The life of mortals is like grass, they flourish like a flower of the field, ¹⁶ then the wind blows on it and it is gone— as though they had never been here. ¹⁷ But for those who revere Me, My love remains forever, and My salvation will extend to the great-grandchildren ¹⁸ of those who are faithful to My covenant, remembering My commandments and obeying them.

¹⁹ For I, the Lord, have established My throne in heaven; from there My kingdom rules over everything. ²⁰ Even My mighty angels praise Me, carrying out My plans, heeding the voice of My word. ²¹ So, give praise all you heavenly hosts, you minsters of Mine, who do My will. ²² Give thanks to Me all My creations, everywhere in My dominion. Praise Me, your Lord, with all your soul!

I AM: VERY POWERFUL

*G*ive praise with all your soul, for I, the Lord your God, am very powerful. I am clothed with splendor and majesty. [2] I wrap myself in light like a garment. I stretch out the starry heavens like a curtain, [3] and lay the rafters of My upper room in the thunderclouds. I make the clouds My chariot and ride upon the wings of the wind. [4] The winds are My messengers and flames of fire, My ministers.

[5] I laid the earth upon its foundations and it can never be moved. [6] I placed the ocean over it like a robe and the waters stood above the mountains. [7] At My rebuke, the waters fled; at the thunder of My voice, they hurried away. [8] The mountains rose and the valleys sank down, to the levels I had decreed for them. [9] I set a boundary the seas can never pass over, so they will never again cover the earth.

[10] I send springs into the valleys and streams flow down from the mountains. [11] They provide water for all the wild animals, for wild donkeys to quench their thirst. [12] The birds of the sky nest by the waters and sing among the branches. [13] From My lofty abode, I water the mountains and the earth is satisfied with the fruit of My works. [14] I make grass grow for the cattle and plants for people to

cultivate, I bring forth food from the earth— 15 wine to gladden their hearts, oil t0 make their faces shine, and bread to strengthen their hearts.

16 My trees are well watered, the cedars of Lebanon, which I planted. 17 The birds build their nests there and the stork has a home among the cypress trees. 18 The high mountains are for the wild goats, their crags are a refuge for the badgers among the rocks. 19 I appointed the moon to mark the seasons and the sun knows when to set. 20 I bring darkness and it becomes night, when all the beasts of the forest prowl. 21 The lions roar for their prey, looking for the food that I, their God, provide. 22 When the sun rises, they steal away, returning to lie down in their dens. 23 Then the people go out to do their work, where they labor until evening.

24 I, the Lord, have made so many things. In wisdom I made them all. The earth is filled with My creatures, 25 even the vast and wide ocean, where innumerable creatures live, both large and small. 26 Where ships sail to and fro, and Leviathan, which I formed, plays. 27 All creatures look to Me to give them food when they need it. 28 When I give it to them, they gather it up; when I open My hand, they are satisfied with good things. 29 And when I hide My face, they are terrified; when I take away their breath, they die and return to the dust. 30 But when I send My Spirit's breath, life is created and I renew the face of the earth.

31 And so, My glory will endure forever, for I am the Lord, and I rejoice in My creations. 32 When I look at the earth, it trembles, when I touch the mountains, they smoke. 33 So, sing to Me as long as you live, sing songs of praise to your last breath. 34 For your meditation is sweet to Me when you find joy in Me. 35 But the sinners will vanish from the earth; the selfish will disappear forever. So, give praise with all your soul. Give thanks to Me, your Lord.

I AM: ALWAYS LEADING YOU

*G*ive thanks to Me, the Lord, call upon My name; tell the whole world what I have done. ² Sing to Me, sing songs to Me. Talk of all My wondrous works. ³ Celebrate My loving name; let all the hearts of those who seek Me rejoice. ⁴ Seek Me when you need strength, continually seek Me. ⁵ Remember the miracles I did, My marvels and judgements. ⁶ For you are the seed of Abraham My servant, you, the children of Jacob, are My chosen ones.

⁷ I am the Lord your God, and My justice extends to every corner of the earth. ⁸ I stand by the promise of My covenant forever, unto a thousand generations. ⁹ The covenant I made with Abraham and My oath to Isaac ¹⁰ was confirmed to Jacob as law and to Israel as a never-ending covenant, ¹¹ when I promised to give him the land of Canaan as his inheritance.

¹² I said this when My people were still few in number and strangers in the land. ¹³ They wandered from country to country, from one kingdom to another; ¹⁴ yet I did not allow anyone to oppress them. For their sake, I rebuked kings, saying, ¹⁵ "Do not touch My chosen people, and do not harm my prophets." ¹⁶ I then

called down famine on the land of Canaan, cutting off its food supply.

¹⁷ Then I sent a man ahead of them to Egypt, Joseph, sold as a slave. ¹⁸ They bruised his feet with shackles, his neck was put in irons, ¹⁹ until the time his dreams came to pass and My word proved him true. ²⁰ So the king of Egypt sent and released him; the ruler of the nation set him free. ²¹ He made him master of his house and ruler of all his possessions, ²² instructing his princes as he pleased and teaching his elders My wisdom.

²³ Then Israel also came to Egypt and Jacob dwelt in the land of Ham. ²⁴ I, the Lord, made My people very fruitful and made them too numerous for their enemies. ²⁵ The hearts of the Egyptians came to hate My people, they began to conspire against My servants. ²⁶ So, I sent My servants Moses and Aaron, who I had chosen. ²⁷ They performed My miracles and wonders among them, in the land of Ham.

²⁸ Because they rebelled against My command to let My people go, I blanketed Egypt in darkness.. ²⁹ I turned their waters into blood and caused their fish to die. ³⁰ Then their land was overrun with frogs, even in the bedrooms of their kings. ³¹ I spoke, and flies and lice swarmed throughout the whole country. ³² I gave them hail for rain and lightning throughout their land. ³³ I struck down their grapevines and fig trees, shattering the trees of their country. ³⁴ I spoke and locusts came, grasshoppers without number; ³⁵ they devoured all the vegetation in their land and ate up all the crops in their fields. ³⁶ I struck down all the first-born in their land, the first-fruits of all they had.

³⁷ This is how I brought My people out of Egypt, laden with silver and gold; and among all of Israel's tribes, not one was feeble or sickly. ³⁸ Egypt was glad when they left, for the fear of Israel had fallen on them. ³⁹ I then spread out a cloud as a covering and fire to give light at night. ⁴⁰ The people asked and I sent them quail

and satisfied them with the manna of heaven. [41] I split the rock and water gushed out, flowing in the desert like a river.

[42] For I remembered My sacred promise to Abraham My servant. [43] Therefore I brought My people out of Egypt with joy, My chosen ones were rejoicing. [44] I gave My people the lands of the corrupt nations, and they harvested crops that others had planted. [45] All this happened so that My people would follow My ways and keep My laws. Therefore, give thanks to Me, your Lord.

106

I AM: PRAISEWORTHY

I, the Lord, am worthy of praise. So, give thanks to Me, for I am good; and My love endures forever. ² Who could possibly list all of My mighty acts or fully declare My glory? ³ There is joy for those who act justly and do what is right! ⁴ I will remember them when I help My people, for I will give them My salvation. ⁵ And they will share in the prosperity of My chosen ones, rejoicing in the gladness of My people, triumphing with those who belong to Me!

⁶ You know you have sinned just like your ancestors did; you have done wrong and have acted selfishly. ⁷ Your ancestors in Egypt took My miracles for granted; they soon forgot My many mercies, and rebelled against Me at the Red Sea. ⁸ Nevertheless I saved them, because of My promise, that I might make My mighty power known. ⁹ So, I rebuked the Red Sea, and it dried up, and I led them through the depths as through a desert. ¹⁰ I saved them from the hand of the foe and redeemed them from the hand of the enemy. ¹¹ The waters covered their enemies, not one of them was left. ¹² Then they believed My words and sang praises to Me.

¹³ But they soon forgot what I had done and did not wait for My plan to unfold. ¹⁴ While in the wilderness, they gave into their

cravings and put Me, their God, to the test. [15] So, I gave them what they asked for, but sent leanness to their soul. [16] Those in the camp grew envious of Moses and Aaron, who were consecrated to Me. [17] So, the earth opened up and swallowed Dathan, and buried the faction of Abiram; [18] fire blazed among their followers and flames consumed the corrupt.

[19] Then at Sinai they made a calf and worshiped a molded idol; [20] they traded My glory for the image of a bull eating grass! [21] They forgot Me, the God who had saved them, who had done such wondrous things in Egypt, [22] all the amazing miracles I performed in the land of Ham! Such powerful things at the Red Sea! [23] Fed up, I would have destroyed them had not Moses, My chosen one, pled for them and stood between us, to keep My anger from destroying them.

[24] Then, because they did not believe My promise to care for them, they refused to enter the promised land! [25] Instead, they complained in their tents and refused to listen to Me, the Lord. [26] So, I raised My hand and swore an oath to them, 'I would let them die in the wilderness [27] and would scatter their descendants among the nations, exiling them to distant lands."

[28] Then at Peor, they joined in the worship of Baal and ate sacrifices offered to the dead! [29] They provoked Me to anger by their actions, so I sent a plague that broke out among them; [30] but Phinehas stood up and intervened and the plague was stopped. [31] Thus he was regarded as a just man ever since, and will be for all time to come.

[32] Again, by the springs of Meribah, they again angered Me, and trouble came to Moses because of them, [33] for they rebelled against My Spirit and rash words came from Moses' lips. [34] Nor did they destroy the corrupt nations, as I, the Lord, had commanded them; [35] instead, they intermarried with them and adopted their pagan ways. [36] They served idols, which became a trap for them. [37] They even sacrificed their sons and their daughters to false gods! [38] They

shed the blood of innocent children, the blood of their sons and daughters, who they sacrificed to the idols of Canaan, and the land was desecrated by their blood!

[39] They defiled themselves by what they did, by their deeds they prostituted themselves. [40] This is why I, the Lord, was angry with My people and abhorred My inheritance. [41] So, I abandoned them to the power of other nations and their foes ruled over them. [42] Their enemies oppressed them and they were in complete subjection to their power. [43] I delivered them many times, but they were bent on rebellion and wasted away in their corruption.

[44] Yet, even then, I pitied them when I heard their cries. [45] For their sake, I remembered My covenant, and because of My great love, I relented. [46] I caused those who carried them away captive to take pity upon them. [47] That's why I, the Lord your God, will save you. I will gather you back from among the nations, that you may give thanks for My loving name and triumph in My goodness. [48] So give praise from everlasting to everlasting. Let all the people say Amen and hallelujah.

BOOK 5

Chapters 107-150
Psalms of Thanksgiving

-NUMBERS-

Alleluiah
Songs of Ascent
Davidic Grouping III
Congregational Praise Grouping II

107

I AM: ANSWERING PRAYER

*G*ive thanks to Me, the Lord, because I am good; My faithful love endures forever. ² Let the redeemed tell the story of how I rescued them from the hand of the enemy. ³ For I gathered them out from the nations, from the east and from the west, from the north and from the south. ⁴ Some of them wandered in the wilderness, lost and far from home. ⁵ Hungry and thirsty, their life was ebbing away. ⁶ So, they cried out to Me in their trouble and I delivered them. ⁷ I led them straight to safety, to a city they could call home. ⁸ O' that they would give thanks for My unfailing love and the wonderful works I have done for them.

⁹ I satisfy the thirsty soul and fill the hungry with good things. ¹⁰ Some were in the darkness of the deepest depression, imprisoned in iron chains of misery, ¹¹ all because they had rebelled against My word and scorned My counsel. ¹² So, I let them become worn out from bitter labor, and when they fell, there was no one there to help them. ¹³ Then in their trouble, they cried out to Me and I saved them from their distress. ¹⁴ I brought them out of their darkness and depression, and I broke their chains in pieces. ¹⁵ So, let them praise Me, the Lord, for My unfailing love, and all the wonderful things I have done for them. ¹⁶ For I broke down their prison gates of bronze and cut the bars of iron in two.

¹⁷ Some were fools, they rebelled and suffered affliction because of their sins. ¹⁸ They couldn't even keep food down and were knocking on death's door. ¹⁹ Then in their trouble they cried out to Me, the Lord, and I saved them from their distress. ²⁰ I sent out My Word and healed them; I rescued them from the grave. ²¹ O' that they would give thanks to Me for My unfailing love, and all the wonderful things I have done for them. ²² Let them offer the sacrifices of thanksgiving and tell of My works with songs of joy!

²³ Some went out on the sea in ships, they were merchants on the mighty waters. ²⁴ They saw what I, the Lord, can do, My wonderful deeds in the deep. ²⁵ For I spoke and stirred up a storm that made huge waves. ²⁶ Their ships were tossed to the heavens and plunged again into the depths. In their terror, their courage melted away. ²⁷ They reeled and staggered like drunkards; they were at their wits end. ²⁸ Then in their trouble they cried out to Me and I brought them out of their distress. ²⁹ I calmed the raging storm to a whisper and the waves of the sea were still. ³⁰ They were glad when it grew calm and I guided them safely to harbor. ³¹ O' that they would give thanks to Me, the Lord, for My great love, and for the wonderful things I have done for them. ³² Let them proclaim My greatness in the assembly of the people and praise Me before the leaders of the nation.

³³ I turned rivers into a desert, flowing springs into thirsty ground. ³⁴ I made fruitful land into a salty wasteland because of the wickedness of those who lived there. ³⁵ But I also turned the desert into pools of water and parched ground into flowing springs of water. ³⁶ I brought the hungry to live there, that they could found a city and settle there. ³⁷ They sowed fields and planted vineyards that yielded a fruitful harvest. ³⁸ I blessed them and they had many children, nor did their herds diminish.

³⁹ But when My people were diminished and brought low through oppression, affliction, and sorrow, ⁴⁰ I poured contempt on their leaders and caused them to wander in empty wastelands. ⁴¹ Yet, I

lifted the needy out of their affliction, and increased their families like a flock. ⁴² The upright saw this and rejoiced while all the corrupt shut their mouths. ⁴³ Whoever is wise will observe these things, and they will understand My lovingkindness, for I am the Lord.

I AM: YOUR VICTORY

I, your God, see your heart is steadfast! You sing and write music with all your soul! ² So, awaken your harp and lute and wake up the dawn! ³ Give thanks to Me, your Lord, among the peoples, and sing praises among the nations. ⁴ My great love is higher than the heavens; My faithfulness reaches to the skies. ⁵ For I am exalted above the heavens and My glory covers all the earth.

⁶ I will save you with My right hand, so that My beloved may be delivered! ⁷ I promise upon My sacred honor, you will rejoice when I parcel out Shechem and distribute the Valley of Succoth to My people. ⁸ Gilead is mine, Manasseh is mine; Ephraim is my helmet and Judah my lawgiver. ⁹ I will use Moab as a wash-pot, I will throw My sandal at Edom, and will shout in triumph over Philistia.

¹⁰ Who will bring you into the fortified city? Who will give you victory over Edom? ¹¹ You have asked, "O God, have you cast us off? Will you no longer go out and fight in our battles?" ¹² I will help you in your trouble, for human help is worthless. ¹³ With My help, you will do mighty things, for I am the One who will defeat your enemies.

I AM: HERE FOR YOU

I, the God who you praise, will not keep silent. ² For the mouth of those who are selfish and deceitful have opened against you; they have spoken against you with lying tongues. ³ With words of hatred they surround you, attacking you for no reason. ⁴ In return for your love, they are your accusers—even as you are praying for them! ⁵ For they have rewarded you evil for good and hatred for your love.

⁶ They curse, saying, "Appoint corrupt judges against them; let accusers stand on their right hand. ⁷ So, when they are tried, they will be found guilty, and their own prayers will condemn them. ⁸ May their days be few; may someone else take their position. ⁹ May their children become orphans, and their spouse, bereaved. ¹⁰ May their children become homeless beggars that are driven out of their ruined homes. ¹¹ May the bank seize all they have, and may strangers plunder the fruits of their labor. ¹² May no one extend kindness to them, nor anyone take pity on their orphaned children. ¹³ May all their descendants be cut off, and may their name be blotted out by the second generation. ¹⁴ May the guilt of their fathers be remembered before the Lord, and their mother's guilt never be forgiven. ¹⁵ May their guilt remain forever before the Lord, and let Him remove all memory of them from the earth."

¹⁶ They have refused to show kindness, persecuting the poor and the needy, and hounding the brokenhearted to death. ¹⁷But as they loved to curse others, so it will come back on them. As they never blessed others, so blessings will be far from them. ¹⁸ Cursing is as natural to them as is clothing, like the water they drink, or the rich foods they eat. ¹⁹ Yet, their own curses will wrap around them like clothing, they will be tied around them like a belt. ²⁰ This is how I will reward the accusers who speak evil of you.

²¹ I, the Sovereign Lord, will help you because I am honorable; out of the goodness of My love, I will deliver you. ²² For you are poor and needy, and your heart is wounded within you. ²³ Like an evening shadow you fade away, you are blown away like an insect. ²⁴ Your knees are weak from fasting; you are nothing but skin and bones. ²⁵ You are an object of scorn to your accusers; when they see you, they shake their heads.

²⁶ I, the Lord your God, will help you; because of My unfailing love, I will save you. ²⁷ And your enemies will know that it is My hand that has done it. ²⁸ They may curse you, but I will bless you. Those who attack you will be put to shame, but My servant will rejoice. ²⁹ Your accusers will be clothed with dishonor; they will wear their own shame like a robe. ³⁰ But you will enthusiastically thank Me and will praise Me in the assembly of the people, ³¹ Because I stand at the right hand of the needy, to save them from those who would condemn them.

I AM: VICTORIOUS

I, the Lord, said to your Lord, "Sit here at My right side until I make Your enemies a footstool under Your feet". ² For I will extend Your mighty scepter from Zion, proclaiming, "Rule in the midst of Your enemies!" ³ Your people will serve You willingly in the day of Your power. Arrayed in loving splendor, your youth will be renewed every day like the morning dew. ⁴ For I have sworn an oath and will not change My mind, "You are a priest forever according to the order of Melchizedek."

⁵ I, the sovereign Lord, will be at Your right hand as You crush kings on the day of judgement. ⁶ You will judge the corrupt nations, filling their lands with the dead; the rulers and military leaders of their nations will lie among them without distinction. ⁷ And when You are finished, You will drink from the brook along the way, and will raise Your head victorious!

I AM: REVERED

*G*ive praise and gratitude with your whole heart as you meet together with My people, for I am the Lord! [2] For My deeds are mighty and all who delight in Me should ponder them. [3] Indeed, My works are honorable and glorious, and My love endures forever.

[4] I have done wondrous miracles to be remembered, for I am gracious and full of compassion. [5] I have provided food for those who revere Me, and I am ever mindful of My covenant. [6] I have shown My people My great power by giving them the lands of corrupt nations. [7] The works of My hands are always faithful and just toward My people and everything I command is trustworthy and sure. [8] They will stand fast forever and ever, for they are done in truth and uprightness.

[9] I provided redemption for My people and I have guaranteed My covenant to be forever. My renown is holy and awe-inspiring. [10] Reverence for Me, the Lord, is the beginning of wisdom. All who follow My commandments will grow in understanding. For My praise endures forever.

I AM: GIVING YOU SUCCESS

*G*ive praise to Me, the Lord. For those who revere Me are blessed, finding great delight in My commandments. ² Their children will be successful; the entire generation of those who are godly will be blessed. ³ Wealth and riches will be in their houses, and their love will endure forever.

⁴ Even in darkness, light will shine for the upright, for they are gracious, full of compassion, and just. ⁵ Good will come to those who are generous and lend freely, who conduct their affairs honestly. ⁶ The loving will never fall; they will be remembered forever. ⁷ They will have no fear of bad tidings, for their hearts are steadfast when they trust in Me, their Lord.

⁸ Their hearts are secure, they have no fear, for in the end, they know they will look in triumph over their foes. ⁹ And so they generously scatter their gifts to those in need. Their righteousness will endure forever, for their strengths will be exalted in honor. ¹⁰ The corrupt will see this and be infuriated; they will gnash their teeth, yet they will waste away, for the desires of the corrupt will come to nothing.

I AM: WORTHY OF PRAISE

*G*ive thanks, for I am the Lord. Give thanks all My servants, come and boast in My name. ² Let My name be celebrated both now and forevermore. ³ From the rising of the sun to the place where it goes down, let My name be lifted up.

⁴ For I am exalted above all nations; My glory is even above the heavens. ⁵ Who is like Me, the Lord your God, the One who sits enthroned on high, ⁶ who humbles Himself to behold the things that are in the sky and on the earth?

⁷ I raise the poor from the dust and lift the needy from the garbage heap. ⁸ I set them among princes, even the princes of My own people. ⁹ I give the barren woman a family, and make her her a happy mother. So, give praise, for I am your Lord!

I AM: YOUR DELIVERANCE

*W*hen Israel came out of Egypt, and Jacob's descendants left that foreign land, ² Judah became My sanctuary, and Israel became My dominion. ³ The sea saw it and fled; even the Jordan River turned back. ⁴ The mountains skipped like rams, and the little hills like lambs.

⁵ What ails you, O' sea, that you fled? And you, O' Jordan, why did you turn back? ⁶ Why, O' mountains, did you skip like rams, and you little hills like lambs? ⁷ Because the earth trembles at My presence, for I am the Lord God of Jacob, ⁸ who turned flint hard rock into flowing fountains and pools of refreshing water.

I AM: REAL

*N*ot to yourself, but to My name give glory, f0r I, the Lord, am loving and faithful. [2] Why should the nations say, "Where is your God?" [3] For I am in heaven doing whatever I choose. [4] But their gods are metal and wood, the work of human hands. [5] They have mouths, but they cannot speak, they have eyes but they cannot see. [6] They have ears, but they cannot hear, they have noses, but they cannot smell. [7] They have hands, but they cannot feel; they have feet, but they cannot walk; nor can their throat make a sound. [8] All those who made them and all those who trust in them will become just like the idols they have made.

[9] O' Israel, trust in Me, your Lord, for I am your help and your shield. [10] O' you priests, trust in Me, for I am your help and your shield. [11] You who revere Me trust in Me, for I am your help and your shield. [12] I remember you and will bless you; I will bless the house of Israel, I will bless the house of My priests. [13] I will bless those who revere Me, the great and the small alike. [14] I will cause you all to flourish more and more, both you and your children.

[15] I, the Maker of heaven and earth, will bless you. [16] For the highest heavens belong to Me, but the earth, I have given to

humanity. [17] The dead cannot sing praise Me, the Lord, for they have gone into the silence of the grave. [18] It is you, the living, who give Me glory, both now and forevermore. So, give thanks to Me, your Lord.

I AM: LISTENING

*Y*ou love Me because I have heard your voice, I heard your prayer for mercy. ² Because I have bent down to listen to you, you have decided to pray to Me as long as you live. ³ For death entangled you in its ropes, the anguish of the grave closed in on you and you were overcome by anxiety and sorrow. ⁴ Then you called on My name, "I beg you Lord, deliver my soul!"

⁵ I am gracious and loving; I, your God, am full of compassion. ⁶ I protect the naive; so when you were brought low, I saved you. ⁷ Let your soul be at rest, for I have been good to you. ⁸ I have delivered your soul from death, your eyes from tears, and your feet from stumbling. ⁹ All so that you can walk in My presence in the land of the living.

¹⁰ You trusted Me when in your anxiety you said, "I am deeply troubled Lord, ¹¹ everyone is telling lies!" ¹² Now you wonder, "how you can repay the Lord for all His goodness?" ¹³ By lifting up the cup of salvation and giving glory to My name! ¹⁴ By fulfilling your vows to Me in the presence of all My people.

¹⁵ For the death of My faithful servants is deeply precious to Me. ¹⁶ And truly, you are My servant; you serve just as your mother did,

and so I freed you from the chains of death. ¹⁷ Therefore give the sacrifice of thankfulness when you call upon My name. ¹⁸ Fulfill what you have committed to Me, the Lord, in the presence of all My people. ¹⁹. In the courts of My house, in the midst of Jerusalem, give a testimony of praise!

I AM: KIND

*G*ive praise all you nations, for I am the Lord! Boast in My name all you peoples! ² For great is My loving kindness towards you, and My truth endures forever. Give praise, for I am the Lord!

I AM: REDEMPTION

*G*ive thanks for I, the Lord, am good, and My love endures forever. ² Let Israel say, "His love endures forever." ³ Let My priests say, "His love endures forever." ⁴ Let all who have reverence for Me say, "His love endures forever."

⁵ In your distress, you called on Me and I answered you and set you free. ⁶ I am with you, so don't be afraid; what can mere mortals do to you? ⁷ I am with you, I am your helper. You will triumph over those who hate you. ⁸ Therefore, it is better to trust in Me than to put your confidence in people. ⁹ It is better to trust in Me than to trust in rulers.

¹⁰ Though hostile nations surrounded you, you defeated them in My name. ¹¹ They were around you on every side; yet you defeated them in My authority. ¹² They swarmed around you like bees, but they were consumed as quickly as a brush fire; you defeated them in My name. ¹³ You were fiercely attacked and about to fall, but I helped you. ¹⁴ For I, the Lord, am your strength and song, and I have become your salvation.

¹⁵ The shouts of joy and victory are in the homes of the godly; for My right hand is valiant; ¹⁶ My right hand is raised in triumph; My right hand has done glorious things! ¹⁷ You will not die; instead,

you will live to proclaim what I have done. [18] Though I have chastened you severely, I have not given you over to death. [19] So, open the gates of righteousness and go in, giving thanks to Me, your Lord. [20] This is the gate through which only the loving may enter.

[21] Give thanks, for I have answered you, and I have become your salvation! [22] For the stone that the builders rejected has become the cornerstone! [23] This is My doing and it is marvelous to behold. [24] This is the day that I, the Lord, have promised; so rejoice and be glad! [25] For I will save you and will grant you success. [26] He who comes in My name is blessed; you will bless Him from My sanctuary.

[27] I, the Lord, am God, and I have given you light. So, bind the sacrifice with cords to the horns of the altar. [28] For I am your God, and you will thank Me; you will exalt in Me! [29] O' give thanks, because I am good and My love endures forever.

I AM: THE LAWGIVER

*M*y Law of Love (א Aleph)

¹ Those who walk with integrity, who live according to My law are filled with joy. ² Those who keep My testimonies, who seek Me, the Lord, with their whole heart are blessed. ³ They do not live perversely, but walk in My ways. ⁴ I gave My precepts, so you would be careful to keep them. ⁵ O' that your actions were consistent in following My teachings. ⁶ Then you would not be ashamed when you contemplate all of My commandments. ⁷ You will thank me with an honest heart, as you learn My laws of love. ⁸ When you keep My teachings, you will never be forsaken.

YOUTH AND MY LAW OF LOVE (ב BETH)

⁹ How can a young person stay on the path of purity? By living according to My word. ¹⁰ When you seek Me with your whole heart, I will not let you stray from My commandments. ¹¹ For you have hidden My word in your heart, that you might not disobey Me. ¹² Therefore I, the Lord, will teach you My ways and you will praise Me. ¹³ With your own lips, you will declare all the laws that

come from My mouth. [14] You rejoice in following My commands as though rejoicing over an immeasurable fortune! [15] You meditate upon My instructions and contemplate My ways, [16] therefore, because you delight in My laws, you will never forget My word.

HAPPINESS IN MY LAW OF LOVE (ג GIMEL)

[17] I will deal bountifully with you, My servant, that you may live and keep My word. [18] I will open your eyes that you may see the wonderful truths in My law. [19] You are only a foreigner on this earth, therefore, I will not hide My teachings from you. [20] Your soul aches with longing for My wise rulings at all times. [21] I rebuke those who are proud and arrogant, who are accursed, and who stray from My commandments. [22] But you have kept My decrees, therefore, I will remove from you their scorn and contempt. [23] Though leaders plot together and slander you, you, My servant, meditate on My teachings, [24] for My instructions are your delight; they are your counselors.

GRACE IN MY LAW OF LOVE (ד DALETH)

[25] Your soul has been laid low in the dust, but I will revive you according to My word. [26] You have told Me your plans and I answered you. I will teach you My ways. [27] I will help you to understand the path of My precepts, that you may meditate on My wonderful works. [28] Your soul is weary with sorrow, but I will strengthen you according to My word. [29] I will keep you from deceitful ways, and in My grace, I will teach you My laws. [30] You have chosen the way of faithfulness and have set your heart on My laws. [31] You cling to My instructions, therefore I, the Lord, will not let you be put to shame. [32] Because you pursue My commandments, I will enlarge your heart with wisdom.

. . .

Revival in My Law of Love (ה He)

³³ I, the Lord, will teach you how to live My law, that you may follow it to the end. ³⁴ I will give you understanding, that you may keep My law, and observe it with your whole heart. ³⁵ I will lead you in the path of My commandments, for you delight in them. ³⁶ I will turn your heart toward My testimonies, and not toward covetousness. ³⁷ I will turn your eyes away from worthless things, and revive you in My word. ³⁸ I will fulfill My promise to you, My servant, for you are devoted to revering Me. ³⁹ Therefore, I will take away the disgrace you fear, for My laws are just and good. ⁴⁰ I see how you long for My teachings, so I will revive you in My love.

Joy in My Law of Love (ו Waw)

⁴¹ I, the Lord, will come to you in unfailing mercy, to give you the salvation I promised; ⁴² then you can answer anyone who taunts you, for you trust in My word. ⁴³ I will never take the word of truth from your mouth, for you have put your hope in My teachings. ⁴⁴ So, keep My law continually, forever and ever, ⁴⁵ and you will walk in freedom because you pursue My precepts. ⁴⁶ Then you will speak My commandments before kings and will not be put to shame. ⁴⁷ For you find joy in My commands because you love them. ⁴⁸ You honor and love My commandments and meditate upon My teachings.

Confidence in My Law of Love (ז Zayin)

⁴⁹ I remember My promise to you, for I have given you hope. ⁵⁰ It brings you comfort in the midst of your troubles; My promise has given you life. ⁵¹ Though the proud mock you unmercifully, you have not departed from My law. ⁵² You remember My ancient laws and they bring you comfort. ⁵³ Outrage grips you because of the selfish who have forsaken My law. ⁵⁴ For My teachings are the

theme of your songs wherever you journey. [55] Even in the night you remember Me, your Lord, that you may keep My law. [56] To keep My teachings has become the rule of your life.

Devotion to My Law of Love (ח Heth)

[57] I, the Lord, will be your portion. You have sworn to keep My word, [58] and have sought My face with all your heart; therefore, I will be gracious to you according to My promise. [59] You have thought about your ways and have turned your steps to follow My instructions. [60] Without delay, you hasten to keep My commandments. [61] When the corrupt try to entangle you in their nets, you have not forgotten My law. [62] Even at midnight you rise and give thanks for My loving wisdom. [63] You are a friend to all who revere Me, to all who keep My teachings. [64] The earth is filled with My love, and so I, the Lord, will teach you My ways.

Value in My Law of Love (ט Teth)

[65] I have kept My word, and have been good to you, My servant. [66] Therefore, I will teach you wisdom and knowledge, because you trust in My commandments. [67] Before you were humbled, you went astray, but now you keep My word. [68] I am good and what I do is good, so I will teach you My ways. [69] Even though the arrogant have smeared you with lies, with your whole heart you have kept My teachings. [70] Their hearts are callous and unfeeling, but you delight in My law. [71] It was good for you to be humbled, so that you could learn My ways. [72] The law from My mouth is now more precious to you than thousands of gold and silver coins.

Comforted by My Law of Love (י Yodh)

[73] My hands made you and formed you and I also gave you intelligence, so that you could learn My commandments. [74] Those

who revere Me find courage when they see you, because you put your hope in My word. ⁷⁵ You know that My laws are loving, and that when I humble you, I do so out of faithfulness. ⁷⁶ So let My mercy-filled love be your comfort, according to what I have promised you, My servant. ⁷⁷ Allow My compassion to surround you, that you may recover; for My law is your joy. ⁷⁸ The arrogant will be put to shame for treating you unjustly without cause, but you meditate upon My teachings. ⁷⁹ Those who revere Me and understand My word will turn to you. ⁸⁰ For when you wholeheartedly follow My teachings, you will never be ashamed.

FAITHFULNESS TO MY LAW OF LOVE (כ KAPH)

⁸¹ Your soul is worn out waiting for My salvation, yet you still place your trust in My word. ⁸² Your eyes are tired from looking for what I promised and you plead, "How long must I wait for You to help me?" ⁸³ You feel as useless as a discarded wineskin, yet you have not forgotten My teachings. ⁸⁴ How much longer must you wait? When will My judgement come to those who persecute you? ⁸⁵ The proud may have dug pitfalls for you, they may flout My law, ⁸⁶ but all My commandments are trustworthy, and I will help you, for you are being persecuted without cause. ⁸⁷ They almost wiped you from earth, yet you did not forsake My precepts. ⁸⁸ In My unfailing love, I will revive you, that you may keep the teachings of My mouth.

PROTECTED BY MY LAW OF LOVE (ל LAMEDH)

⁸⁹ My eternal word is forever settled in the heavens. ⁹⁰ My faithfulness endures throughout all ages; for I established the earth, and it endures. ⁹¹ It endures to this day according to My laws, because they are all My servants. ⁹² If My law had not been your joy, you would have perished in your misery. ⁹³ But you will never forget My commandments, for by them I have preserved

your life. ⁹⁴ I will save you, for you belong to Me, and you have sought to live by My teachings. ⁹⁵ While the selfish are waiting to destroy you, you ponder My laws. ⁹⁶ For you have seen the limits of perfection, but My commands have no limit.

Adoration for My Law of Love (מ Mem)

⁹⁷ Oh, how you love My law! You meditate on it all day long. ⁹⁸ My commands are always with you, and they make you wiser than your enemies. ⁹⁹ You have more understanding than all your teachers, because you meditate on My instructions. ¹⁰⁰ You have greater wisdom than the elders, because you keep My commandments. ¹⁰¹ You have restrained your feet from every selfish path, because you want to obey My word. ¹⁰² You have not departed from My laws because I Myself have taught you. ¹⁰³ My words are sweet to your taste, sweeter than honey to your mouth! ¹⁰⁴ You gain wisdom from My laws, and so you hate every false way.

Light from My Law of Love (נ Nun)

¹⁰⁵ My word is a lamp to your feet and a light for your path. ¹⁰⁶ You made a solemn promise to follow My law of love. ¹⁰⁷ Because of this, you have suffered much; but I, the Lord, will preserve your life, according to My word. ¹⁰⁸ For I will accept your offering of praise, and will teach you My ways. ¹⁰⁹ For though you have constantly put your life at risk, you have not forgotten My law. ¹¹⁰ The corrupt attempt to ensnare you, but you have not strayed from My teachings. ¹¹¹ You have claimed as your eternal inheritance, My commandments; for they are the joy of your heart. ¹¹² So, you have set your heart on keeping My laws, forever, to the very end.

Safety in My Law of Love (ס Samekh)

[113] You despise the double-minded, but you love My law. [114] For I am your hiding place and your shield; you put your hope in My word. [115] You have told the corrupt, "Get out of my life, for I have chosen to keep the commandments of my God". [116] Therefore I, your God, will sustain you according to My word, that you may live. I will not let your hope turn to shame. [117] I will hold you up and you will be safe, for you have always given allegiance to My commands. [118] But I will reject all those who go astray from My laws, for their delusions will come to nothing. [119] I will cast away all the corrupt of the earth like rubbish. But you love My instructions, [120] and your flesh trembles in reverence before Me, because you stand in awe of My judgements.

Obedience to My Law of Love (ע Ayin)

[121] You have done what is just and loving, I would never abandon you to your oppressors! [122] I will ensure My servant's well-being; I will not let the proud oppress you. [123] Though your eyes fail from looking for My salvation, for My promised word, [124] I will provide for you according to My love, and will teach you My ways. [125] For you are My servant, and I will give you discernment, so that you may understand My ways. [126] The time is coming for Me, the Lord, to act, for people have regarded My law as void. [127] But you love My commandments more than gold, more than the finest gold. [128] And because you consider all My teachings to be right, you despise every false path.

Longing to Obey My Law of Love (פ Pe)

[129] My teachings are wonderful; this is why your soul desires to keep them. [130] The unfolding of My word gives light, it imparts understanding to the simple. [131] You pant in expectation, longing for My commandments. [132] Therefore, I will turn to you, and have mercy on you as I do for all those who love My name. [133] I will

direct your steps by My word and I will not let selfishness have dominion over you. [134] I will redeem you from oppression, so you can follow My precepts. [135] I will make My face shine upon you, My servant, and will teach you My ways. [136] For I see the rivers of water running down from your eyes, because My law is not being followed.

The Justice of My Law of Love (צ Tsadhe)

[137] I, the Lord, am loving, and My judgements are just. [138] The commandments that I have given are loving and trustworthy. [139] That is why you are consumed by zeal when your enemies disregard My word. [140] For My word is pure and genuine, that is why you love it. [141] Even though you are lowly and despised, you do not forget My teachings. [142] For My love is everlasting, and My law is truth. [143] And when trouble and distress bear down on you, My commandments bring you joy. [144] The lovingkindness of My teachings are everlasting; they will give you understanding, that you may live.

Seeking My Law of Love (ק Qoph)

[145] With all your heart, you cry out to Me, "Answer Me, Lord, and I will obey your teachings." [146] You cry out to Me, "Save me, and I will keep Your laws." [147] You rise before dawn and cry for help because you have put your hope in My word. [148] All night long you lie awake, meditating on My promises. [149] In My unfailing love, I hear your voice; I, the Lord, will preserve your life in accordance with My love. [150] For those who devise selfish schemes are near, yet they are far away from My law. [151] Yet I am near you, for all My commands are true. [152] Long ago you learned from My laws, that I established them to last forever.

. . .

The Truth of My Law of Love (ר Resh)

¹⁵³ I have looked upon your suffering, and will save you, for you have not forgotten My law. ¹⁵⁴ I will defend your cause and redeem you; I will save you, according to My word. ¹⁵⁵ Salvation is far from the wicked, for they do not seek out My teachings. ¹⁵⁶ But My tender mercies are great; therefore, I the Lord will be just, and will revive your life. ¹⁵⁷ You have many enemies and oppressors, yet you have not turned from My teachings; ¹⁵⁸ when you see these treacherous people you are filled with loathing because they do not follow My word. ¹⁵⁹ I see how you love My instructions; therefore, in accordance with My love, I the Lord will give you life. ¹⁶⁰ For all of My words are truth, and all My laws of love are eternal.

Protected by My Law of Love (ש Shin)

¹⁶¹ Powerful people attack you without a cause, but your heart trembles only at My word. ¹⁶² You rejoice at My promises, like one who finds great treasure! ¹⁶³ You despise and abhor falsehood, but you love My law. ¹⁶⁴ Seven times a day you thank Me for My righteous laws. ¹⁶⁵ For those who love My law have great peace, and there is nothing that can make them stumble. ¹⁶⁶ Therefore, you wait for My salvation, and you follow My commandments. ¹⁶⁷ Your soul keeps My teachings, and you love them greatly. ¹⁶⁸ You obey My precepts and My instructions because everything you do is known to Me.

Hope in My Law of Love (ת Taw)

¹⁶⁹ Your cry has come before Me, the Lord; therefore, I will give you understanding according to My promised word. ¹⁷⁰ Your prayer has come before Me and I will deliver you in faithfulness to My word. ¹⁷¹ Praise will pour from your lips because I will help you learn My laws. ¹⁷² Your tongue will sing of My word because

all My commandments are love. [173] My hand is always ready to help you because you have chosen My teachings. [174] I, the Lord, see that you long for My salvation and that My law gives you delight. [175] I will give life to your soul that you may continue to praise Me, for My wisdom will guide you. [176] Though you have strayed like a lost sheep, I will come and look for you, My servant, for you have not forgotten My commandments.

I AM: PEACE

*I*n your distress, you cried to Me, the Lord, and I heard you. ² I will save you from lying lips and deceitful tongues. ³ What prize shall be given to these liars? What shall be done to these deceivers? ⁴ They can expect a warriors sharp arrows, with red-hot coals from the broom tree. ⁵ For you suffered living in Assyria in the north, and it pains you to live among the tents of Arabia in the south. ⁶ You have lived too long among those who hate peace. ⁷ You are for peace, but when you speak of it, they are for war.

I AM: WATCHING OVER YOU

*Y*ou lift up your eyes to the hills, and ask, "where will My help come from"? [2] Your help will come from Me, the Lord, who made heaven and earth. [3] I will not let your foot slip; I, who watch over you, never slumber. [4] Behold, I, the protector of Israel, neither slumber nor sleep. [5] I the Lord watch over you; ; I am the shade at your right hand. [6] The sun will not harm you by day, nor the moon by night. [7] I will keep you from all harm; I will preserve your soul. [8] I will watch over your coming and going, from this time forth, and forevermore.

I AM: YOUR HOME

*Y*ou rejoiced when they said to you, "Let's go to the house of the Lord." ² And now, here you are, standing within Jerusalems gates. ³ Jerusalem is a well built city, compact and unbreachable. ⁴ All My tribes make their pilgrimage there, giving thanks to My name, as was decreed for Israel. ⁵ For there the thrones of judgement are set up, the thrones of the house of David. ⁶ So, pray for the peace of Jerusalem, that those who love her may prosper. ⁷ O' let there be peace within her walls and safety within her palaces. ⁸ For the sake of your family and friends say, "Peace be within you." ⁹ For the sake of the house of the Lord your God, seek for her to prosper.

I AM: MERCIFUL

*Y*ou lift up your eyes to Me who sits enthroned in the heavens. ² Just as the eyes of servants closely watch the hand of their masters, or as a maid carefully observes the slightest gesture of her mistress, so your eyes look to Me, waiting for the Lord, your God, to have mercy upon you. ³ Therefore, I the Lord will have mercy on you, I will show you mercy; for you have endured enough contempt. ⁴ Your soul has had more than its fill of scorn from the proud, the contempt of the arrogant.

124

I AM: ON YOUR SIDE

*W*hat if I, the Lord, had not been on your side? Answer, O' Israel! ² If it had not been the Lord who was on your side when people attacked you? ³ They would have swallowed you up alive when their anger was kindled against you; ⁴ the flood would have engulfed you, the torrent would have swept over you, ⁵ the raging waters would have swept you away! ⁶ So, give thanks to Me, for I did not leave you to be torn by their fangs. ⁷ Your soul has escaped like a bird from the snare of the fowler; the trap has been broken, and you are free! ⁸ For your help is in My name, the Lord, the maker of the heavens and the earth.

I AM: JUST

*T*hose who trust in Me, the Lord, are like Mount Zion, which cannot be moved, and abides forever. ² As the mountains surround Jerusalem, so I surround My people from this time forth and forever. ³ For the scepter of the wicked will not always rule over the land allotted to the righteous; if they did, the just themselves might reach out their own hands to corruption. ⁴ I, the Lord, will do good for those who are good, to those who are upright in their hearts. ⁵ As for those who abandon My ways, I will lead them away along with the workers of injustice. But peace will be upon Israel!

I AM: DOING GREAT THINGS

When I, the Lord, restored the exiles of Zion, you felt as if you were dreaming. ² Your mouth was filled with laughter, and your tongue with shouts of joy! Then it was said among the nations, "The Lord has done great things for them." ³ Indeed, I have done great things for you, and you rejoiced. ⁴ I will make you prosperous yet again, just as rain brings water back to dry riverbeds. ⁵ Those who sow in tears will reap in joy. ⁶ Those who wept as they went out, bearing precious seed for sowing, will return with rejoicing, bringing in the sheaves of harvest.

I AM: YOUR PROVIDER

*U*nless I, the Lord, build the house, they who build it labor in vain. Unless I protect the city, the guards stand watch in vain. ² It is useless to work so hard, getting up early and going to bed late, anxiously laboring for food to eat, for I provide for those I love, even while they are sleeping.

³ Your children are a heritage from Me; the fruit of the womb is My reward to you. ⁴ Like a warrior with a fistful of arrows, so are the children of one's youth. ⁵ Blessed is the family whose quiver is full of them. They will never be ashamed when they meet their enemies in public.

I AM: GENEROUS

*B*lessed are those who revere Me, the Lord, who walk in My ways. ² You will enjoy the fruit of your labor; you will be happy and it will go well for you. ³ Your wife will be like a fruitful vine in the home, and your children will be like young olive shoots around your table. ⁴ Such are the blessings that I lavish on those who revere Me. ⁵ I, the Lord, will bless you from Zion, that you may see Jerusalem prosper all the days of your life. ⁶ That you may live to see your grandchildren. May peace be upon Israel!

I AM: PROTECTIVE

*I*srael, your enemies have oppressed you many times, from your youth up. ² Ever since you were young, your enemies have afflicted you, yet they have not prevailed against you. ³ The plowers plowed their furrows deep and long down your back. ⁴ But I, the Lord, am loving, and I cut you free from the shackles of the wicked. ⁵ Indeed, all who hate Zion will be driven back in shame. ⁶ They will be like grass growing on a roof which withers before it can grow, ⁷ unfit for harvest by the reaper, nor worth the effort of binding into sheaves. ⁸ Those who pass by will see that I have not blessed them, therefore neither will they bless them in My name.

I AM: UNFAILING

O ut of the depths of your despair, you cry to Me; [2] I can hear your voice. My ears are attentive to your cry for mercy. [3] If I, the Lord, kept a record of your guilt, who could stand? [4] But with Me, there is forgiveness, that's why you respect Me. [5] And so, you wait for Me, the Lord, your soul waits, and My word gives you hope. [6] Your soul waits for Me more eagerly than sentries waiting for the morning, more than the night watchmen wait for the dawn. [7] O' Israel, put your hope in Me, the Lord; for in Me you will find mercy, and in Me you will find abundant redemption. [8] For I, Myself, will redeem Israel from all their sin.

I AM: SEEING YOU

I, the Lord, see that your heart is not proud, nor are your eyes arrogant. You do not meddle with matters far above you, nor with subjects you do not understand. [2] Instead, you have calmed and quieted your soul. As a weaned child lies quietly in its mother's arms, your soul is quiet within you. [3] O' Israel, put your hope in Me from this time forth and forevermore.

I AM: COMMITTED

I, the Lord, remember David and all the sacrifices he endured. ² He swore an oath to Me, he made a vow to the Mighty God of Jacob, saying: ³ "I will not enter my home or go to my bed; ⁴ I will not rest or sleep, ⁵ until I provide a place for the Lord, a home for the mighty One of Jacob." ⁶ When he heard rumors about the Ark of the Covenant in Bethlehem, he found it in a forest meadow. ⁷ He shouted, "Let's take it to the tabernacle and worship before His throne!"

⁸ I, the Lord, will arise and enter My temple, along with the ark, the symbol of My power. ⁹ May My priests be clothed in My righteousness and may My faithful people shout for joy. ¹⁰ For the sake of My servant David, I will not turn away My anointed one. ¹¹ For I swore an oath to David, a truth that I will never revoke: I will place one of his descendants upon his throne. ¹² And if his children keep My covenant, and My teachings, then they will also sit upon his throne forever.

¹³ For I, the Lord, have chosen Zion. I long for it to be My dwelling place. ¹⁴ My resting place, forever and ever. I will live there, for this is the home I have desired. ¹⁵ Then I will richly bless Zion with all she needs; I will satisfy her poor with food. ¹⁶ I will clothe her

priests with salvation, and her faithful people will shout aloud for joy. [17] I will make the strength of David's kingdom grow. My anointed One will be a light for My people. [18] I will clothe his enemies with shame, but his head will be adorned with a radiant crown.

I AM: THE LIFE GIVER

*H*ow wonderful and how pleasant it is when My people live together in unity! [2] It's like precious anointing oil poured on the head, running down on the beard, on Aaron's head and beard, running down over the collar of his robes. [3] It is like the dew of Mount Hermon descending upon Zion's mountains. For that is where I, the Lord, will bestow My blessing of eternal life.

134

I AM: BLESSING YOU

ome, give praise all you who are My servants, who stand ready through the night to serve in My house. ² Raise your hands in prayer in My sanctuary, and give thanks. ³ For I, the Lord, maker of the heavens and the earth, will bless you from Zion!

I AM: THE LIVING GOD

*B*oast in Me, the Lord! Give thanks for who I am; give praise you servants of the Lord, ² you who minister in My house, in the courts of the house of your God! ³ Boast in Me because I am loving; sing to My name, because I am gracious. ⁴ I, the Lord, have chosen Jacob for Myself, the people of Israel are My special treasure.

⁵ You know that I am powerful above all other gods. ⁶ That I can do whatever I wish, in both the heavens and on the earth, in the seas and in all the deep places. ⁷ I bring storm clouds from the ends of the earth, I make lightning for the rain, and I bring the winds out of My treasury.

⁸ In Egypt, I destroyed all the first-born, both people and animals. ⁹ I performed miracles and wonders in the midst of you, O' Egypt, upon Pharaoh and all his officials. ¹⁰ I defeated many corrupt nations and slew powerful kings: ¹¹ Sihon, king of the Amorites of Syria; Og, king of Bashan of the Golan Heights; and all the kings in Canaan, the sons of Ham. ¹² I gave their lands to My people; I gave them to Israel. ¹³ Indeed, My name endures forever; My renown, throughout all ages. ¹⁴ For I, the Lord, will vindicate My people, and will have compassion on My followers.

¹⁵ The idols of the nations are silver and gold, the work of human hands. ¹⁶ They shape mouths for them, but they cannot speak, and they carve eyes, but they do not see. ¹⁷ They place ears on them, but they cannot hear, nor is there any breath in their mouths. ¹⁸ All those who made them and who trust in them will become like the works they have made!

¹⁹ O' Israel give thanks, for I am your Lord; O' My priests give thanks! ²⁰ Give praise, O' house of Levi. All you, who revere Me, give thanks. ²¹ For I am the loving Lord of Zion, and I dwell in Jerusalem! Boast in Me, your Lord!

I AM: EVERLASTING LOVE

O' give thanks, for I the Lord am good, and My love endures forever. ² Give thanks, for I am the God of gods, and My love endures forever. ³ Give thanks, for I am the Lord of lords, and My love endures forever.

⁴ I, alone, perform great miracles, and My love endures forever. ⁵ By My wisdom, I made the heavens, and My love endures forever. ⁶ I spread out the earth above the oceans, and My love endures forever. ⁷ I filled the skies with light, and My love endures forever. ⁸ The sun to rule over the day, and My love endures forever. ⁹ The moon and the stars to rule over the night, and My love endures forever.

¹⁰ I struck down the first-born of Egypt, and My love endures forever. ¹¹ I led the people of Israel out from among them, and My love endures forever. ¹² With a mighty hand and an outstretched arm, and My love endures forever. ¹³ I divided the Red Sea, and My love endures forever. ¹⁴ I led My people through the midst of it, and My love endures forever. ¹⁵ But I swept Pharaoh and his army into the Sea, and My love endures forever. ¹⁶ I led My people through the wilderness, and My love endures forever.

¹⁷ I am He who struck down great kings, and My love endures forever. ¹⁸ I slew famous kings, and My love endures forever. ¹⁹ Sihon, king of the Amorites of Syria, and My love endures forever. ²⁰ And Og, king of Bashan of the Golan Heights, and My love endures forever. ²¹ I gave their lands to My people, and My love endures forever. ²² I gave them as an inheritance for Israel, My servant, and My love endures forever.

²³ I remembered you when you were down, and My love endures forever. ²⁴ I rescued you from your foes, and My love endures forever. ²⁵ I give food to every living creature, and My love endures forever. ²⁶ So give thanks, for I am the God of heaven, and My love endures forever.

I AM: AGAINST BABYLON

*B*y the rivers of Babylon, you sat and wept when you remembered Zion. ² There on the willows you hung up your harps. ³ For there your captors told you to sing; your tormentors asked in mirth, saying, "Sing us one of the songs of Zion!"

⁴ But how could you sing My songs in a foreign land? ⁵ You would rather have your right hand wither than to forget Jerusalem! ⁶ Rather to never sing again than to not remember her, if you did not consider Jerusalem your highest joy.

⁷ I, the Lord, remember what you, Edomites, did on the day Jerusalem fell. "Tear it down," you cried, "Tear it down to its foundations!" ⁸ O' daughter of Babylon, you are doomed to destruction. My people will have justice when they see you repaid according to how you treated them. ⁹ When your own little ones are dashed against the stones, then you will grieve as they did.

I AM: YOUR MAKER

*G*ive thanks to Me, the Lord, with all your heart; sing praise to Me before the angels. ² Look toward My sanctuary and worship, giving thanks for My name, for My lovingkindness and truth are unfailing. And I have exalted My word and My name above everything. ³ For on the day that you cried out, I answered you, and I increased your strength of soul.

⁴ The kings on the earth will give thanks to Me when they have heard the words of My mouth. ⁵ They will marvel at the ways of your Lord, for My glory is very great. ⁶ Yet, even though I am highly exalted, I care for the lowly, but I keep My distance from those filled with arrogant pride.

⁷ Though you walk in the midst of troubles, I will revive you. I will stretch out My hand and strike your enemies, with My right hand I will deliver you. ⁸ I will fulfill My purpose for you, for My steadfast love endures forever. I will not abandon you, for you are the work of My hands.

I AM: LEADING YOU

I, the Lord, have searched your heart and know everything about you. ² I know when you sit down and when you rise up; I know all your thoughts even when you are far away. ³ I watch when you travel and when you rest. I am familiar with everything you do. ⁴ Even before there is a word on your tongue, I already know what you will say. ⁵ I am all around you, on every side; I go before you and follow you, and lay My hand upon your shoulder. ⁶ This knowledge is too wonderful for you; you can't even comprehend it.

⁷ Where can you go from My Spirit? Where can you flee from My presence? ⁸ If you ascend up to the heavens, I am there; if you go down to the grave, I am there. ⁹ If you flew upon the wings of the morning sun, or lived at the farthest ocean, ¹⁰ even there My hand shall lead you, and My right hand will hold you. ¹¹ You might think that you can hide in the dark, when the light around you turns into night, ¹² but even darkness cannot hide you, for the night shines like the day; seeing in the darkness and the light are the same to Me.

¹³ For I formed your inmost parts; I knit you together in your mother's womb. ¹⁴ And, because you are fearfully and

wonderfully made, you praise Me; for all My works are wonderful, and your soul knows it very well. ¹⁵ Nothing about you was hidden from Me, as you took shape in secret, carefully woven together in the heart of the womb. ¹⁶ My eyes saw your unformed body; all the days fashioned for you were written in My book, before any of them even began. ¹⁷ My thoughts and plans are precious to you. The sum of them is vast. ¹⁸ Were you to count them, they would outnumber the grains of sand; yet, when you awake, I, your God, am still near you.

¹⁹ In time, I will destroy the wicked and deliver you from the bloodthirsty. ²⁰ For they speak against Me with evil intent; these adversaries misuse My name. ²¹ I see how you despise those who despise Me. You abhor those who are in rebellion against Me. ²² You have nothing but disdain for them; you regard them as your enemies. ²³ For I, God, search you and know your heart; I test you and know you are anxious. ²⁴ I will point out when there is any offensive way in you, and I will guide you into the way of everlasting life.

I AM: YOUR DEFENSE

I, the Lord, will deliver you from evil people; I will protect you from those who are violent. ² They are always plotting selfishly, always stirring up quarrels. ³ Their tongues are like deadly snakes; their words like a cobra's poison. ⁴ I will guard you from the hands of the wicked, and will keep you safe from the violent people who plot your downfall.

⁵ These arrogant people have hidden traps for you; they have set out nets and snares along your path to catch you. ⁶ You say to Me, the Eternal, "You are my God. Hear my cry for help, Lord!" ⁷ I am your strong deliverer, I shield your head in the day of battle. ⁸ I will not grant evil people their desires; I will not let their plots succeed!

⁹ Those arrogant people who surround you, who make their threats against you, will be destroyed by the very mischief they have planned for you. ¹⁰ Burning coals will fall upon them. They will be cast into the fire of miry pits, never to rise again. ¹¹ These liars will not prosper. Misfortune will overtake the violent and destroy them. ¹² For you know that I, the Lord, defend the cause of the poor and the rights of the needy. ¹³ Surely those who are loving will praise Me, indeed, and the upright will live in My presence.

I AM: WATCHING OVER YOU

*W*hen you cry out to Me, the Lord, I will come quickly to you. I will listen to your voice when you call to Me. ² Your prayers come before Me like incense, and your uplifted hands are like an evening sacrifice.

³ I will keep watch over the door of your lips and I will set a guard over your mouth. ⁴ I will not let your heart be drawn to what is evil, so that you take part in wicked deeds alongside those who are corrupt; I will not let them lure you with their pleasures.

⁵ For when a godly person punishes you, it is done out of kindness. When they rebuke you, it is anointing oil for your head; so don't refuse it. Be in constant prayer against the deeds of the corrupt. ⁶ When those who lead them are killed, the corrupt will know My words were true. ⁷ Like a rock that one breaks apart and shatters on the ground, so shall their bones be scattered at the mouth of the grave.

⁸ But your eyes are turned toward Me, your Sovereign Lord; in Me, you seek refuge; I will not leave you defenseless. ⁹ I will keep you from the traps they have set for you, from the snares of the corrupt. ¹⁰ The wicked will fall into their own traps, while you escape safely.

I AM: HOLDING YOU UP

*Y*ou cry out to Me, the Lord, for help; you plead with Me for mercy. ² You pour out your complaints before Me and tell Me all your troubles. ³ When your spirit is overwhelmed within you, I am the one that watches over your way.

In the path where you walk, your enemies have hidden snares for you. ⁴ When I look beside you, I see that there is no one at your right hand to help; no one even acknowledges you. You have no refuge, no one to care for your soul's well-being. ⁵ You cry to Me, "Lord, You are my refuge. You are all I want in this life. ⁶ Listen to my cry for help, for I am in desperate need".

I will deliver you from your persecutors, for they are much too strong for you. ⁷ I will set your soul free from its prison, that you may praise My name once again; loving people will surround you and I will bless you abundantly.

I AM: YOUR RELIEF

I, the Lord, hear your prayers. In My faithfulness and love, I will come to your relief. [2] I won't enter into judgment against you, My servant, for no one is innocent before Me. [3] The enemy who pursues your soul has crushed you to the ground. He makes you dwell in darkness like those in the grave. [4] Therefore, your spirit has lost hope, and your heart is in deep despair.

[5] But you reflect on the days of old and you meditate on all My works, considering what My hands have done. [6] You lift your hands up to Me in prayer, while your soul thirsts for Me, like a dry parched land. [7] Therefore I, the Lord, will answer you quickly because your spirit is failing. I will not hide My face from you, lest you become like those who go down into the grave.

[8] I will remind you each morning of My stedfast love, for you have put your trust in Me. I will let you know the way you should go, for you have lifted up your soul to Me. [9] I will deliver you from your enemies, for you have hid yourself in Me. [10] I will teach you to do My will, for you have chosen Me as your God. My gracious Spirit will lead you on level ground.

[11] For the sake of My name, I, the Lord, will revive you. In My lovingkindness, I will bring your soul out of trouble. [12] In my unfailing love, I will silence your enemies, and destroy all those who afflict your soul, for you are My servant.

I AM: YOUR VICTORY

*G*ive thanks to Me for I am your rock; I train you for the battle and prepare you for the fight. ² I, your loving God, am your fortress, your stronghold, and your deliverer, your shield, and the One in whom you take refuge. I will subdue the nations under you.

³ What are human beings, that I, the Lord, care for them, mere mortals, that I pay attention to them? ⁴ They're like a breath of air; their days are like a fleeting shadow. ⁵ Yet, I part the heavens and come down, and when I touch the mountains, they smoke. ⁶ I send forth lightning and scatter your enemies; I shoot out My arrows and send them running. ⁷ I will reach down My hand from above and will deliver you; I will rescue you from the mighty waters and the hands of strangers, ⁸ those whose mouths are full of deceit and lie even under oath.

⁹ So sing a new song to Me, your God; make music to Me on the ten-stringed harp. ¹⁰ For I give victory to kings and delivered My servant David. ¹¹ I will rescue you from the deadly sword, I will deliver you from the hand of the stranger, whose mouths are full of deceit, swearing to tell the truth, but they lie instead.

[12] May your sons flourish in their youth like well-nurtured plants. May your daughters be like graceful columns which adorn a beautiful palace. [13] May your barns be filled with produce of every kind. May your sheep increase by the thousands. [14] May your cattle be heavy with young. May there be no breach in your walls, no going into captivity, nor cry of distress in your streets. [15] Joyful are the people for whom this is true; happy are the people who have Me, the Lord, as their God!

I AM: LOVE

*Y*ou will exalt in My greatness, for I am your God and King; you will praise Me forever and ever. ² Every day you will thank Me and will rejoice in My name forever. ³ For I, the Lord, am majestic and am worthy of gratitude; for My majesty is beyond comprehension.

⁴ One generation to the next will celebrate My works and tell of My mighty triumphs. ⁵ They will meditate on the glorious splendor of My majesty and will marvel at My works. ⁶ My awe-inspiring deeds will be on every tongue and they will proclaim My greatness. ⁷ They will celebrate in My abundant goodness and joyfully sing of My love.

⁸ For I, the Lord, am gracious and compassionate, slow to anger, and rich in loving mercy. ⁹ I am good to all and My tender mercies are over all I have made. ¹⁰ All My creatures will rejoice in Me and all My faithful people will give thanks. ¹¹ They will speak of the glory of My kingdom and tell of My power, ¹² so that all nations may know of My mighty deeds and the glorious splendor of My kingdom. ¹³ For My kingdom is an everlasting kingdom and My dominion endures throughout all generations.

I, the Lord, am trustworthy in all that I promise; I am faithful in all that I do. [14] I hold up all those who are falling and lift up all who are broken down. [15] The eyes of all look to Me in hope and I give them their food in due season. [16] I open My hand and satisfy the desires of every living thing.

[17] I, the Lord, am loving in all My ways and faithful in all that I do. [18] I am near to those who call upon Me, to all those who pray to Me in sincerity and truth. [19] I fulfill the desires of those who revere Me; I hear their cries and save them. [20] I watch over all who love Me; but all the wicked will be destroyed. [21] Your mouth will speak in praise and all My creatures will bless My loving name forever and ever.

I AM: FAITHFUL FOREVER

*G*ive praise! Give thanks with all your soul! ² You will praise Me as long as you live. You will sing praises to Me till your dying breath. ³ Do not put your trust in human leaders, in mortals who cannot save you. ⁴ When their breath departs, they return to the dust; on that very day, all their plans come to an end.

⁵ Happy are those who have the God of Jacob to help them, whose hope is in Me, the Lord, their God; ⁶ I am the maker of heaven and earth, the sea, and all that is in them; I am truthful forever. ⁷ I bring justice for the oppressed and give food to the hungry. I set prisoners free ⁸ and give sight to the blind; lifting up all those who are weighed down.

I cherish My loving people. ⁹ I protect foreigners. I sustain the fatherless and the widow. But I turn the plans of the wicked upside down. ¹⁰ For I reign forever; I, your God, O' people of Zion, reign eternal to all generations. So give praise that I am your Lord!

I AM: RESTORING YOU

*G*ive thanks to Me, your Lord. It is delightful when you sing your praise to Me; your gratitude is pleasant and beautiful. ² For I, the Lord, am restoring Jerusalem; I am gathering together the outcasts of Israel, ³ to heal the broken-hearted and bind up their wounds. ⁴ Though I count the number of the stars and call them all by name, ⁵ though I, the Lord, am majestic and mighty in power, and My wisdom is infinite, ⁶ I still support the humble, and cast the corrupt down into the dust. ⁷ So sing to Me, the Lord, a grateful praise; make music for Me on the harp.

⁸ I cover the sky with clouds; I supply the earth with rain, and make grass grow on the hills. ⁹ I provide food for the animals and feed the young ravens when they call. ¹⁰ I do not take pleasure in the strength of a horse, nor in human might. ¹¹ What I, the Lord, delight in, is in those who honor Me, who put their hope in My unfailing love. ¹² So glorify Me, O' Jerusalem. Give thanks to Me, your God, O' Zion. ¹³ For I keep your gates strong and I bless your people. ¹⁴ It is I who grant peace to your borders and satisfy you with the finest wheat.

¹⁵ I send My commands to the earth and My word is done swiftly. ¹⁶ I spread snow like a wool blanket and scatter frost like dust. ¹⁷ When I throw down hail like stones, who can withstand My icy blasts? ¹⁸ When I give My word, the ice melts; when I send the wind, the water flows away. ¹⁹ I have revealed My word to Jacob and My laws and decrees to Israel. ²⁰ I have not done this for any other nation; they do not know My teachings. Therefore, give thanks to Me, your Lord.

I AM: GLORIOUS

*G*ive praise! Let the skies be filled with praise and the highest heavens with the shouts of glory! [2] Let My angels and all My heavenly hosts give praise. [3] Give praise, O' sun and moon; celebrate, O' shining stars. [4] Let the highest heavens and the waters above the skies give praise. [5] Let them all praise My name. For at My command they were created; [6] I established them forever and ever. I issued the decree and it will never pass away.

[7] Praise Me from the earth, you great sea creatures of the ocean depths; [8] lightning and hail, snow and clouds, stormy winds that obey My commands. [9] Praise Me, O' hills and mountains, fruit trees and forests, [10] wild animals and livestock, scurrying animals and birds. [11] Praise Me, O' kings, and all nations, you princes and rulers on earth; [12] young men and young women, old people and children, too.

[13] Let all give thanks to My name. For My name alone is exalted; My glory towers over the earth and the heavens. [14] For I have made My people strong, honoring My faithful ones, for the people of Israel are dear to Me. So, give thanks, for I am your Lord!

I AM: HONORING YOU

$\mathcal{G}$ive thanks to Me, your Lord. Sing a new song. Give praise in the assembly of My faithful people. ² Rejoice in your Maker, O' Israel, let the people of Zion be glad in their King. ³ Praise My name with dancing; make music to Me with drums and harps. ⁴ For I take delight in My people!

I will beautify the humble with salvation. ⁵ So let My faithful people rejoice in this honor and sing for joy on their beds. ⁶ Let them shout high praises to Me, their God, while brandishing swords in wild dances.

⁷ For vengeance will come upon the corrupt nations, a reckoning upon their peoples. ⁸ Their kings will be bound in chains and their leaders in shackles of iron, ⁹ when judgement is executed against them. But all My faithful people will have a seat of honor. So give thanks to Me, your Lord!

I AM: LIMITLESS

*H*allelujah! Praise Me in My sanctuary! Praise Me in the mighty heavens! [2] Praise Me for the mighty things I have done! Praise My infinite majesty! [3] Praise Me with trumpets! Praise Me with the lute and harp! [4] Praise Me with tambourines and dancing! Praise Me with stringed instruments and flutes! [5] Praise Me with cymbals, with loud crashing cymbals! [6] Let everything that has breath sing praise, for I am the Lord! Hallelujah!

BOOK 6

Chapters 151-160
Psalms of Healing

-LOST PSALMS-

Orthodox
Apocryphal
The Dead Sea Scrolls

I AM: ANOINTING YOU

*Y*ou were the smallest of your siblings, the youngest in your father's household, so he made you a shepherd over his flock, to care for his sheep. ² So your hands made a reed flute, and your fingers a small harp, and with them you gave Me glory. ³ You thought to yourself, "Mountains cannot witness to Him, nor can the hills proclaim: 'Lift up His word you trees, and His songs you sheep'. ⁴ And who will recount and declare the deeds of my life?"

⁵ But I, the God of everything, have seen and heard; I have paid attention! ⁶ That's why I sent My prophet Samuel to anoint you, and raise you up. ⁷ Your siblings went out to meet him, handsome of figure, and handsome of appearance. ⁸ Although they were tall, good looking, and had beautiful hair, I the Lord God did not choose them. ⁹ I sent and fetched you from behind the flock and anointed you with oil, making you leader of My people, a ruler over the children of My covenant.

¹⁰ Then, when you saw the Philistine among the ranks of the enemy, uttering insults in the names of his idols, ¹¹ in My strength you cast three stones at him. You hit him in the forehead and felled

him to the earth. [12] Drawing his own sword, you used it to cut off his head, taking away the reproach of the children of Israel.

I AM: YOUR HELPER

I am your God. I will come to your aid! I will help you and save you. I will deliver your soul from the destroyer! ² You will not go down to the grave by the mouth of the lion. The wolf will not be the end of you. ³ Was it not enough for them that they lay in wait for your family's flock, to tear the sheep to pieces from the sheepfold? Now they are even wishing to destroy your life!

⁴ But I, the Lord, will have pity and save My elect; I will save My anointed from destruction, that you may speak of My glory all of your days, and thank My good name. ⁵ I will deliver you from the hands of the destroying lion and the ravenous wolf. I will rescue you from captivity in the hands of these beasts. ⁶ I, your Lord, will quickly send you a deliverer, to draw you out of the gaping abyss that seeks to imprison you in its depths.

I AM: SAVING YOU

*G*ive thanks to Me, the Lord, all you nations; exalt in Me and bless My name! ² I rescued the soul of My chosen from the hands of death, and delivered My anointed from destruction. I saved you from the net cast by the grave, and your soul from the bottomless pit!

³ Before your deliverance came, you were almost torn in two by beasts. ⁴ But I sent My angel and closed their gaping mouths, rescuing your life from destruction. ⁵ Your soul will glorify Me and thank Me because of all the kindnesses I have, and will continue to do for you!

I AM: WISDOM

*E*xalt in Me, your God, with a loud voice, and proclaim My glory in the assembly of the people. ² Glorify My name among the throng of the upright, and celebrate My majesty with the faithful. ³ Unite your soul with the good and the innocent, and rejoice in Me, the Most High God. ⁴ Gather yourselves together and make My salvation known. Don't hesitate in sharing My power and glory with the humble.

⁵ For wisdom has been given that My glory may be known. ⁶ She has been revealed to humanity, that they might understand My ways. ⁷ That the humble may understand My power, and help those who lack wisdom. That they all may comprehend My glory. ⁸ For wisdom is available to all who are far from her gates, and have strayed from her ways.

⁹ Indeed, I am the Most High, the Lord of Jacob, and My majesty is upon all My works. ¹⁰ I accept all those who have reverence, ¹¹ bringing the appropriate offering of the lamb, making the altar full of burnt offerings, for it is a pleasing aroma from the hand of the justified.

¹² Wisdom's voice is heard from the homes of the loving and her song is in the assembly of the upright. ¹³ When they eat until they

are satisfied she is discussed, and when they drink in community together [14] their meditation is on My word. Their conversations are all about making My righteousness known.

[15] Wisdom is far away from the corrupt, her knowledge is distant from all the insolent. [16] But My eyes take pity upon the upright. [17] I, the Lord, give mercy to those who glorify Me, and I will deliver their soul from the time of evil.

[18] I, the Lord, am blessed, for I redeem the humble from the hand of strangers, and deliver the pure from the hand of the corrupt. [19] For I will raise up a deliverer out of Jacob, and a judge of the people from Israel.

I AM: THERE FOR YOU

*Y*ou called to Me, the Lord, and I am listening to you. [2] You lifted up your hands to My loving sanctuary and I inclined My ear to you. I will answer your petition and will not withhold your prayer from Me. [3] I will build up your soul and will not cast it down; I will not abandon you to the wicked. I, the judge of truth, will turn the fate of the corrupt away from you.

[4] I will not judge you according to your guilt, because no one is innocent before Me. [5] I will give you discernment and will teach you My precepts, that all races of the earth may hear of My works, that all the nations may come to revere Me.

[6] I remember you and will not forget you; I would never leave you in unbearable hardship. [7] I will cause the indiscretions of your youth to pass from you and will not discipline you any longer. [8] I, the Lord, will cleanse you from the plague of your self-centeredness, and will not let it return to you. [9] I will dry up its roots from within you, I won't even let it sprout within you. [10] For I am the source of your power, and your prayers are fulfilled in Me.

[11] To whom will you cry that can grant these things to you? What help can be found in the strength of human beings? [12] Your trust is

in Me, your Lord. You cried to Me and I answered you, and I healed the brokenness of your heart. [13] You slumbered and slept as though you were in a dream, but then you woke up and called on Me; [14] and I supported you, because I am your deliverer.

[15] Now you will behold your enemies shame; for you who have trusted in Me will not be ashamed. [16] You will be given honor forever and ever. [17] I, the Lord, will redeem Israel, My elect, and those of the house of Jacob, My chosen ones.

I AM: BENEVOLENT

*T*he dead cannot praise Me, nor can those covered in maggots and worms recount My loving-kindness. [2] But the living are able to thank Me! Even those who stumble will thank Me! For I will reveal My kindness to them, and will show them My righteousness. [3] For the soul of every living being is in My hand; I have given breath to all life.

[4] Therefore, I, your Lord, will deal with you according to My goodness, according to the greatness of My mercy, and the power of My loving deeds. [5] For I listen to the voice of those who love My name, and will not deprive them of My loving-kindness. [6] So give thanks, for I carry out what is just, and crown My upright ones with loving-kindness and mercy.

[7] Your soul explodes with praise for My name, giving thanks with shouts of joy for My mercy. You proclaim My faithfulness, for there is no limit to My gifts. [8] You were near death because of your sins, for your depravity had sold you to the grave. [9] But I, the Lord, saved you in the vastness of My mercy, and the power of My righteous deeds. [10] That is why you have loved My name and found refuge in Me. [11] Whenever you remember My power, your heart is strengthened, for you lean upon My mercy.

¹² I, your Lord, will forgive your guilt, and cleanse you from your sin. ¹³ I will bestow upon you a spirit of faithfulness and knowledge, and will not let you be dishonored in ruin. ¹⁴ I will not let the adversary dominate you; nor will an unclean spirit, or your sinful desires, take possession of your bones. ¹⁵ For I, the Lord, am your source of rejoicing! And in Me you can hope all day long. ¹⁶ For your brethren will rejoice with you, and your family's house will be astounded by My grace! ¹⁷ Indeed, you will have eternity to rejoice!

I AM: LOVING MY PEOPLE

$\mathcal{W}$ hen I bring you to mind, O' Zion, it's in blessings; for with all My strength I have loved you. Your memory will be blessed forever. ² Great is your hope O' Zion, for the peace of My salvation will come! ³ Generation after generation will dwell in you, all the generations of the upright will be your glory. ⁴ Those who longed for the day of Zion's salvation will rejoice in the greatness of her beauty. ⁵ They will suckle on the fullness of My glory and will skip in her beautiful streets. ⁶ In that day, you will tell tales about the powerful deeds of the prophets and you will glory in the deeds of upright!

⁷ So purge violence from your midst; let falsehood and deceit be put away from you. ⁸ That your children may rejoice in your streets, and your loved ones may always be with you. ⁹ O' how the people have hoped for Zion's salvation; O' how My devoted ones have mourned. ¹⁰ But your hope will not perish, nor will your longing be forgotten! ¹¹ For the loving will never perish, but the selfish will not survive. ¹² For each person will be tested according to their choices; each is repaid according to their path. ¹³ Indeed, I will cut off your oppressors O' Zion, all who hate you will been scattered.

[14] Your thanksgiving is such a pleasing aroma floating throughout all the earth. [15] I often think of the blessings I could give you; with all My heart I want to bless you! [16] That you may experience everlasting loving-kindness, and happiness with My glorious ones. [17] Therefore, accept the visions and dreams of prophets given to guide you. [18] Then you will be exalted and grow. At that time, you will exult in glorious thanksgiving to Me, your Redeemer! And I will rejoice in your beauty forever!

I AM: COMING

*I*n the midst of the congregation, let them praise Me, the Lord! ^{2} For I will come to judge every action and will remove evil from the earth, so that the children of corruption will never be found again! ^{3} The heavens will again give their dew and there shall be no drought within her skies. ^{4} The earth will yield its fruit in its season and its produce will never fail. ^{5} The fruit trees will give freely the fruit of its vineyards, and the ground will not cheat on its produce. ^{6} The poor and oppressed will eat their fill, and all those who revere Me, their God, will be content!

159

I AM: ETERNAL

he heavens and the earth shall give praise together. All the stars of evening twilight will give praise. ² Rejoice, O' Judah in your joy! Rejoice and be glad in your happiness, leap and dance! ³ Celebrate your pilgrim festivals and keep your vows, for no longer will the deceiver be in your midst. ⁴ Lift up your hands, for your right hand will prevail. ⁵ Behold, the enemy will perish, and all his despots and villains will be destroyed. ⁶ For I, the Lord, am eternal, and My glory will be forever and ever. Hallelujah!

I AM: THE I AM

I, the Lord, am powerful yet loving, the most sacred of sacred from generation to generation. [2] Majesty goes before Me and the roar of the ocean follows in My train. [3] Loving-kindness and truth surround My face. Truth, wisdom, and justice are the foundation of My government.

[4] Separating light from deep darkness, I established the dawn by the knowledge of My wisdom. [5] All the angels sang aloud when they saw it! [6] I crowned the hills with fruit, with good food for every living being. [7] For I established the world by My wisdom. I stretched out the heaven by My understanding, and brought forth wind from My storehouses. [8] I made lightning for the rain, and raised a mist from the end of the earth. [9] For I, who made the earth by My power, am Love.

EXEGETICAL APPENDIX

Due to the novel nature of attempting to faithfully reverse the perspective of a book of the Bible, while maintaining its spirituality, I thought it wise to offer a more detailed appendices explaining how I approached translating various phrases and verses that may alter the original text to a degree. I attribute these, largely, to readability and perspective, and more importantly, to the nature of God verses the tendencies of human nature; therefore some variations of translation were required, and were in almost every case, due not consciously to preference, but by necessity. Obviously, one can never meet the needs of every possible view on a particular scripture, but none-the-less, I have made an effort to include my methodology and apologetics for various textual anomalies. While this effort can hopefully be expanded upon and the translations better perfected over time (for which I encourage scholars to contact me), you will find the main translations which were of issue, in alphabetical order as follows:

ANGER OF GOD

God is love, not anger. Certainly there are specific circumstances when He will become angry, frustrated, disappointed. But He is our Father. Even caring earthly fathers do not abuse their children when they have made errors. Certainly, we need consequences for our actions. But God is not controlling. He does not intimidate people into doing His will. Rather, He is a loving father who is attempting to prevent His children from running out into the busy street. Consequently, I have muted this harsh language with more paternal language, to reflect God's higher pedagogical motives, rather than human motives of curses, resentment, or control.

Ezekiel 18:32 (NIV) "For I take no pleasure in the death of anyone, declares the Sovereign LORD. Repent and live!" / Ezekiel 33:11 (NIV) "Say to them, 'As surely as I live, declares the Sovereign LORD, I take no pleasure in the death of the wicked, but rather that they turn from their ways and live. Turn! Turn from your evil ways! Why will you die, people of Israel?'"

FEAR THE LORD

The root meaning of the word "fear" in Hebrew implies "reverence" or "honor". Therefore, to "fear-God" is to "respect Him", as you would an elder or mentor that has deep integrity. To "fear" is in reality, a sense of wonder and awe at God's overwhelming beauty and power. A healthy respect is proper when entering the hall of a powerful monarch. How much more then, the King of an entire Universe! For this reason, I have changed the wording of "fear" to reflect a clearer translation of our paternal Heavenly Father as "reverence", rather than what we inaccurately assume is terror. Certainly, being in the presence of God is not devoid of terror, for we are only mortal; indeed, every-time an angel revealed themselves, the prophets would collapse in fear. But the angel never left them in that state, rather, they consistently told them, "Do not be afraid" or "You are favored". God's intention isn't for us to be afraid of Him, but rather, to love and respect Him, on account that He is honorable, and keeps His word. God never uses His power to coerce or enslave, but, rather, to protect and empower.

Fear-iyr'â; feminine form, fear (also used as infinitive); morally, reverence; dreadful, exceedingly, terror as in awesome or terrifying thing, respect, reverence, revered in piety. / Daniel 10:18-19 (NIV) "Again the one who looked like a man touched me and gave me strength. 'Do not be afraid, you who are greatly beloved,' he said. 'Peace! Be strong now; be strong.' When he spoke to me, I was strengthened and said, 'Speak, my lord, since you have given me strength.'" / Jeremiah 31:3 (NIV) "The Lord appeared to us in the past, saying: 'I have loved you with an everlasting love; I have drawn you with unfailing kindness.'" / Exodus 34:6-7 (NOG) "Then Yahweh passed in front of Moses, calling out, 'Yahweh, Yahweh, a compassionate and merciful El, patient, always faithful and ready to forgive. He continues to show his love to thousands of generations, forgiving wrongdoing, disobedience, and sin. And He never lets the corrupt go unpunished.'"

FOR YOUR NAME'S SAKE

"For your name's sake" simply means for the sake of your "reputation". To have a good name is, by implication, to be honorable, to be a person of your word. When the Psalms use this term, it is essentially asking God to "defend His reputation by protecting His people according to His own promises". Therefore, I have rephrased this wording at times to the implied intent found in the Hebrew. It was also a logical necessity, due to God speaking in first-person; showing the immutability of His own integrity: For the sake of "My name", ie: "My integrity / reputation".

Name-šêm; a primitive word for one's name, with the idea of definite and conspicuous position, as a mark or memorial of individuality; by implication, honor, authority, character; name, renown, or fame. / Ezekiel 12:28 (NIV) "Therefore say to them, ''This is what the Sovereign Lord says: None of my words will be delayed any longer; whatever I say will be fulfilled, declares the Sovereign Lord.'" / Jeremiah 1:12 "The Lord said to me, 'You have seen correctly, for I am watching to see that My word is fulfilled.'"

GEOGRAPHY

In the case of long dead ancient cultures and localities, I have taken the liberty to update the locations to where they are located adjacent to the modern world. For example, Mt. Hermon, which is located on the border between Lebanon and Syria, I updated to simply say Syria, or Mt. Hermon in Syria, in order that people will know the locations, or their proximity to Israel. I have only done this selectively as it fit the context, and not exhaustively.

ISRAEL

Israel is not simply a nation, but was originally a given name to Jacob, whose birth-name meant, "heel-holder". From the womb, Jacob was attempting to wrest the spiritual promise from his brother Esau, which eventually led to his being exiled for deceiving his father Isaac. Jacob was eventually given the name, "Israel", by God, meaning, "God prevails"; only because the Angel of the Lord had to physically subdue Jacob with a permanent handicap before he would submit and accept that, God alone was responsible for the promise being fulfilled. Therefore, the true inheritor of God's "promise of salvation", is the one who submits to God in their heart, and not simply because of lineage. As such, I have elected, at limited times, to translate "Israel", as, 'My people". I believe this typological principle to be fully supported in the book of Joshua, where we see that God is not xenophobic, rather, He is the Creator of all humanity. This concept of foreigners and strangers being invited into Israel's spiritual heritage is well established throughout the law and the prophets.

Genesis 32:28 (NKJV) "And He said, 'Your name shall no longer be called Jacob, but Israel; for you have struggled with God and with men, and have prevailed.'" Jacob = "heel holder" or "supplanter"; Israel-iyśrâ'êl; (Aramaic) meaning God prevails / Joshua 5:13-14 (NLT) "When Joshua was near the town of Jericho, he looked up and saw a man standing in front of him with sword in hand. Joshua went up to him and demanded, 'Are you friend or foe?' 'Neither one,' he replied. 'I am the commander of the Lord's army.' At this, Joshua fell with his face to the ground in reverence." / Romans 2:28-29 (NRSV) "For a person is not a Jew who is one outwardly, nor is true circumcision something external and physical. Rather, a person is a Jew who is one inwardly, and real circumcision is a matter of the heart—it is spiritual and not literal. Such a person receives praise not from others, but from God." / Psalms 22:27-28 (GNT) "All nations will remember the Lord. From every part of the world they will turn to Him; all races will worship Him. The Lord is King, and He rules the nations." / Leviticus 19:33-34 (NLT) "Do not take advantage of foreigners who live among you in your land. Treat them like native-born Israelites, and love them as you love yourself. Remember that you were once foreigners living in the land of Egypt. I am the Lord, your God.

JUDAH

Judah was the first born son of Jacob/Israel, the eldest brother of the twelve. As such, he was the one to whom the promise of the "seed", the Messiah, was given; making him the typological father of all those who belong to God through faith. The term "Judah", tends to be overly nationalistic, as it has come to be associated only with the final remaining tribe of the twelve, the "Jews", which is short for Jude, a derivative of Judah. Therefore, as with the term Israel, I chose to translate, at limited times, "Judah", with its spiritual meaning, with terms such as, "My city", or "Zion", or "My people". I did this solely to make the passages more universally applicable to all those who are redeemed through faith in the promised "seed", a promise that actually began, not with Jerusalem, but with Adam and Eve.

Genesis 3:15 (NIV-WS) "And I will put enmity between you and the woman, and between your offspring and hers; he will crush your head, and you will strike his heel." / Genesis 12:2-3 (NIV-WS) "I will make you into a great nation, and I will bless you; I will make your name great, and you will be a blessing. I will bless those who bless you, and whoever curses you, I will curse; and all peoples on earth will be blessed through you." / Genesis 13:14-15 (KJV Strong's) "And the Lord said unto Abram, after Lot was separated from him, Lift up now thine eyes, and look from the place where thou art northward, and southward, and eastward, and westward: For all the land which thou seest, to thee will I give it, and to thy seed for ever." / Jeremiah 33:14-16 (NIV-WS) "'The days are coming,' declares the Lord, 'when I will fulfill the good promise I made to the people of Israel and Judah. In those days, and at that time, I will make a righteous Branch sprout from David's line; he will do what is just and right in the land. In those days, Judah will be saved and Jerusalem will live in safety. This is the name by which it will be called: The Lord, Our Righteous Savior.'" / Psalms 98:2-4 (NIV-WS) "The Lord has made His salvation known and revealed His righteousness to the nations. He has remembered His love and His faithfulness to Israel; all the ends of the earth have seen the salvation of our God. Shout for joy to the Lord, all the earth, burst into jubilant song with music." / Isaiah 65: 17 (NIV) "See, I will create new heavens and a new earth. The former things will not be remembered, nor will they come to mind."

PRAISE

David was definitely a man who was grateful to God. His praise for God is displayed, in that, nearly every Psalm ended on a positive note of praise or trust. Yet, as a first-person statement, the usage of the term "praise" sounds egotistical. Imagine if someone were giving the order, "you will praise Me" or "give praise to Me always" and other such wordings, of which David uses nearly ad-nauseam. It just simply does not work in this form of reinterpretation. Therefore, it was compulsory to reinterpret, at times, the term "praise", with the wider meaning of the Hebrew word, being: "give thanks", or "sing to Me" or "thank Me", and other similar forms. Praise does additionally imply worship, but the context of that worship is in love, gratitude, or of singing about what God has accomplished. Consequently, the re-interpretation works in the context, and is still true to the original Hebrew meaning; however, it is most certainly a broadening of highly esteemed phrases from the Psalms.

Praise-Yâḏâ: to hold out the hand; physically, especially to revere or worship with extended hands; intensively, to confess praise, to give thanks, to make a confession of. / Praise-Ilâ: laudation; specifically a song or hymn of adoration, thanksgiving, for qualities or deeds of attributes of God's renown, fame, or glory.

PSALM DIVISIONS

The reader will note that there are six-book-divisions of the Psalms. (Chapters 1-41: Psalms of Praise, GENESIS, Davidic Grouping I. Chapters 42-72: Psalms of Need, EXODUS, Davidic Grouping II sons of Korah Grouping I. Chapters 73-89: Psalms of Hope, LEVITICUS, Asaph, Sons of Korah Grouping II. Chapters 90-106: Psalms of Deliverance DEUTERONOMY, Congregational Praise Grouping I. Chapters 107-150: Psalms of Thanksgiving, NUMBERS, Alleluiah, Songs of Ascent, Davidic Grouping III, Congregational Praise Grouping II. Chapters 151-160, Psalms of Healing, LOST PSALMS, Orthodox, Apocryphal, The Dead Sea

Scrolls.) There were only five original divisions of the Psalms. I added the apocryphal sixth division. The traditional five-divisions were organized historically by ancient Hebrew scholars to represent the five books of the Torah, with each section ending with a doxology. The term, "Psalm", is derived from the Greek *psalmoi*, meaning "songs of praise" . Therefore, the "Psalms" were essentially what we would consider today, a hymnal. Concurrently, just as in modern hymnals, the attribution of the author was given at the beginning of each book. And, in later christian translations, they attributed the author at the beginning of each Psalm, just as we have with modern hymnals.

PSALM 151-160

While researching the history of the Psalms, I came across a collection of missing Psalms. They would be considered apocryphal writings, what theologians would consider outside of the accepted canon. *(Incidentally, I also stumbled across some possible original music that accompanied a few of the canon Psalms)*. In total, I discovered ten apocryphal Psalms. Psalm 151-155 appear to have some legitimacy, while Psalm 155-160 are highly questionable. Psalm 151 and 154, as well as some fragments, were found among the Dead Sea Scrolls. Limited manuscripts of the Septuagint contain Psalm 151. The Syriac biblical manuscript contains Psalm 152-155. And the Eastern Orthodox Church has always used Psalm 151. To me, these lend plausibility to their existence as a legitimate collection of songs from the ancient Hebrew compilators. This is, of course, subjective, but I thought them of enough interest to include them in the collection.

Sources: The Oxford handbook of the Psalms, William Brown - Oxford University Press - 2014 / 11Q11 Apocryphal Psalms, Logos Edition, Lexham Press - 2011

PSALM 119

As a point of interest, Psalm 119, which is also the longest Psalm, is broken up into 22 sections, one for each letter of the Hebrew alphabet. Hebrew was a language composed entirely of consonants. It is called the Aleph-bet, and each of the letters have a written symbolism within them, similar to Chinese characters; they also have corresponding numerical values and word meanings. In musical poetry, this could lead to all types of double meanings about God and His goodness, if one were to study into it. I, therefore, attributed each letter in the heading of each section of Psalm 119, as well as its contextual subject.

Alef, Bet, Vet (Alef, Bet, Vet) / Gimel, Dalet, Hey (Gimel, Dalet, Hey) / Vav, Zayin, Chet, Tet (Vav, Zayin, Chet, Tet) / Yud, Kaf, Chaf (Yud, Kaf, Chaf) / Lamed, Mem, Nun (Lamed, Mem, Nun) / Samech, Ayin, Pey, Fey (Samech, Ayin, Pey, Fey) / Tzadi, Kuf, Reysh (Tzadi, Kuf, Reysh) / Shin (Shin) / Sin (Sin) / Tav (Tav)

READABILITY

For the reader's knowledge, there are included many random and subtle alterations such as where I removed "The Lord" many times were it was exceedingly redundant; this was never due to intent, but the necessity of readability. Another example would be Psalm 1, where I altered the term, blown away like "chaff" to blown away like "husks". I recognize this can subtly alter the meaning of the terminology, due to chaff being a worthless part of wheat threshing. But, so, few people even comprehend these concepts in the modern world, I prefer to err on the side of a spiritual reading for the uninformed. It is my intent that this translation be read like intimate letters from God, and not simply a collection of theological treatises.

SERVANT

I have translated the term "servant" at times to "My child" or "My chosen". The Hebrew word for "servant" implies a sense of equality, a place of honor, or as an opportunity, as in that of a chosen mutually beneficial indentured slavery of free will, allowing for a life of upward mobility. There is also a servant similar to what we would call today, a public servant. Even those in the military today are those who are called to "serve" their country. Yet, having abolished slavery, the western mind has difficulty understanding the implied meanings in the Hebrew, and for good reason. But David meant this language as in a favored helper, a companion who has the ear of their master, or a surrendering of the heart, and not simply an object under a master's whip. Indeed, Jesus Himself specifically stated, "I call you no longer servants, but I call you friends" John 15:15. So, in the light of the original languages intent, and larger biblical revelation of God's love for His people, I believe the updated translation to be biblically justified.

Ebed: a servant: a chosen bondservant, slave, a subject, worshippers of God, servant in special sense as prophets or priests, servant of Israel or ones nation, servant as form of address between equals.

RIGHTEOUS, RIGHTEOUSNESS, HOLINESS

As I stated in the introduction, there is only two subjects of translation I intentionally paraphrased and altered the wording at times: that is, firstly, in the case of cherished historical terms of righteousness, holiness, godliness, which I changed to love, justice, kindness, and the like. In the larger reading of who God has revealed Himself to be, throughout the entirety of the Bible, it becomes obvious that God is love, that all of His ways are to benefit us and to bless, and that His approbations are intended to protect, not to enslave or control. Therefore, I have reinterpreted this wording to reflect what is the core theme of the gospel; that's is to say, what the fall into sin and what redemption is truly for. In order to properly address my paraphrasing, it will need to take the form of a Bible Study:

- **Scripture states that God is righteous:** Deuteronomy 32:3-4. (NASB) "For I proclaim the name of the Lord; Ascribe greatness to our God! "The Rock! His work is perfect, For all His ways are just; A God of faithfulness and without injustice, righteous and upright is He."

- **It also states that the Law is righteous:** Psalms 119:75-76 (NIV) "I know, Lord, that Your laws are righteous, and that in faithfulness You have afflicted me. May Your unfailing love be my comfort" / Exodus 22:22-23 (NLT) "You must not exploit a widow or an orphan. If you exploit them in any way and they cry out to Me, then I will certainly hear their cry."

- **The Bible also says that God is love:** 1 John 4:7-8 (NKJV) "Beloved, let us love one another, for love is of God; and everyone who loves is born of God and knows God. He who does not love does not know God, for God is love." / James 1:27 (TVB) "Real, true religion from God the Father's perspective is about caring for the orphans and widows who suffer needlessly." / Psalms 82:3-4 (NLT) "Give justice to the poor and the orphan; uphold the rights of the oppressed and the destitute. Rescue the poor and helpless; deliver them from the grasp of evil people."

- **And that the Fulfilling of law is love:** Galatians 5:13-14 (KJV) "For you, brethren, have been called to liberty; only do not use liberty as an opportunity for the flesh, but through love serve one another. For all the law is fulfilled in one word, even in this: "You shall love your neighbor as yourself." / Romans 13:8-10 NKJV "Owe no one anything except to love one another, for he who loves another has fulfilled the law. For the commandments, "You shall not commit adultery," "You shall not murder," "You shall not steal," "You shall not bear false witness," "You shall not covet," and if there is any other commandment, are all summed up in this saying, namely, "You shall love your neighbor as yourself." Love does no harm to a neighbor; therefore love is the fulfillment of the law."

- **And Jesus stated that love is the most important commandment:** Mark 12:28-34 (NIV) One of the teachers of the law came and heard them debating. Noticing that Jesus had given them a good answer, he asked Him, "Of all the commandments, which is the most important?" "The most important one," answered Jesus, "is this: 'Hear, O Israel: The Lord our God, the Lord is one. Love the Lord, your God, with all your heart and with all your soul and with all your mind and with all your strength.' The second is this: 'Love your neighbor as yourself.' There is no commandment greater than these." "Well said, teacher," the man replied. "You are right in saying that God is one and there is no other but Him. To love Him with all your heart, with all your understanding and with all your strength, and to love your neighbor as yourself is more important than all burnt offerings and sacrifices." When Jesus saw that he had answered wisely, He said to him, "You are not far from the kingdom of God."

- **The new law Jesus gave is essentially a summation of the whole law:** John 13:34-35 (NIV) "A new command I give you: Love one another. As I have loved you, so you must love one another. By this, everyone will know that you are My disciples, if you love one another."

Ergo, the inescapable conclusion is that: *righteousness is love*. One need only look to the Cross to see that is true. In the very context of our fall into "sin", God's solution was self-sacrificial love as the means of healing. If we limit spirituality to merely academic literalism, or religious moralism, we fail to grasp the actual spiritual meaning and intent of God and His teachings.

Righteous-Saḏiyq: just, lawful, righteous integrity, righteous or just in governing, right in a just cause , righteous as in justified and vindicated by God, to be right, or correct. / Holiness-Qôḏeš: sacred, consecrated dedicated, hallowed. set-apartness, separateness from sin and the ways of the world

SIN, WICKED, WICKEDNESS

Again, as I stated in the introduction, the only other subject I, at times, intentionally paraphrased and/or altered, is with the cherished terms of sin, wickedness, unrighteousness, etc., to selfishness, corruption, and injustice. The concept of sin has become burdened under mountains of religious cliche and prevents us from truly seeing the nature of evil in our motives. Accordingly, if righteousness is, indeed, love, then sin would logically be the opposite of love. When we read stories in the Bible about people who were unrighteous, ungodly, unholy, sinful, what is it that they have actually done that constitutes sin? Is it not betrayal of their loved ones? Violating others? Using people, or oppressing them? Or worshipping false gods based in lust, violence and self-interest? These are all essentially based in selfishness. The true nature of sin manifests itself in our families, in our relationships, in our social networks, businesses, and governments, does it not? Therefore, again, I will address this in the form of biblical study.

- **What really happened in the Garden?** Genesis 3:7-13 GNB "As soon as they had eaten it, they were given understanding and realized that they were naked; so, they sewed fig leaves together and covered themselves. That evening, they heard the Lord God walking in the garden, and they hid from HIm among the trees. But the Lord God called out to the man, "Where are you?" He answered, "I heard You in the garden; I was afraid and hid from You, because I was naked." "Who told you that you were naked?" God asked. "Did you eat the fruit that I told you not to eat?" The man answered, "The woman you put here with me gave me the fruit, and I ate it." The Lord God asked the woman, "Why did you do this?" She replied, "The snake tricked me into eating it."

The immediate impact of sin wasn't doctrinal, nor was it the destructive global outcomes we see today; no, those are the long-term systemic outcomes of selfishness. The immediate effect of sin was for Adam to shame his wife and to blame God for it. The impact of sin was relational. The love they had in the garden, was replaced by fig leaves of excuse. You see, when Eve "took" the fruit, she violated the very principle that eternal life is based upon: that of giving and receiving. When I have, I give to you, and you give to me, and we both have. But when we take, it leads to someone going without, and if I am without, it will logically lead to some form of conflict, suffering, and death. Hence, sin, i.e. "selfishness" is causal, destroying everything it touches. And that is what God has always been attempting to prevent. Let me illustrate this concept using 1 Corinthians 13:4-8 (NIV):

- Love is patient = Selfishness is impatient
- Love is kind = Selfishness is rude
- Love does not envy = Selfishness is jealous

- Love does not boast = Selfishness brags
- Love is not proud = Selfishness is arrogant
- Love does not dishonor others = Selfishness uses others
- Love is not self-seeking = Selfishness is narcissistic
- Love is not easily angered = Selfishness is hot tempered
- Love keeps no record of wrongs = Selfishness fixates on flaws
- Love does not delight in evil = Selfishness is sadistic
- Love rejoices with the truth = Selfishness lives in denial
- Love always protects = Selfishness abandons others
- Love always trusts = Selfishness is cynical
- Love always hopes = Selfishness is apathetic
- Love always perseveres = Selfishness gives up easy
- Love never fails = Selfishness never follows through

Clearly, sin is based in selfishness, and righteousness, which is opposite of sin, is based in love. This is why I, at times, altered the translations. Because love versus selfishness is the very theme of the conflict between God and Lucifer. Lucifer, the covering cherub, deceived one-third of the angels, and all of humanity, into believing that selfishness (the breaking of God's principles/laws of love), is the true path to enlightenment. And God has allowed this narrative to play itself out, but only for the sake of the long-term stability of the Universe; if God had destroyed Lucifer immediately, the beings throughout His kingdom would have obeyed Him out of fear of being killed if they disobeyed. And, unfortunately, this very same lie, has too often been foisted upon humanity by the church itself.

> *Revelation 12:12 (NLT)* *"Therefore, rejoice, O, heavens! And you who live in the heavens, rejoice! But terror will come on the earth and the sea, for the devil has come down to you in great anger, knowing that he has little time."*

God allowed sin to entirely unmask itself, only, so that everyone would see for themselves that selfishness leads to suffering and death. We had to learn for ourselves what God was trying to protect us from, in acquiring "the knowledge of evil". The laws and teachings God has given, are simply the basis of happiness and love. And He has proven this to us, not just through talk, but through action, by willingly sacrificing His own life, on the Cross.

John 3:16-18 (NLT) *"But this is how God loved the world: He gave His one and only Son, so that everyone who believes in Him will not perish but have eternal life. God sent His Son into the world not to judge the world, but to save the world through Him. There is no judgment against anyone who believes in Him."*

A final note from the Author: If there are areas of significant scholarship, from disparate faith leaders, that you feel could improve the messianic and redemptive nature of the text, please, see my contact info. I would be happy to dialogue and consider your scholarship for future editions. Grace and Peace to you in our Lord Jesus Christ.

-Shayne Mason Vincent

ABOUT THE AUTHOR

Shayne Mason Vincent grew up in the wilds of Northern Minnesota. He has a love for adventure and has traveled extensively. He graduated with a B.A. of Ministry, a B.A. of Counseling, and a Master's of Social Work. He has worked as a Pastor, Chaplain, Therapist, Hospice Bereavement Counselor, and as a Musician. His passions in life include God, family and friends, teaching, travel, free-diving, sailing, motorcycles, cars, and music. His areas of study include philosophy, theology, psychology, politics, history, and music. His writings, poetry, photography, and music can be found at:

www.BaringMySoul.com